THOMAS CARLYLE

Modern Critical Views

These and other titles in preparation

Modern Critical Views

THOMAS CARLYLE

Edited and with an introduction by

Harold Bloom
Sterling Professor of the Humanities
Yale University

CHELSEA HOUSE PUBLISHERS ◇ 1986
New York ◇ New Haven ◇ Philadelphia

© 1986 by Chelsea House Publishers, a division of Chelsea
House Educational Communications, Inc.
   133 Christopher Street, New York, NY 10014
   345 Whitney Avenue, New Haven, CT 06511
   5014 West Chester Pike, Edgemont, PA 19028

Introduction © 1982 by Oxford University Press, Inc., © 1986
by Harold Bloom

Printed and bound in the United States of America

∞ The paper used in this publication meets the minimum
requirements of the American National Standard for
Permanence of Paper for Printed Library Materials,
Z39.48-1984.

Library of Congress Cataloging-in-Publication Data
Thomas Carlyle.
   (Modern critical views)
   Bibliography: p.
   Includes index.
   1. Carlyle, Thomas, 1795–1881—Criticism and
interpretation—Addresses, essays, lectures. I. Title.
II. Series.
PR4434.T46 1986   824'.8   86-2326
ISBN 0-87754-688-6 (alk. paper)

Contents

Editor's Note

This book gathers together a selection of the best criticism yet devoted to the writings of Thomas Carlyle, arranged in the chronological order of its original publication. I am grateful to Frank Menchaca for his aid in research, and for his counsel in judging these essays.

The introduction ranges widely in Carlyle in order to describe some of the revisionary elements in his characteristic rhetorical stance. John Holloway's exegesis of Carlyle's prophetic language begins the chronological sequence, which continues with Albert J. LaValley's strenuous reading of *The French Revolution*, emphasizing that change for Carlyle is "disruptive action," and illuminatingly comparing the book to Conrad's *Nostromo*.

LaValley's invocation of the historical novel is paralleled by the resort to fictional analogues by George Levine in his account of *Sartor Resartus*, and by Brian John in a reading of *Past and Present*. Levine demonstrates that the strength of *Sartor Resartus* depends upon Carlyle's awareness of the distance between himself and his own fictive characters, a distance lost in the later writings. John finds that Carlyle's two crucial personae, as historian and as literary hero, achieve a final synthesis in *Past and Present*.

The image of the hero in Carlylean history is seen by Philip Rosenberg to be a version of the self's triumph over its own destiny. This transcendental overcoming of fate necessarily yields to transcendental despair, which is the focus of the observations upon *The French Revolution* by John P. Farrell. A very different Carlyle, the creative critic, is delineated in Geoffrey H. Hartman's discovery of his true precursor in the enthusiasm of Carlyle's commentaries.

In a final overview of Carlyle, A. Dwight Culler contrasts the prophet to the philosopher John Stuart Mill, as rival representatives of the spirit of the age in Victorian culture. Mill's turn to Romantic sensibility, to the Wordsworthian Sublime, in order to heal the emotional ravages brought

about by the psychological deficiencies of an exclusively Utilitarian perspective, is thus set against Carlyle's passionate rejection of Benthamism,
with its strong conviction that nothing valuable in the past ages of culture
could be permanently lost from the spirit of an age to come.

Introduction

In his early essay "Signs of the Times" (1829), Carlyle prophesied the rise of our own literary culture. A culture becomes literary, for better and for worse, when religion, philosophy, and science accelerate the long process of losing their authority. Carlyle, seer of transcendental possibilities, began as a rebel against the main tradition of British speculation, the empirical line from Bacon to Bentham, and yet his rebellion was more equivocal than he seems to have realized. Protesting the Mechanical Age, Carlyle remained what Nietzsche in *The Twilight of the Gods* mocked him for being, an English atheist who, merely upon principle, declined to be what he truly was.

This hardly damages Carlyle as a writer; perhaps it might yet revive him if his scholars would cease emulating his rhetorical descents into the bathos of High German Transcendentalism. Goethe was for Carlyle a mask and a shield, without which Carlyle would have been a belated British poet, Byronic in verse, Coleridgean in prose. Reading Carlyle's poems of 1823–33 is a gleeful experience for those who seek revenge upon his later prose:

> What is Life? A thawing iceboard
> On a sea with sunny shore;—
> Gay we sail; it melts beneath us;
> We are sunk, and seen no more.

Carlyle's famous portrait of Coleridge in his *Life of John Sterling* (1851) goes back to an 1824 call upon Coleridge in London. Nothing could be more brilliantly unfair than Carlyle's summing-up of his truest precursor, and nothing could be more revelatory of Carlyle himself:

> To the man himself Nature had given, in high measure, the seeds
> of a noble endowment; and to unfold it had been forbidden him.

1

A subtle lynx-eyed intellect, tremulous pious sensibility to all good and all beautiful; truly a ray of empyrean light;—but imbedded in such weak laxity of character, in such indolences and esuriences as had made strange work with it. Once more, the tragic story of a high endowment with an insufficient will. An eye to discern the divineness of the Heaven's splendours and lightnings, the insatiable wish to revel in their godlike radiances and brilliances; but no heart to front the scathing terrors of them, which is the first condition of your conquering an abiding place there. The courage necessary for him, above all things, had been denied this man. His life, with such ray of the empyrean in it, was great and terrible to him; and he had not valiantly grappled with it, he had fled from it; sought refuge in vague day-dreams, hollow compromises, in opium, in theosophic metaphysics. Harsh pain, danger, necessity, slavish harnessed toil, were of all things abhorrent to him. And so the empyrean element, lying smothered under the terrene, and yet inextinguishable there, made sad writhings. For pain, danger, difficulty, steady slaving toil, and other highly disagreeable behests of destiny, shall in no wise be shirked by any brightest mortal that will approve himself loyal to his mission in this world; nay precisely the higher he is, the deeper will be the disagreeableness, and the detestability to flesh and blood, of the tasks laid on him; and the heavier too, and more tragic, his penalties if he neglect them.

Carlyle is the courageous titan with the heart to front pain, danger, difficulty, and steady slaving toil. Poor Coleridge attempted to steal into heaven, and Carlyle, too canny to believe in an outworn logos, mocks his precursor's pieties of self-deception:

What the light of your mind, which is the direct inspiration of the Almighty, pronounces incredible,—that, in God's name, leave uncredited; at your peril do not try believing that. No subtlest hocus-pocus of "reason" *versus* "understanding" will avail for that feat;—and it is terribly perilous to try it in these provinces!

These provinces are empirical, the lands of Bacon and Locke, Hume and Bentham, and the Mills. Carlyle's anxiety is that he may become irresolute or self-deceived, that he may become Coleridge. Carlyle has no Supreme Fiction, but only what in his early "Corn-Law Rhymes" (1832) he calls the knowing that comes through his work, a knowing that is strength, force, seeing, and "a certain Originality." The ultimate instance of this knowing is Shakespeare, about whom Carlyle writes with rare insight in *On Heroes and Hero-Worship* (1841). Far better than the entire history of formal Shakespeare criticism is Carlyle's fundamental realization that Shakespeare's true power is cognitive:

> For, in fact, I say the degree of vision that dwells in a man is a correct measure of the man. If called to define Shakspeare's faculty, I should say superiority of Intellect, and think I had included all under that. What indeed are faculties? We talk of faculties as if they were distinct, things separable; as if a man had intellect, imagination, fancy, etc., as he has hands, feet, and arms. That is a capital error. Then again, we hear of a man's "intellectual nature," and of his "moral nature," as if these again were divisible, and existed apart. Necessities of language do perhaps prescribe such forms of utterance; we must speak, I am aware, in that way, if we are to speak at all. But words ought not to harden into things for us. It seems to me, our apprehension of this matter is, for the most part, radically falsified thereby. We ought to know withal, and to keep for ever in mind, that these divisions are at bottom but *names*; that man's spiritual nature, the vital Force which dwells in him, is essentially one and indivisible; that what we call imagination, fancy, understanding, and so forth, are but different figures of the same Power of Insight, all indissolubly connected with each other, physiognomically related; that if we knew one of them, we might know all of them. Morality itself, what we call the moral quality of a man, what is this but another *side* of the one vital Force whereby he is and works? All that a man does is physiognomical of him. You may see how a man would fight, by the way in which he sings; his courage, or want of courage, is visible in the word he utters, in the opinion he has formed, no less than in the stroke he strikes. He is *one*; and preaches the same Self abroad in all these ways.

What Carlyle teaches us is that Shakespeare's cognitive originality has altered every mode available to us for representing cognition in language, including the one we now ascribe to Freud. Reading Carlyle on Shakespeare, we see that Freud's map of the mind codifies and rationalizes Shakespeare's. An extraordinary further outburst of Carlyle's rhetoric is evocative of Shakespeare's deepest influence upon us:

> If I say therefore, that Shakspeare is the greatest of Intellects, I have said all concerning him. But there is more in Shakspeare's

intellect than we have yet seen. It is what I call an unconscious
intellect; there is more virtue in it than he himself is aware of.
Novalis beautifully remarks of him, that those Dramas of his are
Products of Nature too, deep as Nature herself. I find a great
truth in this saying. Shakspeare's Art is not Artifice; the noblest
worth of it is not there by plan or precontrivance. It grows-up
from the deeps of Nature, through this noble sincere soul, who
is a voice of Nature. The latest generations of men will find new
meanings in Shakspeare, new elucidations of their own human
being; "new harmonies with the infinite structure of the Universe;
concurrences with later ideas, affinities with the higher powers
and senses of man." This well deserves meditating. It is Nature's
highest reward to a true simple great soul, that he get thus to be
a part of herself. Such a man's works whatsoever he with utmost
conscious exertion and forethought shall accomplish, grow up
withal *un*consciously, from the unknown deeps in him;—as the
oaktree grows from the Earth's bosom, as the mountains and
waters shape themselves; with a symmetry grounded on Nature's
own laws, conformable to all Truth whatsoever. How much in
Shakspeare lies hid; his sorrows, his silent struggles known to
himself; much that was not known at all, not speakable at all:
like *roots*, like sap and forces working underground! Speech is
great; but Silence is greater.

By "unconscious intellect" Carlyle primarily means mind at its least
tendentious, or as he says later, at its most prophetic. Attempting prophecy,
Carlyle himself became wholly tendentious. Too strong to admit the reproach
he felt in Shakespeare, Carlyle was also too honest not to be made uneasy.
For him, Shakespeare was religious writing, a new Bible to replace Old and
New Testament alike. We can learn from Carlyle also that the distinction
between religious and secular writing is merely political and not critical.
Critically, all writing is religious, or all writing is secular; Carlyle sees that
Shakespeare has abolished the distinction, and has become the second Bible
of the West.

II

What in the nineteenth and twentieth centuries *is* religious writing?
What can it be? Which of these passages, setting their polemics aside, is
better described as religious writing?

People say to me, that it is but a dream to suppose that Christianity should regain the organic power in human society which once it possessed. I cannot help that; I never said it could. I am not a politician; I am proposing no measures, but exposing a fallacy, and resisting a pretence. Let Benthamism reign, if men dare no aspirations; but do not tell them to be romantic, and then solace them with glory; do not attempt by philosophy what was once done by religion. The ascendancy of Faith may be impracticable, but the reign of Knowledge is incomprehensible.

He that has done nothing has known nothing. Vain is it to sit scheming and plausibly discoursing: up and be doing! If thy knowledge be real, put it forth from thee: grapple with real Nature; try thy theories there, and see how they hold out. *Do* one thing, for the first time in thy life do a thing; a new light will rise to thee on the doing of all things whatsoever.

I have taken these passages randomly enough; they lay near by. The distinguished first extract is both truly religious and wonderfully written, but the second is religious writing. Newman, in the first, from *The Tamworth Reading Room* (1841), knows both the truth and his own mind, and the relation between the two. Carlyle, in the second, from "Corn-Law Rhymes" (1832), knows only his own knowing, and sets that above both Newman's contraries, religion and philosophy. "Corn-Law Rhymes" became a precursor text for Emerson because he could recognize what had to be religious writing for the nineteenth century, and to that recognition, which alone would not have sufficed, Emerson added the American difference, which Carlyle could not ever understand. Subtle as this difference is, another intertextual juxtaposition can help reveal it:

"But it is with man's Soul as it was with Nature: the beginning of Creation is—Light. Till the eye have vision, the whole members are in bonds. Divine moment, when over the tempest-tost Soul, as once over the wild-weltering Chaos, it is spoken: Let there be Light! Ever to the greatest that has felt such moment, is it not miraculous and God-announcing; even as, under simpler figures, to the simplest and least. The mad primeval Discord is hushed; the rudely-jumbled conflicting elements bind themselves into separate Firmaments: deep silent rock-foundations are built beneath; and the skyey vault with its everlasting Luminaries above: instead of a dark wasteful Chaos, we have a blooming, fertile, heaven-encompassed World."

"Nature is not fixed but fluid. Spirit alters, moulds, makes it. The immobility or bruteness of nature, is the absence of spirit; to pure spirit, it is fluid, it is volatile, it is obedient. Every spirit builds itself a house; and beyond its house a world; and beyond its world, a heaven. Know then, that the world exists for you. For you is the phenomenon perfect. What we are, that only can we see. . . . Build, therefore, your own world. As fast as you conform your life to the pure idea in your mind, that will unfold its great proportions. . . . The kingdom of man over nature, which cometh not with observation,—a dominion such as now is beyond his dream of God,—he shall enter without more wonder than the blind man feels who is gradually restored to perfect sight."

This juxtaposition is central, because the passages are. The first rhapsody is Carlyle's Teufelsdröckh uttering his Everlasting Yea in *Sartor Resartus*; the second is Emerson's Orphic poet chanting the conclusion of *Nature*. Carlyle's seeing soul triumphs over the Abyss, until he can say to himself: "Be no longer a Chaos, but a World, or even Worldkin. Produce! Produce!" The Abyss is bondage, the production is freedom, somehow still "in God's name!" Emerson, despite his supposed discipleship to Carlyle in *Nature*, has his seeing soul proclaim a world so metamorphic and beyond natural metamorphosis that its status is radically *prior* to that of the existent universe. For the earth is only part of the blind man's "dream of God." Carlyle's imagination remains orthodox, and rejects Chaos. Emerson's seeing, beyond observation, is more theosophical than Germanic Transcendental. The freedom to imagine "the pure idea in your mind" is the heretical absolute freedom of the Gnostic who identified his mind's purest idea with the original Abyss. American freedom, in the context of Emerson's American religion, indeed might be called "Abyss-radiance."

I return to the question of what, in the nineteenth century, makes writing *religious*. Having set Carlyle in the midst, between Newman and Emerson, I cite next the step in religious writing beyond even Emerson:

we have an interval, and then our place knows us no more. Some spend this interval in listlessness, some in high passions, the wisest, at least among "the children of this world," in art and song. For our one chance lies in expanding that interval, in getting as many pulsations as possible into the given time.

Pater, concluding *The Renaissance*, plays audaciously against Luke 16:8, where "the children of this world are in their generation wiser than the children of light." Literalizing the Gospel's irony, Pater insinuates that in his generation the children of this world are the only children of light. Light expands our fiction of duration, our interval or place in art, by a concealed allusion to the Blakean trope that also fascinated Yeats; the pulsation of an artery in which the poet's work is done. Pater sinuously murmurs his credo, which elsewhere in *The Renaissance* is truly intimated to be "a strange rival religion" opposed to warring orthodoxies, fit for "those who are neither for Jehovah nor for His enemies."

To name Emerson and Pater as truly "religious writers" is to call into question very nearly everything that phrase usually implies. More interestingly, this naming also questions that mode of displacement M. H. Abrams analyzes in his strong study *Natural Supernaturalism*: "not . . . the deletion and replacement of religious ideas but rather the assimilation and reinterpretation of religious ideas." I believe that the following remarks of Abrams touch their limit precisely where Carlyle and Emerson part, on the American difference, and also where Carlyle and Ruskin part from Pater and what comes after. The story Abrams tells has been questioned by J. Hillis Miller, from a Nietzschean linguistic or Deconstructive perspective, so that Miller dissents from Abrams exactly where Nietzsche himself chose to attack Carlyle (which I cite below). But there is a more ancient perspective to turn against Abrams's patterns-of-displacement, an argument as to whether poetry did not inform religion before religion ever instructed poetry. And beyond this argument, there is the Gnostic critique of creation-theories both Hebraic and Platonic, a critique that relies always upon the awesome trope of the primal Abyss.

Abrams states his "displacement" thesis in a rhetoric of continuity:

> Much of what distinguishes writers I call "Romantic" derives from the fact that they undertook, whatever their religious creed or lack of creed, to save traditional concepts, schemes, and values which had been based on the relation of the Creator to his creature and creation, but to reformulate them within the prevailing two-term system of subject and object, ego and non-ego, the human mind or consciousness and its transactions with nature. Despite their displacement from a supernatural to a natural frame of reference, however, the ancient problems, terminology, and ways of thinking about human nature and history survived, as the implicit distinctions and categories through which even radically secular writers saw themselves and their world.

Such "displacement" is a rather benign process, as though the incarnation of the Poetic Character and the Incarnation proper could be assimilated
to one another, or the former serve as the reinterpretation of the latter. But
what if poetry as such is always a counter-theology, or Gentile Mythus, as
Vico believed? Abrams, not unlike Matthew Arnold, reads religion as abiding
in poetry, as though the poem were a saving remnant. But perhaps the saving
remnant *of poetry* is the only force of what we call theology? And what can
theology be except what Geoffrey Hartman anxiously terms it: "a vast,
intricate domain of psychopoetic events," another litany of evasions? Poems
are the original lies-against-time, as the Gnostics understood when they
turned their dialectics to revisionary interpretations not only of the Bible
and Plato, but of Homer as well. Gnosticism was the inaugural and most
powerful of Deconstructions because it undid all genealogies, scrambled all
hierarchies, allegorized every microcosm/macrocosm relation, and rejected
every representation of divinity as non-referential.

Carlyle, though he gave Abrams both the scheme of displacement and
the title-phrase of "natural supernaturalism," seems to me less and less self-
deceived as he progressed onwards in life and work, which I think accounts
for his always growing fury. Here I follow Nietzsche, in the twelfth "Skir-
mish" of *Twilight of the Idols* where he leaves us not much of the supposedly
exemplary life of Carlyle:

> this unconscious and involuntary farce, this heroic-moralistic
> interpretation of dyspeptic states. Carlyle: a man of strong words
> and attitudes, a rhetor from *need*, constantly lured by the craving
> for a strong faith and the feeling of his incapacity for it (in this
> respect, a typical romantic!). The craving for a strong faith is no
> proof of a strong faith, but quite the contrary. If one has such a
> faith, then one can afford the beautiful luxury of skepticism; one
> is sure enough, firm enough, has ties enough for that. Carlyle
> drugs something in himself with the fortissimo of his veneration
> of men of strong faith and with his rage against the less simple
> minded: he *requires* noise. A constant passionate dishonesty
> against himself—that is his *proprium*; in this respect he is and
> remains interesting. Of course, in England he is admired precisely
> for his honesty. Well, that is English; and in view of the fact that
> the English are the people of consummate cant, it is even as it
> should be, and not only comprehensible. At bottom, Carlyle is
> an English atheist who makes it a point of honor not to be one.

It seems merely just to observe, following Nietzsche's formidable wit, that Carlyle contrived to be a religious writer without being a religious man. His clear sense of the signs and characteristics of the times taught him that the authentic nineteenth-century writer had to be religious *qua* writer. The burden, as Carlyle knew, was not so much godlessness as belatedness, which compels a turn to Carlyle (and Emerson) on history.

III

Carlyle, with grim cheerfulness, tells us that history is an unreadable text, indeed a "complex Manuscript, covered over with formless inextricably-entangled unknown characters,—nay, which is a *Palimpsest*, and had once prophetic writing, still dimly legible there. . . ." We can see emerging in this dark observation the basis for *The French Revolution*, and even for *Past and Present*. But that was Carlyle "On History" in 1830, just before the advent of Diogenes Teufelsdröckh, the author of "On History Again" in 1833, where the unreadable is read as Autobiography repressed by all Mankind: "a like unconscious talent of remembering and of forgetting again does the work here." The great instance of this hyperbolic or Sublime repression is surely Goethe, whose superb self-confidence breathes fiercely in his couplet cited by Carlyle as the first epigraph to *Sartor Resartus*:

> Mein Vermächtniss, wie herrlich weit und breit!
> Die Zeit ist mein Vermächtniss, mein Acker ist die Zeit.
>
> [My inheritance, how splendidly wide and broad!
> Time is my inheritance, my seed-field is time.]

Goethe's splendid, wide, and broad inheritance is time itself, the seed-field that has the glory of having grown Goethe! But then, Goethe had no precursors in his own language, or none at least that could make him anxious. Carlyle trumpets his German inheritance: Goethe, Schiller, Fichte, Novalis, Kant, Schelling. His English inheritance was more troublesome to him, and the vehemence of his portrait of Coleridge reveals an unresolved relationship. This unacknowledged debt to Coleridge, with its too-conscious swerve away from Coleridge and into decisiveness and overt courage, pain accepted and work deified, may be the hidden basis for the paradoxes of Carlyle on time, at once resented with a Gnostic passion and worshipped as the seed-bed of a Goethean greatness made possible for the self. It is a liberation to know the American difference again when the reader turns from Carlyle's two essays on history to "History," placed first of the *Essays* (1841) of Emerson:

This human mind wrote history, and this must read it. The Sphinx must solve her own riddle. If the whole of history is in one man, it is all to be explained from individual experience. . . .

Property also holds of the soul, covers great spiritual facts, and instinctively we at first hold to it with swords and laws, and wide and complex combinations. The obscure consciousness of this fact is the light of all our day, the claim of claims; the plea for education, for justice, for charity, the foundation of friendship and love, and of the heroism and grandeur which belong to acts of self-reliance. It is remarkable that involuntarily we always read as superior beings. . . .

The student is to read history actively and not passively; to esteem his own life the text, and books the commentary.

So much then for Carlyle on history; so much indeed for history. The text is not interpretable? But there is no text! There is only your own life, and the Wordsworthian light of all our day turns out to be: self-reliance. Emerson, in describing an 1847 quarrel with Carlyle in London, gave a vivid sense of his enforcing the American difference, somewhat at the expense of a friendship that was never the same again:

Carlyle . . . had grown impatient of opposition, especially when talking of Cromwell. I differed from him . . . in his estimate of Cromwell's character, and he rose like a great Norse giant from his chair—and, drawing a line with his finger across the table, said, with terrible fierceness: "Then, sir, there is a line of separation between you and me as wide as that, and as deep as the pit."

Hardly a hyperbole, the reader will reflect, when he reads what two years later Carlyle printed as "The Nigger Question." This remarkable performance doubtless was aimed against "Christian Philanthropy" and related hypocrisies, but the abominable greatness of the tract stems from its undeniable madness. The astonished reader discovers not fascism, but a terrible sexual hysteria rising up from poor Carlyle, as the repressed returns in the extraordinary trope of black pumpkin-eating:

far over the sea, we have a few black persons rendered extremely "free" indeed. Sitting yonder with their beautiful muzzles up to the ears in pumpkins, imbibing sweet pulps and juices; the grinder and incisor teeth ready for ever new work, and the pumpkins cheap as grass in those rich climates: while the sugar-crops rot round them uncut, because labour cannot be hired, so cheap are the pumpkins. . . .

and beautiful Blacks sitting there up to the ears in pumpkins, and doleful Whites sitting here without potatoes to eat. . . .

The fortunate Black man, very swiftly does he settle *his* account with supply and demand:—not so swiftly the less fortunate White man of those tropical localities. A bad case, his, just now. He himself cannot work; and his black neighbour, rich in pumpkin, is in no haste to help him. Sunk to the ears in pumpkin, imbibing saccharine juices, and much at his ease in the Creation, he can listen to the less fortunate white man's "demand" and take his own time in supplying it. . . .

An idle White gentleman is not pleasant to me; though I confess the real work for him is not easy to find, in these our epochs; and perhaps he is seeking, poor soul, and may find at last. But what say you to an idle Black gentleman, with his rum-bottle in his hand (for a little additional pumpkin you can have red-herrings and rum, in Demerara),—rum-bottle in his hand, no breeches on his body, pumpkin at discretion. . . .

Before the West Indies could grow a pumpkin for any Negro, how much European heroism had to spend itself in obscure battle; to sink, in mortal agony, before the jungles, the putrescences and waste savageries could become arable, and the Devils be in some measure chained there! . . . A bit of the great Protector's own life lies there; beneath those pumpkins lies a bit of the life that was Oliver Cromwell's.

I have cited only a few passages out of this veritable procession of pumpkins, culminating in the vision of Carlyle's greatest hero pushing up the pumpkins so that unbreeched Blacks might exercise their potent teeth. Mere racism does not yield so pungent a phantasmagoria, and indeed I cannot credit it to Carlyle's likely impotence either. This pumpkin litany is Carlyle's demi-Gnosticism at its worst, for here time is no fair seed-bed but rather devouring time, Kronos chewing us up as so many pumpkins, the time of "Getting Under Way" in *Sartor Resartus*:

"Me, however, as a Son of Time, unhappier than some others, was Time threatening to eat quite prematurely; for, strive as I might, there was no good Running, so obstructed was the path, so gyved were the feet."

IV

Sartor Resartus, rather than *Past and Present* or *The French Revolution*, seems now to be Carlyle's great accomplishment, though alas it seems fated also to lack readers, now and in the future. A little application of Carlyle to current American society would do wonders. Envision a House of Representatives and a Senate required to deliberate absolutely naked (presumably in a sufficiently heated Capitol). Clearly the quality of legislation would rise, and the quantity of rhetoric would fall. Envision professors, quite naked, instructing equally naked classes. The intellectual level might not be elevated, but the issue of authority would be clarified. Envision our president, naked on television, smilingly charming us with his customary amiable incoherence. We might be no less moved, but reality would have a way of breaking in upon him, and even upon us.

Teufelsdröckh's Theorem, "Society founded upon cloth," is sublimely illustrated in one of Carlyle's happiest conceits:

> "What would Majesty do, could such an accident befall in reality; should the buttons all simultaneously start, and the solid wool evaporate, in very Deed, as here in Dream? *Ach Gott*! How each skulks into the nearest hiding-place; their high State Tragedy (*Haupt- und Staats-Action*) becomes a Pickleherring-Farce to weep at, which is the worst kind of Farce; *the tables* (according to Horace), and with them, the whole fabric of Government, Legislation, Property, Police, and Civilised Society, *are dissolved*, in wails and howls."

Lives the man that can figure a naked Duke of Windlestraw addressing a naked House of Lords? Imagination, choked as in mephitic air, recoils on itself, and will not forward with the picture. The Woolsack, the Ministerial, the Opposition Benches—*infandum*! *infandum*! And yet why is the thing impossible? Was not every soul, or rather every body, of these Guardians of our Liberties, naked, or nearly so, last night; "a forked Radish with a head fantastically carved"? And why might he not, did our stern fate so order it, walk out to St. Stephen's, as well as into bed, in that no-fashion; and there, with other similar Radishes, hold a Bed of Justice? "Solace of those afflicted with the like!" Unhappy Teufelsdröckh, had man ever such a "physical or psychical infirmity" before? And now how many, perhaps, may thy unparalleled confession (which we, even to the sounder British world, and goaded-on by Critical and Biographical duty,

grudge to reimpart) incurably infect therewith! Art thou the ma-
lignest of Sansculottists, or only the maddest?

"It will remain to be examined," adds the inexorable Teufelsdröckh, "in how far the SCARECROW, as a Clothed Person, is
not also entitled to benefit of clergy, and English trial by jury:
nay perhaps, considering his high function (for is not he too a
Defender of Property, and Sovereign armed with the *terrors* of
the Law?), to a certain royal Immunity and Inviolability; which,
however, misers and the meaner class of persons are not always
voluntarily disposed to grant him." * * * * "O my friends, we
are (in Yorick Sterne's words) but as 'turkeys driven, with a stick
and red clout, to the market': or if some drivers, as they do in
Norfolk, take a dried bladder and put peas in it, the rattle thereof
terrifies the boldest!"

Carlyle is in the tradition of Rabelais, Voltaire, and Swift, so far as his
genre (or non-genre) can be determined, but he is less a satirist than the seer
of a grotesque phantasmagoria. *Sartor Resartus* is an outrageous and excessive
fiction, and requires a very active reading. Its enigma is the paradox that
Nietzsche superbly attacked, Carlyle's faithless faith, which is expounded
in book 3, chapter 8, "Natural Supernaturalism":

"O Heaven, it is mysterious, it is awful to consider that we not
only carry each a future Ghost within Him; but are, in very deed,
Ghosts! These Limbs, whence had we them; this stormy Force;
this life-blood with its burning Passion? They are dust and
shadow; a Shadow-system gathered round our ME; wherein,
through some moments or years, the Divine Essence is to be
revealed in the Flesh. The warrior on his strong war-horse, fire
flashes through his eyes; force dwells in his arm and heart: but
warrior and war-horse are a vision; a revealed Force, nothing
more. Stately they tread the Earth, as if it were a firm substance:
fool! the Earth is but a film; it cracks in twain, and warrior and
war-horse sink beyond plummet's sounding. Plummet's? Fantasy
herself will not follow them. A little while ago, they were not; a
little while, and they are not, their very ashes are not.

"So has it been from the beginning, so will it be to the end.
Generation after generation takes to itself the Form of a Body;
and forth-issuing from Cimmerian Night, on Heaven's mission
APPEARS. What Force and Fire is in each he expends: one

grinding in the mill of Industry; one hunter-like climbing the giddy Alpine heights of Science; one madly dashed in pieces on the rocks of Strife, in war with his fellow:—and then the Heaven-sent is recalled; his earthly Vesture falls away, and soon even to sense becomes a vanished Shadow. Thus, like some wild-flaming, wild-thundering train of Heaven's Artillery, does this mysterious MANKIND thunder and flame, in long-drawn, quick-succeeding grandeur, through the unknown Deep. Thus, like a God-created, fire-breathing Spirit-host, we emerge from the Inane; haste storm-fully across the astonished Earth; then plunge again into the Inane. Earth's mountains are levelled, and her seas filled up, in our passage: can the Earth, which is but dead and a vision, resist Spirits which have reality and are alive? On the hardest adamant some footprint of us is stamped-in; the last Rear of the host will read traces of the earliest Van. But whence?—O Heaven, whither? Sense knows not; Faith knows not; only that it is through Mystery to Mystery, from God and to God.

> 'We *are such stuff*
> As dreams are made of, and our little Life
> Is rounded with a sleep!' "

Carlyle's "Natural Supernaturalism" has the presumed merit of ren-dering our lives into so many dramatic poems, but is there any cognitive force in his passionate assertions? Lionel Trilling called Natural Supernat-uralism a new form of belief or "a secular spirituality." It is however an outcropping, as I have indicated, of the most ancient of heresies, Gnosticism. Its one originality surpasses all paradox, because it is a pantheistic gnosis, and every ancient Gnosticism posited an alien God, wholly cut off from our cosmos. Weirdly, Carlyle imports the alien God into nature, while estranging mankind from itself. This rather dubiously gives us just the reverse of Blake's apocalyptic humanism; we become an almost unredeemable entity confront-ing an already more-than-redeemed nature.

Carlyle's later decline is prefigured in his characteristic valorization of nature over what Blake had called "the Human Form Divine." In his pro-found anxiety to overturn the empirical view of the cosmos as a vast machine, Carlyle divinized nature and debased man. It is Carlyle, and not his critic Nietzsche, who is the true forerunner of twentieth-century Fascism, with its mystical exaltation of the state and its obliteration of compassion and the rights of the individual. That shadow cannot be removed from the later Carlyle, author of such efforts as "The Nigger Question" (1849) and "Shooting Niagara: and After?" (1867), and uncritical idolator of those iron men, Oliver Cromwell and Frederick the Great. It is the Carlyle who wrote during the fifteen years from 1828 to 1843 who still matters to us. The author of "Signs of the Times" (1829) and "Characteristics" (1831), of *Sartor Resartus* (completed 1831) and *Past and Present* (1843) remains the sage who fathered Ruskin, inspired Emerson, and stimulated the social prophecy of William Morris. If time has darkened Carlyle, it has shown also that there is a perpetual remnant of value in him, a voice that still rises out of the wilderness.

JOHN HOLLOWAY

The Life of Carlyle's Language

"LIFE-PHILOSOPHY" KNOWLEDGE

In aim if not in method Carlyle is typical of the writers studied in [my book *The Victorian Sage*]. He wants to state, and to clinch, the basic tenets of a "Life-Philosophy," of something that will veritably transform men's outlook. "We shall awaken; and find ourselves in a world greatly widened." "Pray that your eyes be opened that you may see what is before them! The whole world is built, as it were, on Light and Glory." He is writing for "these mean days that have no sacred word"; he envies the preacher his pulpit, and he does so because he feels that his own message has an almost sacred quality. "What am I? What *is* this unfathomable Thing I live in, which men name Universe? What is Life; what is Death? What am I to believe? What am I to do?" Carlyle puts these questions into the mouth of the Young Mahomet; he means to answer them himself.

Insight into "the sacred mystery of the Universe" is not, in Carlyle's view, hard to get. It is the " *'open* secret,'—open to all"; and it is open to all because everyone has the conclusive evidence for it of introspection. "Men at one time read it in their Bible. . . . And if no man could now see it by any Bible, there is written in the heart of every man an authentic copy of it direct from Heaven itself: there, if he have learnt to decipher Heaven's writing . . . every born man may still find some copy of it." In his later books Carlyle tends to call this power of knowledge "conscience"; in the earlier ones Goethe's influence is more prominent, and he discredits clear utterance, rigid argument, and "mere logic" instead. It is at this time that he writes "not our Logical, Mensurative faculty, but our Imaginative one is

From *The Victorian Sage: Studies in Argument.* © 1953 by John Holloway. Macmillan, 1953. Originally entitled "Carlyle."

King over us." But to call this power of knowledge Imagination or Conscience is hardly important, so long as it is steadily contrasted with the knowledge that comes from strict logic and abstract argument.

But this account is an exaggeration. Insight did not come, in Carlyle's opinion, quite so easily. The secret, though "open to all" was "seen by almost none." A man must be of "loyal heart," as he says; and even if he is, "to *know*; to get into the truth of anything, is ever a mystic act," bringing not any facile through-and-through comprehension, but an imperfect glimpse of some basic puzzling truth. "Believe it thou must; understand it thou canst not." Moreover, there must be an initial leap. The effort precedes the insight. Knowledge of God comes from confident belief in him; and if we want to discover what our duties are, we must first actually set our hand to the duty which seems to be the nearest. Whether we are willing to pay this price is no trivial matter. In the search for ultimate truth, the Imagination is one of only two things: "Priest and Prophet to lead us heavenward; or Magician and Wizard to lead us hellward." But if it is allowed to operate correctly it will transform our lives, for the state of illumination, of truly understanding the fundamentals about man and the world, is to ordinary life as waking is to sleeping, or open to closed eyes; and indeed, these contrasts are among Carlyle's favourites.

THE LIVE COSMOS

The philosophy of Carlyle is simple, and it hardly changes all through his life. It is a revolt; or rather, a counter-revolution. In a word, it is *anti-mechanism*. Its main tenets are:

1. the universe is fundamentally not an inert automatism, but the expression or indeed incarnation of a cosmic spiritual life;
2. every single thing in the universe manifests this life, or at least could do so;
3. between the things that do and those that do not there is no intermediate position, but a gap that is infinite;
4. the principle of cosmic life is progressively eliminating from the universe everything alien to it; and man's duty is to further this process, even at the cost of his own happiness.

Such is Carlyle's outlook in brief—regardless of the apparent inconsistencies latent in it at certain points. Its sources do not matter, except that one of them provided him with an invaluable means of expressing this outlook in a really vivid and telling way, expounding what he had to say and simultaneously making it convincing. The doctrine of self-renunciation may recall Carlyle's admiration for Goethe, and the belief that what the senses show of the world is not reality but only appearance recalls Fichte and the German Idealists; but judged as a whole, Carlyle's view of life is enormously indebted to Scottish Calvinism. The omnipotence and omnipresence of God, a universe governed everywhere by relentless necessity, a final division between elect and damned, renunciation of temporal pleasures, and the delusiveness (in a non-philosophical sense) of the shows of the world are Calvin's tenets; and of course they were largely accepted in the England of Carlyle's time, so far as this was nonconformist or evangelical, and have indeed some measure of affinity with Christianity of any and every kind. It was therefore a powerful weapon for Carlyle, to write in a language which is influenced through and through by that of the Authorized Version. This revived a whole world of associations that were deeply rooted in his readers' minds. Even if they had become dissatisfied (as Carlyle was himself) with orthodox Church Christianity, Biblical language might still mean a great deal to them, and its use by Carlyle could attach his outlook to an elaborately developed world view with which his readers would be deeply familiar, and for which they would probably have a deep though perhaps a qualified sympathy. Actually, by using this Biblical language and at the same time often sharply criticizing conventional religion, Carlyle gets the best of both worlds.

The following extract from *Sartor Resartus*, purporting to be the opinions of the mythical Professor Teufelsdröckh, is typical of Carlyle's wildest rhetoric. It will be seen that the specific parallels given from the Authorized Version by no means exhaust the echoes of Biblical style or thought:

There is in man a Higher than Love of Happiness: he can do without
    "Behold, a greater than Solomon is here" (Matt. 12:42)
Happiness, and instead thereof find Blessedness! Was it not
    "thou shalt . . . find the knowledge of God" (Prov. 2:5)
    "that we may . . . find grace" (Heb. 4:16)
to preach-forth this same Higher that Sages and Martyrs, the Poet
"to preach   Jesus Christ" (Acts 5:42)
and the Priest, in all times, have spoken and suffered;
"I will bless the Lord at all   "If I yet preach circumcision, why do
times" (Psa. 34:1)   I yet suffer persecution?" (Gal. 5:11)
bearing testimony, through life and through death, of the Godlike
"bare record . . . of the testimony of Jesus" (Rev. 1: 2; cf. John 8: 17–18).
that is in Man, and how in the Godlike only has he Strength and
"he knew what was in man"   "in the Lord have I righteousness and
(John 2:25)

Freedom? Which God-inspired Doctrine art thou also honoured to be
strength" (Isa. 45:24)
taught; O Heavens! and broken with
"I am broken with their whorish heart" (Ezek. 6:9)
                                                        "in heaviness through
manifold merciful Afflictions, even till thou become contrite, and
manifold temptations" (I Peter 1:6)
"thy manifold mercies" (Neh. 9:19) "even until now" (Gen. 46:34)
"his merciful kindness is great" (Psa. 117:2)
"your manifold transgressions" (Amos 5:12)
learn it! O, thank thy Destiny for these; thankfully bear what
yet remain: thou hadst need of them; the Self in thee needed to be
                    "what things ye have need of" (Matt. 6:8)
annihilated. By benignant fever-paroxysms is Life rooting out the
deep-seated chronic Disease, and triumphs over Death. On the
              "Death is swallowed up in victory" (I Cor. 15:54)
                                                        (cf. Isa. 25:8)
roaring billows of Time, thou art not engulfed, but borne aloft
              "the righteous runneth . . . and is set on high" (Prov. 18:10)
into the azure of Eternity. Love not Pleasure; Love God. This is
              "Lovers of pleasures more than lovers of God"
                                                        (II Tim. 3:4)
the Everlasting Yea, wherein all contradiction is solved: wherein
whoso walks and works, it is well with him.
"whether they will walk   "when it shall be well with thee"
in my law" (Exod. 16:4)   (Gen. 40:14)
"whosoever doeth work therein" (Exod. 35:2)
"ye shall . . . keep mine ordinances, to walk therein" (Lev. 18:3)
        And again: small is it that thou canst trample the Earth with its
"Seemeth it a small thing unto   "the young lion and the dragon
you" (Ezek. 34:18) (cf. Isa. 7:13)   "lest they trample them under
injuries under thy feet, as old Greek Zeno trained thee: thou canst
shalt thou trample under feet" (Psa. 91:13)
their feet" (Matt. 7:6)
love the Earth while it injures thee, and even because it injures thee:
for this a Greater than Zeno was needed, and he too was sent.
"a greater than Solomon" (Matt. 12:42) "them which are sent" (Matt. 23:37)
                            "a messenger was sent" (Ezek. 23:40)
Knowest thou that 'Worship of Sorrow'? The Temple thereof, founded
"Knowest thou not that I have a   "the foundation of the Lord's temple
power to crucify thee?" (John 19:10)   was laid" (Hag. 2:18)
              "A man of Sorrows" (Isa. 53:3)
some eighteen centuries ago, now lies in ruins, overgrown with jungle,

the habitation of doleful creatures: nevertheless, venture forward;
"an habitation of dragons" (Isa. 34:13)
"their houses . . . full of doleful creatures" (Isa. 13:21)
in a low crypt, arched out of falling fragments, thou findest the
Altar still there, and its sacred Lamp perennially burning.
"the fire shall be ever burning upon the altar" (Lev. 6:13)
"the salvation . . . as a lamp that burneth" (Isa. 62:1)
"to cause the lamp to burn always" (Exod. 27:20).

Readers of Goethe or of the German Romantic philosophers will notice other influences at work in this curious stylistic medley. But these are not relevant to the present issue, which is how the texture of Carlyle's writing very often draws unconsciously on the associations and on the whole cosmic outlook of the Bible; and in doing so, of course, it encourages belief in the first of the guiding principles mentioned above, that the universe is not a mechanism but expresses a principle of cosmic life.

But it is important to remember what this principle meant, and upon what part of that meaning Carlyle wanted to insist. The universe was not a mechanism, but it was still governed by law. "I, too, must believe . . . that God . . . does indeed never change; that Nature . . . does move by the most unalterable rules." But they were rules of a distinctive kind, and Carlyle goes on, "What are the Laws of Nature? To me perhaps the rising of one from the dead were no violation of these Laws, but a confirmation; were some far deeper Law, now first penetrated into, and by Spiritual Force, even as the rest have all been, brought to bear on us with its Material Force." "Even as the rest have all been"; this is the crucial phrase. Carlyle wrote for those all too ready, perhaps, to believe that the rules of Nature were unalterable; for him it was of more significance to show that these laws expressed a "Spiritual Force."

At the expense, it must be admitted, of leaving little or no impression of system, there is much in Carlyle's language to suggest this life in the universe. It is possible to distinguish three devices whereby he seeks this effect, and two of these can be discussed quite briefly. First, at the simplest level, is his style: a wild, passionate energy runs through it, disorderly and even chaotic, but leaving an indelible impression of life, force, vitality. The main units of sense and still more of the phrases are brief; punctuation is heavy, expression marks are used in lavish profusion. On the other hand there is little of sustained or close-knit argument demanding concentrated, dispassionate study; the reader is hurried, as if by an all-pervading and irresistible violence, from one problem to another.

Second comes another device, which might be called the dramatization of discussions. Carlyle does not always speak in his own person; his discussion is enlivened by a variety of characters, most fictitious and some not, who interrupt the author, confirm his outlook, defend their own, contradict him, and illustrate the points of view that he wishes to commend or condemn. *Sartor Resartus* is entirely based on this technique: Carlyle merely introduces and comments on the manuscripts of a mythical German Professor Teufelsdröckh, who appears as the real author of the Clothes-Philosophy. Teufelsdröckh comes again in *Past and Present*, this time with "Sauerteig" (of the Pig-Philosophy), and the "Houndsditch Indicator." The same device is employed in the Introduction to *Cromwell's Letters and Speeches*, where the second speaker, "my impatient friend," is anonymous although clearly he is a mouthpiece for Carlyle; and a variety of unidentified speakers, together with "Sauerteig," "Crabbe" of the "Intermittent Reflector," the "Department of Woods and Forests," "John Bull," "Ben Brace," "Gathercoal," and the egregious "M'Crowdy," all do something to diversify the pages of *Latter-Day Pamphlets*. This method tends to be naive and crude, though not without effect. It seems to have grown on Carlyle until he used it for its own sake, but its intrinsic tendency to make the style more varied, violent, surprising, and forceful is indisputable, especially since Carlyle often employed his mythical personages to deliver the wildest passages of rhetoric.

The third feature is Carlyle's use of figurative language. It is probably the most influential of all. In different ways, figurative language operates through both its content and its organization. The importance of its content is easily seen. Time and again Carlyle's images are of some power or force or energy, disorderly perhaps, but passionate, violent, irrepressible. First, the image of fire runs like a bright thread through everything he wrote. Its contribution in this respect is self-evident. "As I rode through the Schwarz-wald, I said to myself: That little fire which glows starlike across the dark-growing moor, where the sooty smith bends over his anvil . . . is it a de-tached, separated speck, cut-off from the whole Universe? Thou fool, that smithy-fire was (primarily) kindled at the sun . . . it is a little . . . nervous centre, in the great vital system of Immensity"; "that fire-development of the Universal Spiritual Electricity . . . Love"; "the Great Man was always as lightning out of Heaven; the rest of men waited for him like fuel, and then they too would flame"; "the blessed glow of Labour . . . is it not as purifying fire?"; "that autograph Letter, it was once all luminous as a burning beacon, every word of it a live coal . . . it was once a piece of the general fire and light of Human Life"; "the age of Miracles had come back! 'Behold the World-Phoenix, in fire-consummation and fire-creation.' " Fire—and light too—becomes almost the permanent context of Carlyle's argument, appearing in the least expected and most trivial places. In *Cromwell*, for example, he even speaks of "editing" documents "by fire," when he simply means destroying those that are useless.

Two other kinds of image acquire this contextual function in varying degrees: those of moving water and of animal life. Sometimes these are fused with images of fire or light; "the inner fountains of life may again begin, like eternal Light-fountains"; "this Planet, I find, is but an inconsiderable sand-grain in the continents of Being . . . that eternal Light-Sea and Flame-Sea." But images of water are frequent alone: "the roaring Billows of Time"; "a life-purpose . . . like an ever-deepening river . . . it runs and flows"; "the undiscovered Sea of Time"; "the Scotch people . . . look into a sea of troubles, shoreless, starless, on which there seems no navigation possible." The different uses to which Carlyle puts the images of *stream* and *ocean* are not relevant at present; both suggest a world that is all power and life, whether clear and purposeful like a stream, or turbulent and confused like a stormy sea.

Perhaps Carlyle's animal imagery also contributes something, by its astonishing frequency and variety. His work is a veritable verbal menagerie: within a mere sixty pages of *Latter-Day Pamphlets*, for example, the ape, wolf, ox, dog, pig, ass, hyena, dragon, serpent, sparrow, python, buzzard, eagle, owl, mouse, horse, mole, rat, beaver, spider, wren and canary all make their appearance in metaphorical uses, many of them several times over. Elsewhere, there are Kilkenny cats, beetles, lions, crows, bees, beagles, boa-constrictors, ostriches, cormorants, camels, lynxes, krakens, hydras, centaurs, chimeras, megatherions, and a multitude of anonymous monsters. The ass chews a thistle, the boa-constrictor wrestles with the lion, the Kilkenny cats are at their legendary occupation, the own screeches, the apes gibber and chatter. Whether his images enlighten us about the good things in the world or the bad, this effect is equally present: everything seems busy with a restless, overwhelming life.

The impression is accentuated: images that do not suggest life and energy by themselves can do so through their sequence. This is conspicuous in the chapter on "Natural Supernaturalism" of *Sartor Resartus*. Here Carlyle's purpose is exactly that now under discussion—to convince his readers that the universe pulsates with life. We are dealing here with a mixture, in fact, of metaphors or comparisons, and simple vivid images: but what they contribute to the book lies partly in what supervenes upon them because they all come so close together. It is their extraordinary sequence which hurries the reader first to the day on which the world was created, then to "Sirius and the Pleiades," then under the sea, then to the planets in their courses, then from the laws of Nature as "celestial hieroglyphics" to the laws of Nature as an "inexhaustible Domestic-Cookery Book," then to the inside of the human body, then to the surface of the earth, the "habitable flowery Earth-rind," then back to the Creation and forward to the Cataclysm, then to "stretch forth my hand and clutch the Sun," then down into Hell, at least by implication ("Orpheus" and "a huge Troglodyte Chasm") and up to Heaven and at last (should we have retained breath enough to follow so far) "like some wild-flaming, wild-thundering train of Heaven's Artillery, does this mysterious MANKIND thunder and flame, in long-drawn, quick-succeeding grandeur, through the unknown Deep . . . like a God-created, fire-breathing Spirit-host, we emerge from the Inane; haste stormfully across the astonished Earth; then plunge again into the Inane. Earth's mountains are levelled, and her seas filled up, in our passage." That seems almost to happen in this passage too. It is the astonished reader who is made to hasten stormfully throughout the Cosmos, and by a well-known process of association to transfer the violence of his journey to the Cosmos through which in imagination he journeys.

THE OCEAN ROLLING ROUND THE ISLET

So much for how Carlyle gives expression to the first principle, that the world is filled with cosmic life. The second was that this spiritual life might be manifested by everything in the universe, however apparently humble it may be. Vivifying this doctrine was a very important part of Carlyle's purpose. Ultimately, like every other writer of his kind, he wants to make the reader see familiar things in a new way, to dwell on and emphasize aspects of them that were overlooked or neglected before. Things are more than the casual eye takes in: the lowest resembles and indeed is in continuity with the highest. Explicit statements of the view are frequent enough in Carlyle. But hints and reminders and particular illustrations pervade his work like an atmosphere, and Carlyle thereby achieves a twin purpose: he spreads the character of those things agreed to be noble or exalted to everything in the universe, and thus he emphatically reinforces our impression that this universe is a giant system moving according to a single pattern.

It is fanciful, perhaps, but not unilluminating, to compare this technique with the form of a *passacaglia* in music. Sooner or later one hears the theme unadorned; but in various modified forms it runs without interruption, the unadorned version audible below. Carlyle approximates to the plain statement in, for example, the words he gives King William Rufus in an attack upon the rigidities of medieval Catholicism: "Behold . . . the world is *wider* than any of us think . . . there are . . . immeasurable Sacrednesses in this that you call . . . Secularity." The variations are numerous: "Sooty Manchester,—it too is built on the infinite Abysses; overspanned by the skyey Firmaments . . . every whit as wonderful . . . as the oldest Salem or Prophetic City." "The Present Time, youngest-born of Eternity, child and heir of all the Past Times with their good and evil." In these the intention and the effect are clear. Greater interest attaches to passages which at first sight seem like nothing more than idyllic descriptive interludes. For example, from *Cromwell's Letters and Speeches*, "Oliver farmed part or whole of these . . . lands . . . past which the river Ouse slumberously rolls . . . his cattle grazed here, his ploughs tilled here"—so far the passage is plain description; but Carlyle continues "the heavenly skies and infernal abysses overarched and underarched him here"; or from the description of the monastery of Edmundsbury in *Past and Present*: "These old St. Edmundsbury walls . . . For twenty generations . . . bells tolled to prayers; and men, of many humours, various thoughts, chanted vespers, matins;—and round the little islet of their life rolled for ever (as round ours still rolls, though we are blind and deaf) the illimitable Ocean, tinting all things with *its* eternal hues and reflexes."

Often, in Carlyle, the lightest touches remind the reader that the world is wider than it seems. For example, he is fond of imagery of green landscapes; and it does not come without its influence. "The green foliage and blossoming fruit-trees of Today . . . the leafy blossoming Present Time"; "Man's life . . . no idle promenade through fragrant orange-groves and green flowery spaces"; "Work is Worship . . . *its* Cathedral . . . coped with the star-galaxies; paved with the green mosaic of land and ocean"; "Chaos is dark . . . let light be, and there is instead a green and flowery world"; "Wisdom . . . rests there, as on its dark foundations does a habitable flowery Earth-rind." Thus a thought of the whole earth and of all the living things that spread over it is worked more intimately still into the texture of the argument. Ultimately, these passages set every immediate and restricted topic in a wider context, in the context of the whole earth, or indeed the whole universe; and they modify the reader's attitude until he tends to think of any small thing as like the grandest and most beautiful and most alive things he knows, and as influenced by them through a direct and genuine continuity. Carlyle's argument is a foreground that is developed against a background; and by sustaining an ever-present sense that this background is grand and awe-inspiring, he is able, without explicit reference, to diffuse our attitude towards it until we have the same attitude towards his immediate subject.

Carlyle's intention in this respect is most clearly seen in his use of the word "miracle." He wishes to say that every existing thing is miraculous;

this indeed is almost his central tenet. "Daily life is girt with Wonder, and based on Wonder, and thy very blankets and breeches are Miracles." What we have been exploring is a device which makes us see things under the influence of those other more portentous things that they are girt with.

SHAMS AND DIABOLISMS

Between the second and the third of Carlyle's central tenets there is perhaps a latent contradiction, for the second explains how everything reflects the cosmic life, and the third how some things in the universe most emphatically lack it. Our problem, however, is not whether he solves this contradiction in logical terms, but how the two parts of it are developed and amplified and made emotionally convincing. And certainly, in pursuing this problem, we discover two contrasting techniques: for the second tenet was conveyed to the reader by devices that hinted at unsuspected affinities, while the third is constantly reinforced through expressions which crystallize a single, pervasive, fundamental dichotomy in the world.

Consider first the plain statement of this dichotomy, and then the direct devices that keep the reader attuned to it. Carlyle praises Dante, for example, because he "felt Good and Evil to be the two polar elements of this Creation, on which it all turns; that these two differ not by *preferability* of one to the other, but by incompatibility absolute and infinite; that the one is excellent and high as light and Heaven, the other hideous, black as Gehenna and the Pit of Hell." Absolute contrasts of this kind attract Carlyle: Revenge is a divine feeling, *but its excess is diabolic*; historical periods differ not merely greatly, *but infinitely*. All good, and all bad things are assimilated: "at bottom the Great Man, as he comes from the hand of Nature, is ever the same kind of thing," while "independence, in all kinds, is rebellion," and untruths are all the Devil's.

This contrast runs sharply through Carlyle's work, because the vocabulary he uses for comment and evaluation tends always to draw upon it. The first quotation from *Heroes and Hero-Worship* above did so by comparing the good to Heaven and Light, the bad to Hell and darkness. The other quotations illustrate Carlyle's use of the contrast between what is divine and what is diabolic, but the contrast between light and dark is perhaps more prominent still. Cromwell's work was for "the Protestant world of struggling light against the Papist world of potent darkness." Elsewhere, Cromwell is as a "luminous body . . . crossing a dark Country, a dark Century"; and— a hint of the same—the intellect of the Younger Vane is "atrabiliar." Carlyle rings many changes, but the guiding principle is simply that there are contrasting extremes and nothing whatever between them. Occasionally he cannot avoid speaking of something good but imperfect; even so he retains the contrast as sharply as he can by employing the usual metaphor in a modified way: perfect religion is like light, imperfect religion (at least in some cases) like "red smoky scorching fire." It can be purified into light, and "Is not Light grander than Fire? It is *the same element* in a state of purity." Thus it is that Carlyle manages to say something of intermediates within a vocabulary that draws the advantages of precluding them.

But the contrast is equally fundamental if made between *true* light and *false* or factitious light. The contrast between the "true" and the "sham" in Carlyle is worked out for light in expressions like "a poor paper-lantern with a candle-end in it," and in the attack on those who believe that "Heroism means gas-lighted Histrionism; that seen with "clear eyes" (as they call Valet-eyes), no man is a Hero." This quotation introduces two new methods employed by Carlyle to emphasize his basic contrast. The "seeing eye" is a frequent alternative for light: "Thor red-bearded, with his blue sun-eyes," and then the contrast is made, for example, in passages like this about Mirabeau: "he has an *eye*, he is a reality; while others are formulas and *eye-glasses*" (alternatives elsewhere to the eye-glass are glass-eyes and spectacles). In view of this, the expressions above, "gas-lighted Histrionism" and "Valet-eyes," are exactly comparable in Carlyle's vocabulary, and they introduce, as two further illustrations of the ultimate contrast, the contrast of real life with acting, and that of master with servant. The first takes many different forms: "Well may the buckram masks start together, terror-struck . . . let whosoever is but buckram and a phantasm look to it"; "considering the Treaty mainly as a piece of Dramaturgy, which must . . . leave a good impression on the Public." The contrast between master and servant is conspicuous in Carlyle's frequent tirades against flunkies and valets and "Valetism, the *reverse* of Heroism"; "England will . . . learn to reverence its Heroes and distinguish them from its Sham-heroes and Valets and gas-lighted Histrios."

Another slash at actors introduces a fresh contrast. Government, says Carlyle, in *Latter-Day Pamphlets*, is "really a heroic work, and cannot be done by histrios, and dexterous talkers having the honour to be"; and many times the contrast of good with bad is likened to that of deed with mere word. "Not a better Talking-Apparatus . . . but an infinitely better Acting-Apparatus" (that is, Doing-Apparatus) is wanted. This explains the innumerable attacks on "cant" and "jargon"; and the tirades against quacks too, for a quack is one who talks of his healing powers but cannot do anything—this is brought out in the words "Sir Jabesh Windbag . . . or what other Cagliostro." The attacks on "dilettantes" serve the same purpose—"unserious Dilettantism . . . grinning with inarticulate incredulous incredible jargon about all things."

The next comparison represents good by the human, and bad by the animal. The type appears in the "dusky potent insatiable animalism" of a "Chartist Notability" (the word "dusky" hints, of course, at the analogy with darkness). It is best illustrated in the analogy between cynics and "Apes . . . *gibbering and chattering* very genuine nonsense . . . they sit . . . with their wizened *smoke*-dried visages . . . looking out through those *blinking smoke-bleared eyes* of theirs, into the wonderfulest universal *smoky Twilight* and undecipherable disordered Dusk of Things." In this passage of intricate rhetoric, the cynic is belittled first by the analogy with the sub-human, and then through the hints of idle chatter, smoke, defective eyes, and darkness. All these metaphors have their established and characteristic function in Carlyle, and here their fusion and interaction is plain.

THE GROWTH OF METAPHOR

Figurative language in Carlyle is so elaborate that a question arises which is really prior to that of its use; for his work displays not merely its use, but its creation. The valet, the eye-glass, the smoke, the buckram mask—these metaphors are scarcely intelligible unless sooner or later they are "cashed," and their significance explained. They are "technical-term" metaphors, effective through other metaphors used prior to them and effective of themselves. But once a connection is made between metaphors that need an introduction and those that need none, the former can vary and amplify the latter. Carlyle uses this method elaborately. He develops a figurative language that becomes more and more esoteric; and the developments do not occur in isolation, but interconnect and sometimes fuse.

Since, of necessity, this has already been a good deal illustrated, it will be enough here to give two examples which display the whole process of image-creation. Consider first how the metaphor of darkness is elaborated. Carlyle asserts that the surviving materials for a life of Cromwell are the "dreariest continent of shot-rubbish the eye ever saw . . . in *lurid twilight* . . . peopled only by *somnabulant* Pedants . . . and doleful creatures . . . by *Nightmares*, pasteboard Norroys, griffins, wiverns and chimeras dire." The sleep-metaphor, as an adjunct to darkness, reappears: "Such darkness, thick sluggish clouds of cowardice . . . thickening as if towards the eternal sleep." What of the griffins and wiverns? They echo another extension of the darkness-metaphor, to be seen in the "thousand-fold wrestle with pythons and mud-demons . . . enormous Megatherions, as were ever born of mud, loom huge and hideous out of the twilight Future" of *Latter-Day Pamphlets*. In this work the same figure is plentiful: "British industrial existence . . . one huge poison-swamp of reeking pestilence . . . communicating with the Nether

Deeps . . . that putrefying well of abominations . . . the universal Stygian quagmire of British industrial life." These passages, besides utilizing the idea that darkness gives rise to monsters, also fuse the metaphor of darkness with that of the swamp, contrast to the fresh flowing stream of healthy life. Later in the same work comes "a dim horn-eyed owl-population." The owl, with these same associations, appears often enough: "a too miserable screech-owl phantasm of talk and struggle" (here "screech-owl" is reminiscent of "darkness" and also "jargon"); "the human Owl, living in his perennial London fog, in his Twilight of all imaginable corrupt exhalations." Already, in an earlier passage, we have been given a hint as to what these exhalations may include: "accumulated owl-droppings and foul guano-mountains," which once more fuses the darkness and the swamp. Sleep, the owl and the swamp, reappear in *Latter-Day Pamphlets*: "twenty-seven millions of my fellow-countrymen, sunk deep in Lethean sleep, with mere owl-dreams of Political Economy . . . in this pacific thrice-infernal slush-element." Thus it becomes clear that the metaphor of darkness is used to *coin* metaphors of sleep, monsters, the owl and the muddy swamp; and through the guano and the mud, owl and swamp share more of each other's qualities than a joint affinity with darkness, and jointly contrast with Carlyle's image of flowing water with its characteristic meaning.

The concept of "silence" also illustrates how Carlyle develops and utilizes a whole interconnected vocabulary of figurative expressions. In one way or another, it serves to amplify each of the three basic tenets discussed so far. It expresses, first, the belief that the universe possesses a mysterious life: "It is fit that we *say* nothing, that we think only in silence; for what words are there! The Age of Miracles past? The Age of Miracles is forever here!—." Second, it reminds us that the universe is vast in space; and by doing so is a symbol that everything, however trivial apparently, has really something of the greatness of those spaces: "The SILENCE of deep Eternities, of Worlds from beyond the morning-stars, does it not speak to thee? . . . the Stars in their never-resting courses, all Space and all Time, proclaim it to thee in continual silent admonition." Sometimes these two ideas are fused: "The divine Skies all silent." Third, silence is an antithesis of speech, and serves in the rich vocabulary that contrasts the sham and the true: "Silence . . . here and there . . . how eloquent in answer to . . . jargon."

This concept re-occurs in expressions like "it is an authentic, altogether quiet fact," or "poor Manchester operatives . . . they put their huge inarticulate question 'What do you mean to do with us?' " or "England in her own big dumb heart." That these are sympathetic descriptions would not be altogether clear, did not Carlyle prepare us for them elsewhere. But the most interesting extension from the concept of silence is Carlyle's occasional use of the word "open." Sometimes he links this with silence directly— "while the world lay yet silent, and the heart true and open"; and sometimes there is an indirect link, through the word "secret": "SILENCE and SECRECY! Altars might still be raised to them"; and "the open secret." Then the concept "open" is used for all the three tasks which "silence" proved to carry out: reminding us, that is, of the world's mysterious life, of its vast extent in space, and of the contrast between real and sham. It recalls (1) the mysterious life of the world in such a phrase as "the sacred mystery of the universe; what Goethe calls " 'the open secret' ". But (2) the secret is open because the mystic force shows itself everywhere throughout the world. "That divine mystery," Carlyle continues, "which lies everywhere in all Beings . . . of which all Appearance, from the starry sky to the grass of the field, but especially the Appearance of Man and his work, is but the *vesture*, the embodiment that renders it visible." Finally (3), the *opened* heart is something true and real, not a sham: "Wholly a blessed time: when jargon might abate, and here and there some genuine speech begin. When to the noble opened heart . . . the difference between . . . true and false, between work and sham-work, between speech and jargon, was once more . . . infinite."

These then, are some of the methods whereby Carlyle preserves, throughout the whole texture of his work, an ultimate and absolute contrast between what in his view is good and what bad. They are methods embedded so deeply and intimately in his language that, so far at least as they are successful, they permanently sustain the attitude that Carlyle desires in the reader. The general effect of this basic contrast is plain enough: it makes Carlyle's philosophy simple, and makes it emphatic. Palliation disappears. The normal judgment to pass on anything is one of outright commendation or censure; qualified judgments, if any, preserve abstract accuracy, but tend to evoke the same attitudes as they would if unqualified.

This irreducible distinction is worked into the texture of Carlyle's argument in another way. Like Newman, Carlyle believes the universe to be a system; but what makes it a system for him must largely be explained through this contrast, since he sees the system of the world as two great movements that spread the good in the world everywhere and annihilate the bad. Thus the third tenet is what gives content to the fourth. Destiny is "Didactic Destiny" and the universe is "a Temple and Hall of Doom"; what destiny teaches being that "a divine message, or eternal regulation of the Universe there verily is, in regard to every conceivable procedure and affair of man: faithfully following this, said procedure or affair will prosper, and have the whole Universe to second it, and carry it, across the fluctuating contradictions, towards a victorious goal; not following this; mistaking this, disregarding this, destruction and wreck are certain for every affair." Certainly, this has its optimistic side. There is an "inevitable necessity . . . in the nature of things" for human progress; "a man is right and invincible . . . while he joins himself to the great deep Law of the World." But there is a pessimistic side too: "no world, or thing here below, ever fell into misery, without having first fallen into folly, into sin against the Supreme Ruler of it, by adopting as a law of conduct what was not a law, but the reverse of one." In one direction or the other, however, the event must turn: "the Highest did of a surety dwell in this Nation . . . leading . . . this Nation heavenward . . . or else the terrible *inverse*." Vice and Virtue have, one as much as the other, their ultimate, uncompromising rewards.

ALBERT J. LaVALLEY

The French Revolution: *Change and Historical Consciousness*

Like *Sartor* [*Resartus*], *The French Revolution* employs the organic metaphor as a background for hope of stability and direction, but it is difficult to detect its presence in the foreground of the book's action. Book One alone seems to promise the emergence of new social vestures and to mark off definite stages of development in Patriotism. In Books Two and Three, with their portrayal of the futilities of Constitutionalism, the internecine quarrels of Patriotism, and the Terror, what has flowered conforms to no traditional organic formulas. Throughout the three volumes, as in *Sartor*, the depiction of dislocation and upheaval, of man's bewilderment in a world from which all the old hierarchy and guideposts have disappeared, is striking. Change appears not so much as organic growth but as disruptive action begetting a new world that is basically characterized by the fluidity of change, the loss of social institutions, and a bewildering complex of multiple and ever-shifting points of view. The picture of Paris struck to fury and demanding arms on the eve of the destruction of the Bastille sets both the problematic tone of wonder, awe, and bewilderment and terror of the new.

> What a Paris, when the darkness fell! A European metropolitan City hurled suddenly forth from its old combinations and arrangements; to crash tumultuously together, seeking new. Use and wont will no longer direct any man; each man, with what of originality he has, must begin thinking; or following those that think. Seven hundred thousand individuals, on the sudden, find

From *Carlyle and the Idea of the Modern: Studies in Carlyle's Prophetic Literature and Its Relation to Blake, Nietzsche, Marx, and Others.* © 1968 by Yale University. Yale University Press, 1968.

> all their old paths, old ways of acting and deciding, vanish from under their feet. And so there go they, with clangour and terror, they know not as yet whether running, swimming, or flying,— headlong into the New Era.

The sense of dislocation and bewilderment belongs not only to the people of Paris but also to the narrator. For Carlyle is also the man of the "new era," the heir of this original act of change and its dislocation of old institutions. His tone of awe and wonder—and even of acceptance—is not the narrow fright of the Revolutionists, however, but an extension of that fright to wider implications. Carlyle is distant in history from the Revolutionists, but only partially, for the new institutions promised by the Revolution have not yet come into being and the same sense of suddenly living without the legitimacy of the old individual and social sanctions still prevails.

Thus, the conclusion of the above description—dashes followed by a swift summing up ("—headlong into the New Era")—conveys no finality of resolution. A frequent technique in the narrative, this device points to Carlyle's superior view of the action, a view possible only with a separation in time. As always, however, the intended resolution is a highly qualified and ironic one, devoid of complete fulfillment in action or omniscience on Carlyle's part. The new era is itself characterized by all that goes before it, a bewilderment about direction and movement, the giddy sense of a headlong plunge. These qualities are as important as the element of finality contained in the words "new" and "era."

Carlyle's awareness of the testament of giant social change, of multiplicity and complexity in individuals and society, casts its spell over the three volumes. This awareness more than any other factor contributes the problematic tone of the history, its strange mixture of hope and futility, wonder and bewilderment, excitement and pity. Far more than his reservations about the questions of belief and the madness of the unconscious energies, the problem of change tempers the enthusiasm of his commitments. Carlyle not only sees what a long battle awaits the Revolutionists; but also envisions his own role as their successor in the nineteenth century and man's similar pitiable plight under industrialism. It is the problem of change, in the Revolutionary past and in the world of the 1830s in England, which gives the book its peculiar urgency, wildness, and vibrancy, the manifestation of Carlyle's own deep involvement. For him the book was a private revolution, a "calcination" as he later said, a descent into hell, the difficult measuring of the personal cost of change and of commitment to the new era.

The complexity of change makes Carlyle impatient with his own fixed theories about the Revolution. Disdaining any simple structure for his book, he utilizes a shifting "point of vision," which "seeking light from all possible sources . . . whithersoever vision or glimpse of vision can be had" may solve his problem in "some tolerably approximate way." As in *Sartor*, theories and fixed structure dissolve, to be replaced by randomness, prodigality, and variety. Now Carlyle is with one group of forces, now with another, throwing his readers suddenly against individuals pitted against other individuals, then just as suddenly against whole groups. At one moment he is within his characters, listening to their turbulent thoughts; at another he is watching them from a relatively changeless position, yet only emphasizing thereby the violent change of the Revolution. The sudden emphasis on ticking clocks that go about their normal task as the Bastille falls and on an empty Versailles underscores the thematic use of this device of focus. Characters who appear as patriots in Book One are led to the guillotine in Book Three, so that within the book the process of change is madly accelerated. And each procession of Louis through Paris is contrasted with its predecessor, the shortness of time between them carefully noted.

But nowhere is the problem of change so visible as in the marked peculiarities of the style. Whereas *Sartor* used the Clothes Philosophy to dislocate conventional vision and gain a flexibility of insight and a new way of approaching reality, *The French Revolution* relies far more strongly on its own special style. Narrative moments are rendered with a pell-mell haste, incident rolling upon incident all in the present tense. The exclamation points and question marks that dot the text create excitement and bewilderment in the immediacy of terrifying and complex situations. Sentences start, suddenly stop, or turn back on themselves, are contradicted, and frequently end with a Carlylean irony that underscores the limits of control and heightens the grim force of the Revolution. For instance, "Loménie has removed the evil, then? Not at all: not so much as the symptom of the evil; scarcely the *twelfth* part of the symptom, and exasperated the other eleven!"; or, "Your Revolution, like jelly, sufficiently *boiled*, needs only to be poured into *shapes*, of Constitution, and 'consolidated' therein? Could it, indeed, contrive to *cool*; which last, however, is precisely the doubtful thing, or even the not doubtful!" Action is subjected to a grimly ironic voice, questioned, and shown as limited and finally futile in the face of revolutionary power. With further irony, the limited human action itself participates in a dialectic, goading the revolutionary powers onward.

As the sentences turn about and new qualities of voice are brought to bear on the material, the reader's own judgments are manipulated and he becomes a bewildered participant in and onlooker at a complex phenomenon. A single paragraph of the narrative may carry him from deep involvement to the most remote of detached viewpoints, from a single individual to a

large group and thence to indifferent nature. In a tumultuous world, he is
left without a resting place and no viewpoint is intended to be final. For
instance, when Lafayette harangues a mob that insists on marching to Versailles and demanding bread, thus upsetting the slower workings of the new
government, even the epic "Scipio-Americanus" bestowed on him provides
no stability but is itself coated with irony.

> The great Scipio-Americanus can do nothing; not so much as
> escape. "*Morbleu, mon Général*," cry the Grenadiers serrying their
> ranks as the white charger makes a motion that way, "you will
> not leave us, you will abide with us!" A perilous juncture: Mayor
> Bailly and the Municipals sit quaking within doors; my General
> is prisoner without; the Place de Grève, with its thirty-thousand
> Regulars, its whole irregular Saint-Antoine and Saint-Marceau,
> is one minatory mass of clear or rusty steel; all hearts set, with
> a moody fixedness, on one object. Moody, fixed are all hearts:
> tranquil is no heart,—if it be not that of the white charger, who
> paws there, with arched neck, composedly champing his bit, as
> if no World, with its Dynasties and Eras, were now rushing
> down. The drizzly day bends westward; the cry is still: "To
> Versailles!"

At other times, the action can suddenly turn into its opposite within the
space of a single sentence. At the reception of Louison Chabray, who has
petitioned the king of behalf on the Menadic women and has been assured
that "grains shall circulate free as air . . . and nothing be left wrong which
a Restorer of French Liberty can right," she gives the news with joy; then
we are moved rapidly to the moment-by-moment workings of the mob:

> Good news these; but to wet Menads, all-too incredible! There
> seems no proof, then? *Words* of comfort,—they are words only;
> which will feed nothing. O miserable People, betrayed by Aris-
> tocrats, who corrupt thy very messengers! In his royal arms,
> Mademoiselle Louison? In his arms? Thou shameless minx, wor-
> thy of a name—that shall be nameless! Yes, thy skin is soft, ours
> is rough with hardship; and well wetted, waiting here in the rain.

The broken sentences express each moment of perception and the growth
of doubt as it changes to anger and finally to violent antagonism, fury, and
the assertion of power and genuine grievances. Louison is suddenly hauled
off "to the lanterne," but just as suddenly saved by two bodyguards of
royalty.

Yet the book as a whole is not, as I have repeatedly stressed, merely a chaotic whirlwind of endlessly reversing actions, for behind these scenes can be sensed an inevitability and power in the revolutionary forces and a growing assurance of victory in their conflicts with royalty. The declaration of freedom, the power of belief, and the trust in unconscious energies all act as a check to disintegration and flux and afford some stability as a central dynamic. Furthermore, the language of change is used not only to give the moment-by-moment turbulence of the revolutionary drama, but also to come to grips with the very variety of the Revolution and thereby to afford some measure of control and some understanding of the problem of change itself.

Carlyle believes in the powers of the Revolution and their ultimate triumph and destiny, yet he knows that these powers are themselves clouded with the problems of change, the sense of complexity involved in living with the inheritance of the Revolution, its bequest of limitless freedom and awesome multiplicity. Carlyle's variety of viewpoint is intended both to ride the whirlwind and to be encyclopedic, to come to grips with the fullness of revolutionary action, to understand not only how each individual felt at the moment of action but also to provide as much of an assessment and judgment of that action as is possible and to relate it to the central dynamic. The elliptical nature of the style, its sheer density, and the irony and "partial" nature of the more auctorial voice point to this complex inheritance of change, to the immense difficulty of living close to individual passion as a guide without the easier categories and guideposts of the past. Change renders fact itself complex and makes doubly difficult man's attempt to detect its meaning and to embrace it in a realistic historical consciousness.

> And now . . . when History, ceasing to shriek, would try rather to include under her old Forms of speech or speculation this new amazing Thing; that so some accredited scientific Law of Nature might suffice for the unexpected Product of Nature, and History might get to speak of it articulately, and draw inferences and profit from it; in this new stage, History, we must say, babbles and flounders perhaps in a still painfuller manner. . . .
>
> But what if History were to admit, for once, that all the Names and Theorems known to her fall short? That this grand Product of Nature was even grand, and new, in that it came not to range itself under old recorded Laws of Nature at all, but to disclose new ones? In that case, History, renouncing the pretension to *name* it at present, will *look* honestly at it, and name what she can of it!

Even the language of "Nature," with its "Laws," "Problems," and "Theorems," seems to disintegrate under the problem of change and the historically new, leaving Carlyle without a vocabulary. His overall view of the Revolution and its inheritance as a giant change in individual and social consciousness provides no resolution of problems, but only their full recognition.

The problem of change must be viewed in the context of Carlyle's literary intentions. He certainly intended to write an epic for the modern age, one that would be both ultimate and full in its recognition of man's deepest drives but would also be different from all previous epics, unresolved and problematic, like the process of history itself. The resemblance of *The French Revolution* to traditional epic is overt, and Carlyle underscores this quality by the frequency of his allusions to the epics of Homer, Virgil, Milton, and Dante and by his highly conscious imitation of their epic devices. It is part of his intention that all the traditional purposes of the old epic shall be subsumed into the new, and he appropriates and imitates epic devices to give to his drama the range, depth, scope, and importance of the great masterpieces.

The frequency of these devices is surprising, because in general *The French Revolution* gives a strong impression of artlessness and direct action, with little indication of literary imitation or the conscious epic manner of Virgil or Milton. Yet there are a number of direct quotations from Homer and Dante in the original languages: geographical allusions to exotic places extend the range of the action much as they do in Milton (Louis' Acapulco ship, the Sahara sand waltz); many of the characters are given heroic epithets or phrases (the sea green, incorruptible Robespierre; brawny Titan Danton; Lafayette, the Hero of Two Worlds); the leaders are likened to gods or heroic figures from Greek mythology (Mirabeau as Hercules, Danton as Atlas); and their haranguing of the multitudes is often deliberately modeled and placed in the manner of the heroic speeches of *The Iliad* and *Paradise Lost*.

There is even the familiar tripartite world of epic with royalty and nobility acting the role of Olympian gods and Versailles as Mt. Ida overlooking the Troy town of Paris. Beneath human society are the Titans, Furies, Eumenides, bacchantes, Menads, Megaeras, and other figures of primitive myth; finally there is a spectral underworld, a kingdom of Dis with its watchdog of Erebus, and Book Three reenacts the traditional epic visit to the underworld: "O fuliginous confused Kingdom of Dis, with thy Tantalus-Ixion toils." Around the universe there is the traditional threat of chaos, of Cimmerian Night in the massed armies of Brunswick and the European powers; deep within there is the figure of Chaos and Old Night in the figure of sooty, blear-eyed Marat. Lastly, there is even "epical machinery" for a scientific age, preternatural states of mind that grip men and whirl them out of control and which Carlyle significantly—as though anticipating the Cambridge classicists—links to the role of godlike forces in the traditional epic.

> May we not predict that a people, with such a width of Credulity and of Incredulity (the proper union of which makes Suspicion, and indeed unreason generally), will see Shapes enough of Immortals fighting in its battle-ranks, and never want for Epical Machinery?

In even broader terms, the expansiveness and the very subject matter of *The French Revolution* also seem modeled on epic. What Thomas Greene says in his chapter "The Norms of Epic" seems true of Carlyle's work:

> The subject of all epic poetry might thus be said to be politics, but a politics not limited to society, a politics embracing the natural and fabulous worlds, embracing even the moral or spiritual worlds they sometimes shadow forth, and involving ultimately the divine. The implications expand to suggest, if not frankly to assert, a cosmic power struggle.

Even though Carlyle uses these parallels and associations to reinforce the weight of his story, he is fundamentally interested in the enormous difference between his book and all previous epics. The parallels exist fundamentally to point out that difference. For instance, the epical machinery is intended to surpass its classical counterpart in the sweeping power of its action. Suspicion is no longer an abstraction with a capital letter, but a genuine force generated by men, seizing them and pitching them into revolutionary terror. Carlyle makes it clear that there is no room for supernatural action in his epic of man and his history. For Carlyle and his age, "True History is the only possible Epic," and even the changing of the gods into metaphors and their attendant armies into human passions will not, Carlyle affirms, lessen its power. Instead, his universe unquestionably seems more of one piece than that of previous epics; from the lowest to the highest action, there is one human force, now appearing in individuals, now in giant masses of men. Carlyle's upper and nether worlds become a part of man's passions, and even when man seems to be the victim of forces beyond his control, he is still a participant in a distinctly human universe. With his preternatural machinery of passions and his metaphors of subterranean powers and Olympian gods, Carlyle achieves a universe that is modern in the implications of the rich interrelationships it manifests.

Not only do the devices and their uses differ from traditional epic; so also does Carlyle's fundamental purpose. His epic for moderns is also a heightened version of mock-epic, a true epic-in-reverse, in which the Titans war upon the Olympian gods and dethrone them forever. The Titanic forces of Patriotism have the real power, energy, and drive toward freedom, and the Olympian court of Louis is but a false mockery of that power: "It was the Titans warring with Olympus; and they, scarcely crediting it, have *conquered*; prodigy of prodigies; delirious—as it could not but be." Versailles may think it is still directing the country, but the gods within it are upon a "cloudy Ida." Carlyle pictures Louis' court in a language of soft surfaces, diffuse sentimentalism, and frivolous activity. Where real activities are concerned, an air of futile remedial measures—a parade of finance ministers— prevails without any attempt to answer new problems, reform existing institutions, or recognize the threat of revolution. Versailles is a playland, as Olympus sometimes is in *The Iliad*, but there is no Jove to give it any power when power is necessary. Carlyle calls its rule an age of paper, underscoring both its spiritual insubstantiality and its poor economic policies. Its fittest emblem is Montgolfier's balloon, symbol of silly diversions, light-headedness, emptiness, and the possibility of a quick descent. The real power is in the Titanic rising of the city of Paris: "Alas, it is no Montgolfier rising there today; but Drudgery, Rascality, and the Suburb that is rising!"

In the face of this uprising, the Olympian gods are ineffectual. Usher de Brézé, who displaces the third Estate from its meeting hall by improvised construction work, is an ineffectual Mercury, for the Third Estate meets in the tennis court of the king and utters the famous oath. De Broglie is an equally ineffectual Mars, since after he fails to deliver the whiff of grapeshot that will put the patriots down, the Bastille is soon conquered. Carlyle's Olympian gods have no connection with nature or man's elemental powers or needs; it is the Titans, man in the mass, who carry for mankind the hope of freedom and the recognition of needs, even if violence and revolution are the necessary prelude to that end. Carlyle reverses the original victory of the Olympians over the Titans, not merely as an isolated metaphor but as a statement of the general significance of his epic structure: the inversion of all previous epics and the complete overturning of society, a grounding of society in its primitive basis of nature and fact, and the promise of a new social order that will recognize that grounding.

The ancient quality of the myth, its very pre-civilized "feel," enhances the sense of a return to a primitive ground that is ultimate and all-powerful. Carlyle wants his readers to feel that the Revolution, though an overturning of venerable Olympian institutions, is nevertheless a final and true destructive act. Like the Titans, it is filled with mad furies and strengths but also in touch with the ultimate forces behind man and the universe. The myth of the Titans and the Olympians is used as a metaphor but, in the rich significance of its reversal, it permeates both the structure and content of the book.

Thus the new epic provides an overarching structure embracing the drive toward freedom and national ideals, the released force of unconscious energies, and a world in dislocation and transition. Like them, it is both ultimate and problematic.

The new epic, though an anti-epic, is marked by finality; at last, society has been returned to its foundations in nature, and the new society emerging promises to be consonant with man's economic and instinctual necessities. Homer, the very Father of Epics, is unseated, for the taking of the Bastille makes the taking of Troy town seem as "gossamer." The new epic appropriates the finality of archetypal and religious language: the Menads, petitioning for bread, are simply "Maternity" or "Judiths" and "Eve's Daughters"; the taking of the Bastille, while diminishing the taking of Troy, is more like the miraculous overturning of the city of Jericho; the Procession of the Estates-General is "the baptism day of Democracy"; the Revolution has its own Night of Pentecost when it abolishes Feudalism and its privileges; the age of miracles returns; and the drive to freedom is like a Sinai vision. The strong use of such religious terms seems to suggest that for Carlyle the Revolution does not merely reincarnate ancient biblical goals, but actually establishes a new religion for a new era. If at first Carlyle associates some of these terms with Rousseau's gospel, as he does the Night of Pentecost, the phrase soon leaps into an independence, when reiterated, that secures for it a biblical basis of comparison and ultimately the supersession of the original event.

The new epic overturns or overshadows all previous epics not only in its finality and the truth of its social reversal but also by its problematic quality. The new epic powers working their way to victory threaten to go awry in their fierceness, for no simple and coherent social expression of them is available. Once unleashed, they threaten to blaze into madness.

> O mad Sansculottism, hast thou risen, in thy mad darkness, in thy soot and rags; unexpectedly, like an Enceladus, living-buried, from under his Trinacria? They that would make grass be eaten do now eat grass, in *this* manner? After long dumb-groaning generations, has the turn suddenly become thine?

Similarly, when Lafayette, who sides with the grievances of the Third Estate, tries to act as a force of moderatism, he is helpless. His traditionally epic appearance on a white charger and his epithet "Hero of Two Worlds" reflect an epic nostalgia that underscores his outmodedness.

> Hitherto, in all tempests, Lafayette, like some divine Sea-ruler, raises his serene head: the upper Aeolus blasts fly back to their caves, like foolish unbidden winds: the under sea-billows they had vexed into froth allay themselves. But if, as we often write, the *sub*marine Titanic Fire-powers came into play, the Ocean-bed from beneath being *burst?* If they hurled Poseidon Lafayette and his Constitution out of Space; and in the Titanic melly, sea were mixed with sky?

Carlyle's epic by its very subject matter and its reversal must accommodate itself to the threats of anarchy, chaos, destruction, and the end of Universal History. By choosing and then reversing the Titan myth, Carlyle seeks both a new finality and a new problematic.

Carlyle seems to draw on an analogy to Pope's *Dunciad* to reinforce these aspects. Like Pope, he acknowledges the terrible power of the threat and the inevitable strength embodied in the "dunces" as they blot out all learning and civilization, but, unlike Pope, he welcomes the overturning; his dunces are oppressed men, kept in ignorance and hunger, who are now asserting their natural might. The awkward gambolings of the giant Sansculottism bear not only a mock-epic quality when compared with Homer but also a strong resemblance to the comic and threatening picture of the dunces in Pope's mock-epic vision. Rascality pitched from the royal horses "amid peals of laughter" and a senate of Menadic women passing enactments reverse Homer and confirm the threat of the mock-epic *Dunciad*. "Thus they, chewing tough sausages, discussing the Penal Code, make night hideous."

Even his heroes possess none of the formal dignity associated with the high style of the traditional epic; they are rude, crude, filled with turbulent energy, not masters of the full scope of the action but only pitches of power in a whirlwind. In Book Three the reversal seems most frightening and complete: with the wild kingdom of Dis, the universal power, the nation is plunged into a saturnalia, a mad carmagnole dance, a Sahara waltz that seems destructive not only of the old order but of all order. A whole nation is stripped naked; Sansculottism seems to have become a term ready-made for the Clothes Philosopher as it acts out its logical destiny into nakedness.

Yet neither the work nor the world is ever completely out of control. A new epic voice comes to the fore to meet both the finality of the new powers and their unprecedented problems.

> The "destructive wrath" of Sansculottism: this is what we speak, having unhappily no voice for singing. . . . Surely a great Phe-nomenon: nay it is a *transcendental* one, overstepping all rules and experience; the crowning Phenomenon of our Modern Time.

The voice cannot sing because the possibility of ancient epic has gone. All triumph is now tinged with a measure of futility and bewilderment, for the new social power is not yet realized. No single high style is possible, since the epic artist cannot be detached from his work when he is so deeply involved in the very historical forces set in motion by his actors. To judge these actors is difficult—except by outmoded Puritan categories—for truth is complex and relative in the world of historical fact and human passion. Stable moral and social categories dissolve, and there seems to be no single language, only a shifting vision, which can recognize with adequacy the mixed quality of the Revolution: "Transcendent things of all sorts, as in the general outburst of multitudinous Passion, are huddled together; the ludicrous, nay the ridiculous, with the horrible."

An epic of fact will of necessity be rough-edged like fact itself. The artist must "speak" to accommodate himself best to the variety of fact. Each event admits of many influences, perspectives, and interpretations; each person is a swarm of passions that can scarcely be disentangled. How then can any individual or single event be judged? The new artist will not preserve true epic distance, measuring his characters against fixed goals and standards, but, instead, will identify with the very thought processes of characters and the moment-by-moment action of the historical drama, judging as best he can, seeking what distance is possible, and remembering his trust in man's powers, his drive toward freedom, and the need for change and revolution. The new epic voice is not one of noble austerity but one of questioning and bewilderment; loyal to its trusts and not abandoning hope, it is nevertheless an ironic mixture of pity and futility.

More than anything else in the book, Carlyle's treatment of constitutional assemblies and feasts underscores this irony. As matters of traditional epic, important in the foundation of the new social order, they are in Carlyle signs of men's folly, their undue hopes of triumph, their overly early abandonment of the complexity of fact and the multiplicity of the new era. Carlyle has little use for the making of the Constitution, though inevitably it must provide a center of the drama since the major revolutionary actors are drawn to it. But for Carlyle it formulates paper theorems out of touch with the real mights of men; the real drama is in the countless complex influences bearing down upon each representative.

The famed gathering on the Champ de Mars with all Paris digging in preparation for the feast merits regard as a kind of symbolism, and Carlyle seems to welcome both the activity and the confounding of class distinctions. Yet, though his language offers encouragement, it becomes clear that he is less than enthusiastic. The actual feast on the Champ de Mars is just another human theatricality, a paper celebration akin to the actions of nobility: "In comparison with unpremediated outbursts of Nature, such as an Insurrection of Women, how foisonless, unedifying, undelightful; like small ale palled, like an effervescence that has effervesced!" His irony increases as he watches two hundred individuals in white albs with "Benjamin Franklin" rods and Talleyrand at their head trying to bring heaven's blessing on the new order; finally he treats with evident satiric relish the sudden rainstorm that droops the General's sash, the flags, the ostrich feathers of fashion and the goddess of Beauty herself. Part of his attitude no doubt stems from his Puritan background, a fear of blasphemy and hatred of ceremony and superstition; but the irony is more strongly justified contextually as a check on men who want finality without the attendant complexity and suffering. He soon goes on to treat, almost as a dialectical outgrowth of the Feast of Pikes, the rebellion at Nanci, "the unsightly *wrong-side* of that thrice glorious Feast of Pikes." The voice of irony is the voice of realism and admits no incident as final and totally affirmative. Far beyond his actors, Carlyle sees the complex interweavings of the Revolution in space and time.

Yet, however limited the revolutionary figures are, they are never treated with sharp satire or an irony that is merely destructive. A mild benevolent irony, tinged with pity, encompasses all human action. Anarcharsis Clootz is, for instance, a ridiculous figure, trailed by representatives of all nations taking their oath to mankind, but ultimately he is more pathetic and silly than opportunistic, and he is certainly not malign. The author's voice clearly judges his folly, but its generality adds a note of pity and even self-reflection.

> Whereby at least we may judge of one thing; what a humour the once sniffing mocking City of Paris and Baron Clootz had got into; when such an exhibition could appear a propriety, next door to a sublimity . . . But so it is; and truly as strange things may happen when a whole People goes mumming and miming.

Robespierre is also ironically treated as a narrow fanatic steeped in vinegar and self-righteousness, the very parody of the Puritan formalist, and his Feast of the Supreme Being is, by comparison with that of the Champ de Mars, futile and silly: a Mahomet Robespierre, "powdered to perfection," setting his torch to "Atheism and Company, which are but made of pasteboard steeped in turpentine" and watching his "Statue of Wisdom" arise by machinery "besmoked a little." Afterwards he is shown with his delusions of grandeur, nursing the hope of being the Christ of the Second Coming that an aged crone claims he is. Carlyle's judgment is succinct: "Mumbo is Mumbo, and Robespierre is his Prophet."

Yet Robespierre emerges neither as fool nor villain; in Carlyle's fully rounded view he is both pathetic and threatening. Though he is the most fanatical and frightening figure in *The French Revolution*, Carlyle's voice, ironically placing him against actors and action, succeeds surprisingly in encompassing him with humanity.

Furthermore, by gently satirizing these feasts and triumphs as part of a mock-epic pattern, Carlyle draws attention to the true action of the Revolution and its complexity. As millennial hopes are shattered, more realistic ones, based on a conscious assessment of real powers, emerge. Carlyle's humor brings him back to reality and introduces that very flexibility and pity which he demanded of it in his essay on Richter. The sudden vision of the Goddess of Reason in her kitchen after her crowning in Notre Dame restores an essential humanity to the revolutionary scene and reinforces the true realism of the central drama.

> But there is one thing we should like almost better to understand than any other: what Reason herself thought of it all the while. What articulate words poor Mrs. Momoro, for example, uttered; when she had become ungoddessed again, and the Bibliopolist and she sat quiet at home, at supper? For he was an earnest man, Bookseller Momoro; and had notions of Agrarian Law. Mrs. Momoro, it is admitted, made one of the best Goddesses of Reason; though her teeth were a little defective.

Like his treatment of feasts and worshippers, Carlyle's handling of his heroes also reinforces the realistic and anti-epic nature of his narrative. Nowhere, in fact, does *The French Revolution* show such a distinct difference from traditional epic than in its refusal to offer a heroic focus for the political action. Though both Mirabeau and Danton, with their Titanic energies and grim, crude powers, seem to offer possibilities of a new and natural epic hero—and obviously prelude Carlyle's later fascination with heroes in *On Heroes and Hero Worship* and the histories of Cromwell and Frederick—they never stand at the center of the action for more than a few pages. They exercise scarcely any real control over the action, achieve only a minimum of their objectives, and are finally thrown down, not by enemies, but by the very forces with which they are working.

Mirabeau alone seems to bear the closest resemblance to a figure of traditional epic heroism, but his trust in his own individual powers is precisely that which gives him a certain epic outmodedness, makes him fail to be really at one with the masses, and is ultimately the cause of his destruction. The forces set in motion by the Revolution are simply too powerful for one man's will. His attempt to meet with Marie Antoinette, who for Carlyle is royalty's most decisive and heroic figure, is fraught with epic possibilities; a new synthesis of powers seems to be emerging as the result of Mirabeau's heroic individual action. The scene is one of the most exciting and memorable in Book Two, promising a whole different history of France and of the world. But no single individual can shoulder such burdens in the new age; Mirabeau is exhausted by his efforts and dies.

> The fierce wear and tear of such an existence has wasted out the giant oaken strength of Mirabeau. A fret and fever that keeps heart and brain on fire; excess of effort, of excitement; excess of all kinds: labor incessant, almost beyond credibility!

> This brother man, if not Epic for us, is Tragic; if not great, is large, large in his qualities, world-large in his destinies.

Mirabeau's attempt to save both monarchy and republic is later interpreted as a royalist plot and leads to his subsequent defamation and removal from the Pantheon of Heroes which ironically he was the first to inhabit. The meeting with Marie Antoinette which seemed so full of heroic daring and individual hopes now pales before the grim inevitability of the Revolution. Granted the power of the Revolution and royalty's tenacity in its refusal to change, one is left wondering what possible epic result could have issued from Mirabeau's action.

Danton has even fewer moments of greatness than Mirabeau, though he is described as a man of "wider gulp" and appears far more fierce in his energies. But his powerful voice, which mobilizes the citizens into their death-defiant plunge against the European powers, is no help when pitted against Robespierre's paltry accusations. Danton is destroyed by his own companions in the Revolution and is led to the guillotine. Furthermore, his generalized message "*to dare, to dare*" lacks the specificity, individuality, and concreteness of real heroic action. His demand is for a subordination of the individual to the headlong plunge of revolutionary action against European enemies—in short, to a kind of fanaticism. Carlyle's preface to the fiery activity of Book Three hovers over all the heroic actions it chronicles, depriving them of a sense of full individuation and giving them a collective dimension.

> For a man, once committed headlong to republican or any other Transcendentalism, and fighting and fanaticising amid a Nation of his like, becomes as it were enveloped in an ambient atmosphere of Transcendentalism and Delirium: his individual self is lost in

something that is not himself, but foreign though inseparable
from him . . . It is a wonderful, tragic predicament . . . Volition
bursts forth involuntary-voluntary; rapt along; the movement
of free human minds becomes a raging tornado of fatalism, blind
as the winds; and Mountain and Gironde, when they recover
themselves, are alike astounded to see *where* it has flung and dropt
them.

The real moments of individualism and heroism that do occur, more
tragic than epic, are the scaffold gestures of bewildered figures, ranging from
revolutionists to royalty, and these provide the human drama of Book Three.
Marie Antoinette, Danton, Charlotte Corday, King Louis, Madame Roland,
and a host of others demonstrate the courage of equanimity, a refusal to
despair, and an assertion of their individual personalities at the guillotine.
Before forces that seem inevitable and beyond their control, they manage to
keep their essential selfhood inviolable. Robespierre's piercing scream as the
bandages are pulled from his wounded jaw contrasts sharply with the equanimity of the other figures at the guillotine, placing them in a heroic light
and shedding its own note of hysteria and horror over the previous actions
of the Terror.

A world without heroes in control is an uncomfortable one—and one
that Carlyle was unable to tolerate for long—but this is the legacy of the
Revolution. The old carefully structured world, with its hierarchy of val-
uations, allowed for individual heroism of a high kind, but in the new world,
with its complexity of forces, the threats to a minimal definition of personality
are immense.

Book Three also underscores, more than the preceding volumes, the
final problematic nature of any epic realization. At the very moment when
Sansculottism is locked in death-grips with the European powers and proving
its innate strength ("There is an Unconquerable in man, when he stands on
his Rights of Man," it also releases its deepest difficulties. The second stage
of the Revolution, once the king has been killed and some minimal gains
have been made, is a stage of violence, terror, and fanaticism, disruptive of
all possibilities of order and positive moral significance.

To believe in the drive of the Revolution, Carlyle must justify—or at
least make some attempt to understand—the frightful actions of the Terror.
He must deal with the butcherings of the Septemberers

a name of some note and lucency,—but lucency of the Nether-
fire sort; very different from that of our Bastille Heroes, who
shone, disputable by no Friend of Freedom, as in Heavenly light-

radiance: to such phasis of the business have we advanced since
then!

He must tell the story of massacres, drownings of humans in packed ships,
fusilladings, the making of wigs from the dead, and finally the tanning of
human skins. He must deal with the revolutionists' quarrels with themselves
and their own group feuds, with Jacobinism turning against the Gironde,
and, finally, with the Revolution devouring its own.

Granted these difficulties, Carlyle succeeds admirably. He avoids both
the Scylla of voicing horror and outrage at the Terror and the equally
dangerous Charybdis of excusing every action. He admits that the Terror
was indeed terrible but sees that it cannot be shrieked away; "it is painful
to look on; and yet which cannot, and indeed which should not, be forgotten."
The Terror is at the heart of the Revolution, a testimony to its ultimate
power and a warning to future history—especially to Carlyle's England—
that no government will be tolerated that does not recognize the needs of
millions who suffer from hunger and oppression.

> Yet our Life is not a Lie; yet our Hunger and Misery is not a
> Lie! Behold we lift up, one and all, our Twenty-five million right
> hands; and take the Heavens, and the Earth and also the Pit of
> Tophet to witness, that either ye shall be abolished or else we
> shall be abolished!
>
> No inconsiderable Oath, truly; forming, as has been often said,
> the most remarkable transaction in these last thousand years.
> Wherefrom likewise there follow, and will follow, results. The
> fulfillment of the Oath; that is to say, the black desperate battle
> of Men against their whole Condition and Environment . . . :
> this is the Reign of Terror. Transcendental despair was the pur-
> port of it, though not consciously so. False hopes, of Fraternity,
> Political Millenium, and what not, we have always seen: but the
> unseen heart of the whole, the transcendental despair, was not
> false; neither has it been of no effect. Despair, pushed far enough,
> completes the circle, so to speak; and becomes a kind of genuine
> productive hope again.

The Terror must be measured by its circumstances, its relation to
revolutionary hopes, the psychology of the people who lived through it, and
its ultimate implications of hope for other ages. Carlyle abandons all rigorous
moral categories and brings to the Terror a flexibility of judgment that places
it in various lights without abandoning its centrality in the Revolution.

His first act, as always, is to look and see rather than to theorize and judge. The primary act of sympathy, the realization that these were men fighting against an unjust condition, makes much that might seem inhuman human.

> One thing therefore History will do: pity them all; for it went hard with them all. Not even the sea-green Incorruptible but shall have some pity, some human love, though it takes an effort. And now, so much one thoroughly attained, the rest will become easier. To the eye of equal brotherly pity, innumerable perversions dissipate themselves; exaggerations and execrations fall off, of their own accord. Standing wistfully on the safe shore, we will look, and see, what is of interest to us, what is adapted to us.

The pity will not only embrace Louis and Robespierre; but will also attempt to understand what it was like to live in fear, suspicion, and want. From the perspective of Carlyle's time, the killing of the king may seem a cruel and unnecessary act, but by making the situation of the revolutionists come alive with their fear, Carlyle places the act in a totally different light.

> But, on the whole, we will remark here that this business of Louis looks altogether different now, as seen over Seas at the distance of forty-four years, from what it looked then, in France, and struggling confused all round one . . . For observe, always one most important element is surreptitiously (we not noticing it) withdrawn from the Past Time: the haggard element of Fear! Not *there* does Fear dwell, nor Uncertainty, nor Anxiety; but it dwells *here*; haunting us, tracking us; running like an accursed ground-discord through all the music-tones of our Existence;— making the Tense a mere Present one! Just so it is with this of Louis. Why smite the fallen? asks Magnanimity, out of danger now . . . So argues retrospective Magnanimity: but Pusillanimity, present, prospective? Reader, thou hast never lived, for months, under the rustle of Prussian gallows-ropes; never wert thou portion of a National Sahara-waltz, Twenty-five millions running distracted to fight Brunswick! . . . The French Nation . . . has pulled down the most dread Goliath, huge with the growth of ten centuries; and cannot believe, though his giant bulk, covering acres, lies prostrate . . . that he will not rise again, man devouring . . . Terror has its scepticism; miraculous victory its rage of vengeance.

Carlyle's eye for the human drama, his psychological sense, renders events that might seem cruel and inexplicable human, immediate, and real. His all-comprehensive viewpoint refuses to let him rest in a narrow interpretation of any event; the Terror is to be seen as an intensification of the manifoldness of the modern world.

> Terror is as a sable ground, on which the most variegated of scenes paints itself. In startling transitions, in colours, all intensated, the sublime, the ludicrous, the horrible succeed one another; or rather, in crowding tumult, accompany one another.

In keeping with this multiplicity, a sudden switch in perspective can color incidents with a totally different value: "That same fervour of Jacobinism, which internally fills France with hatreds, suspicions, scaffolds and Reason-worship, does, on the Frontiers, show itself as a glorious *Pro patria mori*. The Terror at home is only one side of a different kind of Terror on the frontiers, action which Carlyle denominates "the soul of the whole."

In his final judgment on the Terror, Carlyle answers the historian Mont-gaillard with an irony that diminishes the horrors of the Terror in history and validates once again the aims and rights of Sansculottism.

> It was the frightfulest thing ever born of Time? One of the frightfulest . . . It is a horrible sum of human lives, M. l'Abbe:— some ten times as many shot rightly on a field of battle, and one might have had his Glorious Victory with *Te Deum*. It is not far from the two-hundredth part of what perished in the entire Seven-Years War. By which Seven-Years War, did not the great Fritz wrench Silesia from the great Theresa; and a Pompadour, stung by epigrams, satisfy herself that she could not be an Agnès Sorel? The head of man is a strange vacant sounding-shell, M. l'Abbé; and studies Cocker to small purpose . . . There is no period to be met with, in which the general Twenty-five Millions of France suffered *less* than in this period which they name Reign of Terror! But it was not the Dumb Millions that suffered here; it was the Speaking Thousands, and Hundreds, and Units; who shrieked and published, and made the world ring with their wail.

Nevertheless, the Terror presents definite problems for Carlyle. Though a fundamental testimony of the depth and seriousness of the revolutionary instinct, its relationship to the legacy of Sansculottism is unclear. If Carlyle seems somewhat unappalled at the human cost of the Terror (there is, I feel, a sadomasochistic edge to his detailing of the noyadings), he is by no means so unflinching in the face of its anarchic implications. How the new social order emerges from ultimate Sansculottic disorder remains unclarified as Carlyle reverts to the "mystery" language of body and soul to describe the epic legacy.

> And yet a meaning lay in it: Sansculottism verily was alive, a New-Birth of TIME; nay, it still lives, and is not dead but changed. The *soul* of it still lives; still works far and wide, through one bodily shape into another less amorphous, as is the way of cunning Time with his New-Births:—till, in some perfected shape, it embrace the whole circuit of the world! . . . But as for the body of Sansculottism, that is dead and buried,—and, one hopes, need not reappear, in primary amorphous shape, for another thousand years.

Both hope and social realization are present here, but the connection between historical fact (the death of the body of Sansculottism) and historical inheritance (the soul of Sansculottism) is nebulous. The soul-body dichotomy does not help in healing that split. And there is also fright at precisely that aspect of the Terror which creates the ambivalences of Book Three, its "primary amorphous shape."

Book Three, far more than the preceding volumes, is riddled with ambivalent feelings, ambiguities, and contradictions that do not and cannot fall within the scope of the "problematic" epic—the shifting viewpoint and the variety of voice that offered control of the new epic in Books One and Two. In the absence of the drama of patriots against crown, it suffers from a lack of focus and an absence of rigorous and mounting dialectic. Carlyle finds himself bewildered and without a central structure, and Book Three is especially marked by a desperation in its search for order. Nearly every circumstance that could provide a focus is soon hailed as a new center or order and a principle of organization for the revolutionary drama. Yet this desperation only intensifies Carlyle's feeling for the historical facts—that they are enveloped in madness, fanaticism, and chaos.

Apparently recoiling from the threat of such chaos, Carlyle loses some of his faith in the possibilities of his voice to engage such disruption. Though the Terror attests to the Revolution's fundamental might and right, he oddly weakens his case by associating the actual historical quelling of Sansculottism with its death. And though he labels this a death of the body only, he nevertheless thereby further harms his initial and overriding sense of existence as the process of historical existence. Such terms as "nether fire," "chaos," "anarchy," and "Tophet" gradually resume purely negative mean-

ings, however positive their momentary intrusion into the surface of historical existence may be. Consequently, Sansculottism must die, anarchy like
death must be self-devouring, and there must be a "Consummation of
Sansculottism."

Carlyle's vision of the death of Sansculottism leaves little room for its
continuity except as a moral warning to a later age. As we might expect,
the historical method of the book is thus disrupted in the final pages with
metaphysical—or at least metahistorical—discourses on the Gaelic and Teutonic fire that Sansculottism kindled, the figures chosen to represent that fire
being drawn mainly from history prior to the French Revolution. A moralistic tone associated with Carlyle's harsh Puritanism also intrudes and even
begins to dominate when the Gironde are rather suddenly accused of being
strangers to the people, men of formulas, and lovers of luxury. Those qualities are again accentuated in the Republic of the Luxuries, with its Grecian
dandies and Cabarus balls, that succeeds the Revolution. The historical
narrative is by no means abandoned, but the warning to contemporary England seems to have the upper hand. The "Aristocracy of the Moneybag"
that appears after the demise of Sansculottism is obviously not merely a base
historical successor to the revolutionary impulse but also and primarily an
image of the present social situation: "It is the course through which all
European Societies are, at this hour, travelling. Apparently a still baser sort
of Aristocracy? An infinitely baser; the basest yet known." The new Republic
of Mammon blots out the truth of Sansculottism's legacy at the very moment
when some attempt at historical connection is being made; the legacy is
reduced to a mere warning against contemporary shams, a cudgel with which
Carlyle can threaten the money society of his own time.

Even within the actual historical narrative of Book Three there is a
similar flight from disorder and complexity. The fear of chaos and madness
generates a distrust of the capacities of the varied voice and prompts an
occasional search for the finality of order at any price. Carlyle's very for-
mulation of this order shows that it is a last-ditch measure, a desperate
reaction to the disorder that he is chronicling. As if sickened by the mad
whirl of the Terror, he welcomes the order of the army that will halt such
chaos, but the subjunctive mood of his welcome underscores his hesitation.

> For Arrangement is indispensable to man; Arrangement, were it
> grounded only on that old primary Evangel of Force, with Sceptre
> in the shape of Hammer! Be there method, be there order, cry
> all men; were it that of the Drill-sergeant!

> Let there be Order, were it under the Soldier's Sword.

The army, however, offers other fascinations for Carlyle besides the assurance of order. He admires its force so quickly put into operation, its structure of swift command and obedience, and its daring headlong plunge beyond all morality and personal consideration. The army is Carlyle's mob under a species of control. Early in Book Three he explains that in the shrieking confusion of a soldiery "and not elsewhere, lies the first germ of returning Order for France!" The army of millions hurling themselves against Brunswick later becomes the grand fact of the Revolution that history has overlooked and ultimately a justification for the Terror and a means for both affirming and controlling its wild force.

Carlyle has already laid a foundation for the importance of the army in the earlier volumes. Throughout the Revolution, he had always regarded it as the "very implement of rule and restraint, whereby all the rest was managed and held in order." And he will offer praise to anyone who maintains the soldier's code regardless of his side. Bouillé, a royalist officer, is the great recipient of Carlyle's admiration; in his heroic defiance of the insurrectionary troops on the staircase at Metz, he becomes an unforgettable symbol of power and the best of the royalists, fit to be mentioned as a possible ruler with Mirabeau. Similarly, since the worst and most unqualified evil is insurrection in the army, Louis' greatest fault is his indecision and his worst action the order of cease-fire given to the Swiss Guard who are then destroyed in the Insurrection of August 10.

Fundamentally, the triumph of army order and the accompanying delight in the rush of military might must be seen with the triumph of the Mammon world as a blurring of the legacy of Sansculottism. Though Napoleon appears throughout the three volumes as a possible hero, his connection with the central drama remains peripheral. At the end of Book Three, however, he appears on the scene as the major actor, the successor to Danton, and with the whiff of grapeshot that Broglie failed to deliver against the patriots at the beginning of the Revolution in Book One, he ends the Revolution and becomes, rather oddly, the inheritor of its power. As the chief figure of the new army sending its conflagration across the world in a series of kingdom-toppling shock waves, he ultimately joins with the tougher Teutonic fire "which no known thing will put out" and to which Carlyle is presumably heir.

> And even so it [the Gaelic fire] will blaze and run; scorching all things; and, from Cadiz to Archangel, mad Sansculottism, drilled now into Soldiership, led on by some "armed Soldier of Democracy" (say, that monosyllabic Artillery-Officer), will set its foot cruelly on the necks of its enemies; and its shouting and their

shrieking shall fill the world!—Rash Coalised Kings, such a fire
have yet kindled . . . it is begun, and will not end.

The center of Carlyle's history, the grievances of the masses, their
human sense of oppression, seems to be forgotten. Destruction and a kind
of delight in destruction now made orderly by the army usurp the focus.
With the army Carlyle seems to indulge in feelings of sublimity and triumph
over all obstacles; man is viewed under the impersonality of force and becomes a force of nature and history, impersonal and inexorable.

Ironically, the finality of the army and its structure of command and
obedience point to a regression to the structure of the old order whose demise
Carlyle has been so intensely urging. For, despite the rebellious quality of
his book, scattered through it are frequent moments of nostalgia for the old
order, especially for its hierarchy of authorities with its sense of degrees and
the possibility of "transmitting and translating *gradually*, from degree to
degree, the command of the one into the obedience of the other; rendering
command and obedience still possible." Such nostalgia is part of the theme
of loss and contributes strongly to the mood of bafflement and bewilderment.
For Carlyle the new era is characterized by negativity, what it has lost, just
as easily as it is by positive affirmation. The severest censure is reserved for
the nobles, who should have known what to surrender, what to hold, but
instead emigrated and acted fatally on France. The army then functions in
part as a means of punishing them for abandoning France, in part as a
reinstitution of the structure of command and obedience that they once
constituted. Similarly, the yearning for epic heroes, for someone to command
men—and Napoleon alone is seen as Danton's possible spiritual heir—is also
a nostalgia for an older world and an older structure of existence that most
of *The French Revolution* denies. Here then are the first signs of Carlyle's
preoccupation with a philosophy of heroism in conjunction with army order,
materials that will play an important role in his later writings. In *The French
Revolution* such concerns are minor, and it is still possible to argue that the
appearance of the army is a seal of victory set upon the rights and mights
of Sansculottism and the guarantor of its spiritual continuance.

GEORGE LEVINE

Sartor Resartus
and the Balance of Fiction

In his 1832 essay on "Biography," almost two years before the serial publication of *Sartor Resartus*, Carlyle made one of his most famous attacks on
fiction. Or rather, the author of *Aesthetische Springwurzeln*, Gottfried Sauerteig, made the attack: "Fiction," says Sauerteig, "while the feigner of it knows
that he is feigning, partakes, more than we suspect, of the nature of *lying*."
It is no accident that Carlyle placed these anti-fictional remarks in the mouth
of a fictional character. His own attitude toward fiction was essentially am-
biguous. His early readers, had they known that Sauerteig was a fiction,
would have sensed the ambiguity.

Although he turned increasingly through the years away from fiction,
Carlyle never could entirely repudiate it. Some kinds of fictional devices, he
thought, could safely be used without perverting the truth. Many writers
have noted that Carlyle used fictional characters for the expression of his
most radical ideas in order to protect himself from the public disapproval
he expected. But this could hardly be the whole reason for his using Sauerteig
in 1832 as the mouthpiece of his rejection of fiction. Fictions operate throughout his works in complex and devious ways, and at their best—as in *Sartor
Resartus*—they are an extremely important part of Carlyle's full meaning.
Like many other Victorians, Carlyle seems to have found that certain things
could only be said through indirection and could best be expressed, therefore,
through fiction. This need for indirection seems to me one of the most
interesting phenomena of the Victorian experience; and one might be able
to make some headway in explaining it by working out why (even to the

From *The Boundaries of Fiction: Carlyle, Macaulay, Newman*. © 1968 by Princeton
University Press.

end of his career, when his various disguises were well known) fictional
devices were so attractive to Carlyle.

Sartor Resartus, the book in which his fictions operate most persuasively
and most successfully, though always regarded as one of the primary texts
for tracing the shift from Romanticism to Victorianism, is only now beginning to receive the kind of attention it deserves as a work of art. If Carlyle
had achieved, at the period of the writing of *Sartor*, a broader tolerance than
he was ever again to have, he sustained it in that book by means of art. The
art which went into the creation and manipulation of fictions allowed him
a richness of vision not yet impoverished by what appeared in his later years
to be a myopic and often brutal secular Calvinism. Thus, although it may
appear that for most of his writing life Carlyle merely repeated what he had
already said in *Sartor*, the sheer literary brilliance of that book belies that
notion. The manner profoundly affects the matter so that in it ideas which
emerge later, as in the *Latter-Day Pamphlets* and *Shooting Niagara: and After?*,
bitterly interfused with Carlyle's increasing self-deception, need to be taken
seriously.

Sartor Resartus is, in fact, a work of fiction, although it can only be
regarded as a novel in a very special sense. Until the appearance of G. B.
Tennyson's book, consideration of *Sartor* as a novel had almost inevitably
led to misreading. Mr. Tennyson rightly argues, however, that if we accept
a minimal definition of "novel" as "an extended piece of prose fiction," there
is nothing to hinder acceptance of *Sartor* as a novel, especially as Carlyle
himself called it a "Didactic novel." Lying behind the refusal of readers to
accept *Sartor* as a novel is, Mr. Tennyson acutely perceives, "the tradition
of the English realistic novel." He points out that "The real obstacle to seeing
Sartor as a novel is, paradoxically, that portion of the book that critics have
been willing to call a novel even while dispensing with the rest—Book Two."
Early readers were able to delude themselves into thinking that Blumine had
been so richly drawn that she was recognizable as a distinct human figure,
worthy to join the ranks of the great romantic heroines of English literature.
She is, however, barely a shadow. The point surely is, as Mr. Tennyson
argues, that any attempt to see *Sartor* as a work fitting within the dominant
tradition of the English novel, realistic, full of extensive characterization,
governed by a plot which issues in a satisfying denouement, will inevitably
fail. *Sartor* is a fiction whose form is not governed by the demands of either
plot or character development. It is not concerned with verisimilitude, or
with the construction of social modes or manners. Rather it is controlled
thematically and by means of symbols and images; it is concerned exclusively
with subjective states; and its aim is largely satirical and therefore didactic.

I prefer, therefore, in order to avoid the confusion that the word "novel" when used in this way inevitably brings with it, to consider *Sartor* as a fiction belonging to the complex class of "confession-anatomy-romance." Carlyle's incapacity as a novelist has been thoroughly demonstrated, and even the briefest glance at his abortive attempt at a novel, *Wotton Reinfred*, will confirm the view that it is of interest "if for no other reason . . . as evidence of Carlyle's entire unfitness for the writing of fiction."

Nevertheless, the success of *Sartor* is largely the result of its fictions. I shall try to show that this suggests how powerful were the forces which went to the making of the novel as the supreme Victorian art (and which turned poetry so largely to the dramatic monologue and long narrative). These forces increasingly (though never entirely) lost their power with Carlyle, and for this reason *Sartor*'s success can help explain Carlyle's later failures; it can also throw light on certain special but universal kinds of failure in Victorian art. The usual criticisms of much Victorian fiction are that it is prudish or sentimental or pompously moralistic; each of these charges assumes that the novel ought to be faithful to ordinary experience and widely tolerant of it, and to remain sufficiently open to the harshness of reality not to be distorted by need or will. In almost every case I think it can be seen that these are Victorian assumptions as well; and when the great Victorian novelists fail it is usually because they are unequal to their own assumptions. We can see through the example of Carlyle how fiction tended to open experience, not close it; to increase tolerance, not diminish it; to transcend moral conventions, not succumb to them. . . .

Almost every aspect of Carlyle's style, as it was developed in *Sartor*, and many elements in his worldview, suggest his incapacity for fiction. This incapacity was demonstrated fully in the early work, and most critics would agree with [Carlisle] Moore that Carlyle suffered from a "special inaptitude for fiction."

It is therefore doubly significant that when Carlyle used his mature ideas in an independent literary work, he did not altogether abandon fiction; indeed, this form grew naturally out of the idea with which he began (Moore). What needs to be considered now is why, for a man of Carlyle's temperament and intellectual outlook, fiction provided the inescapable framework for his ideas. And to answer this question it will be necessary to consider carefully some of the ways in which fiction operates in *Sartor*.

It will not do to answer the question simply by pointing to what Moore shows to be one of the few traits which Carlyle did not seem to recognize in himself—the love of hoaxing; for this itself requires explanation. Teu-felsdröckh made his appearance on the English literary scene over a year before the publication of *Sartor*, in an essay called "Goethe's Works," although this essay was written after *Sartor* was completed. As far back as 1828, in another essay on Goethe, Carlyle had engaged playfully in quoting himself and treating the quotation with critical detachment. Indeed, his commentary on himself falls into a style rather similar to later Carlylese, with its unnecessary synonyms, its ironic and defensive self-deprecation. Even in his later more violent works, Carlyle insists on the hoax. So "The Nigger Question" purports to be a talk ("no speaker named")

> in the handwriting of the so-called "Doctor," properly "Ab-sconded Reporter," Dr. Phelim M'Quirk, whose singular powers of reporting, and also whose debts, extravagancies and sorrowful insidious finance-operations, now winded-up by a sudden dis-appearance, to the grief of many poor tradespeople, are making too much noise in the police-offices at present! Of M'Quirk's composition we by no means suppose it to be; but from M'Quirk, as the last traceable source, it comes to us;—offered, in fact, by his respectable unfortunate landlady, desirous to make-up part of her losses in this way.

The hoax is perpetuated throughout by parenthetical notations of the audience's response. Once again, the dramatization of the response of his audience, the defensive self-consciousness combined with an implicit sense of his own superiority, and the awareness of his own excesses are all characteristically Carlylean. And they do what little can be done to save that outrageously intolerant performance. Indeed, as a work of art, much might be said for "The Nigger Question."

Carlyle's love of hoax was not merely paradoxically and inexplicably inconsistent with his Calvinist views. One can see in *Sartor*, his most extended hoax, that it relates to the difficulties of a sensitive and intelligent man in coming to terms with his times and working out the means by which he might most effectively communicate to them his sense of truth. Carlyle saw the age as one of crisis and revolution, the long world-historical process engaged in shucking off the husks of the old way. He felt passionately the injustice which allowed for the starving of thousands of workers in a world richer than ever before, an injustice condoned by the "gamekeeping" aristocracy and by respectable, rationalistic, middle-class theory. Nothing was stable; nothing could be counted on. He had himself just emerged from a kind of crisis which would shortly be seen as typical of the period. Thrown back on his own resources by the disintegration of the old values under the shock of rational analysis, and finding the Calvinism of his father insupportable without some new intelligent justification, he had worked his way through the Germans to rediscover the eternal verities in a new guise. Under the stress of near poverty and a sense of his own personal inadequacies he had tried to reshape the world by sheer force of will so as to make it meaningful and therefore inhabitable again. But the effort had cost him, as a similar effort had cost his times, dearly. However firmly he believed in the doctrines at which he finally arrived, he had too full a sense of the division of the modern world to expect—although he could not avoid hoping—to succeed in making those doctrines universally acceptable. He could reassert wonder and reverence only by going through a stage which, after the effects of his conversion wore off, came perilously close to reasserting itself—descendentalism; a stage, that is, in which all things, man included, are reduced to trivia in the face of a vast impersonal world process. He could only reassert man's dignity and importance by renouncing the possibility of rationally understanding anything, by insisting on blind activity and the total renunciation of one's own desires. The alternatives to these views, as Teufelsdröckh suggests, are for the sensitive man to "Establish himself in Bedlam; begin writing Satanic Poetry; or blow-out his brains." The times had made self-consciousness inescapable, had created "a fascination with and uncertainty about oneself" which reopened all the old fundamental questions—about the relation of man to society, nature, God, and himself.

Under these circumstances, Carlyle had shopped about to find an adequate mode of expression. Having failed as both poet and novelist, he had served one of the longest apprenticeships in English literary history. "I never know or can even guess what or who my audience is, or whether I have any audience," he explained to Mill, and thus he wrote *Sartor* on a "Devil-may-care principle" (*Letters to Mill*). "Caring," in ignorance of what he might expect from his audience, would have been altogether fruitless. He had only two genuine certitudes: that England was dangerously close to violent revolution, and that he was obliged to promulgate those doctrines which might save her—and himself. Those doctrines were largely religious in nature.

John Sterling, whose biography Carlyle was later to write, described movingly and precisely the position in which Carlyle found himself and how he responded to it:

> [Luther] could speak out heartily and devoutly in the full confidence of faithful, humble reception from his hearers; but in our days we find the no less fervid utterance of an equally practical

and positive spirit turning back in irony upon himself, and by
his tone of caustic rather than poignant self-mockery giving the
most peculiar and emphatic expression to all his teaching. Luther's
irony, when he does resort to it, is all polemical—a sword to
attack. The Englishman's is generally self-repressive—even more
than self-defensive—as a mantle in which he would wrap his head,
and shut out the images of his own zeal and indignation.

This is the mode, in the absence of confidence in a "faithful, humble reception," that Carlyle felt obliged to adopt in order to speak at all. Fiction was
his only protection, and the only valid representation of his own
uncertainties.

Thus two people, not one, announce the doctrine of *Sartor*, and thus
the literal surface of that book is never wholehearted and unambiguous. By
and large the Editor does sympathize with Teufelsdröckh's views, but he
does not, even at the end, express unqualified assent. Instead, he mockingly
dismisses his "irritated" English audience, and ironically expresses his grat-
itude to William Maginn ("Oliver Yorke"), the real, though undesignated,
editor of *Fraser's* [*Magazine*]. The whole structure of the book reveals a painful
struggle against self-division and uncertainty about the audience (an uncertainty largely confirmed by the violent antagonism aroused by *Sartor*'s serial
publication).

In one aspect, the Editor is intended to represent the audience, and thus
to mediate between Carlyle's ideas and the audience whose antagonism he
could anticipate. The manipulation of the Editor is an attempt at the manipulation of the audience (like the manipulation later in "The Nigger Question"), and to achieve this Carlyle is forced to give the Editor an independent
character. It is, however, an oversimplification to insist that the Editor "serves
as a model for the reader—British, bristlingly empirical, anti-metaphysical
and almost anti-German." As the quotations which follow suggest, he is not
representatively English but rather begins with a recognition of the barren-
ness of English thought and goes as far in the direction of Teufelsdröckh as
possible without alienating his audience. Then, though boasting himself "a
man of confirmed speculative habits, and perhaps discursive enough," the
Editor had never thought of the philosophy of Clothes until the arrival of
Teufelsdröckh's book. While insisting on the usefulness of remaining anonymous, he tries to assure his readers that he is loyal to England, "animated
with a true though perhaps a feeble attachment to the Institutions of our
Ancestors; and minded to defend these, according to ability, at all hazards."
And for the sake of softening up the opposition, he is made to argue that he

has undertaken the presentation of the Clothes philosophy "partly with a view to such defence." Interestingly enough for proof of the point that Carlyle uses him as a tool for manipulation of his anticipated audience, the Editor goes on to assure his readers that he will take up exactly the attitude he urges on them. To them he says, "strive to keep a free, open sense; cleared from the mists of prejudice, above all from the paralysis of cant; and directed rather to the Book itself than to the Editor of the Book." Of himself he says, "be it nowise apprehended, that any personal connection of ours with Teufelsdröckh . . . can pervert our judgment, or sway us to extenuate or exaggerate. . . . Teufelsdröckh is our friend, Truth is our divinity." Although his attitudes are not always consistent, through the rest of the book he demonstrates his willingness to attack Teufelsdröckh, sometimes quite sensibly, and always maintaining the pose of the dispassionate judge, engaged in a difficult task not for his own sake but for the sake of England. In so doing he represents Carlyle sitting in dispassionate judgment on himself.

The whole elaborate device may be taken as a symbolic expression of Carlyle's recognition of the foreignness of his ideas to English life. From this point of view it is clear why Carlyle's spokesmen are almost always foreign; their Germanness is, of course, a recognition of his debt to German thought. His usual fictional trick is to establish some kind of initial antagonism to this foreignness, here in the person of the Editor, hoping to show that if one sensible Englishman can profit from these foreign notions, so might any other Englishman. The problem Carlyle faced is put precisely in the Editor's words: "how could the philosophy of Clothes and the Author of such Philosophy, be brought home, in any measure, to the business and bosoms of our own English Nation?" The answer, Carlyle discovered, was to dramatize his own experience with the Germans, he having initially shared an enthusiasm for Hume and eighteenth-century skepticism. The conflict, then, is between the apocalyptic vision he aspired to (in Teufelsdröckh) and the critical intelligence he could not escape (in the Editor).

Carlyle's initial confusion about means, about self, and about audience thus turned him to fiction. But the traditional emphasis on Carlyle's merely defensive uses of fiction does not adequately explain how it works, because in *Sartor* it offers the best method for expounding Carlyle's ideas. Indeed, as in all good fiction, many of the ideas could only have been precisely formulated in terms of fiction.

This is especially true of his notion of the inescapably partial nature of man's perceptions and knowledge which, as Froude says, "lay at the bottom of all his thoughts about man and man's doing in the world." In his 1830 essay, "On History," Carlyle says that "The old story of Walter Raleigh's looking from his prison-window, on some street tumult, which afterwards three witnesses reported in three different ways, himself differing from them all, is still a true lesson for us." He continues later:

> Truly, if History is Philosophy teaching by Experience, the writer fitted to compose History is hitherto an unknown man. The experience itself would require All-knowledge to record it,— were the All-wisdom needful for such Philosophy as would interpret it, to be had for asking. Better were it that mere earthly Historians should lower such pretensions, more suitable for Omniscience than for human science; and aiming only at some picture of the things acted, which picture itself will at best be a poor approximation, leave the inscrutable purport of them an acknowledged secret; or at most, in reverent Faith, far different from that teaching of Philosophy, pause over the mysterious vestiges of Him, whose path is the great deep of Time, whom History indeed reveals, but only all History, and in Eternity, will clearly reveal.

Teufelsdröckh takes up nearly the same position, rejecting a "Cause-and-Effect Philosophy of Clothes, as of Laws," on the implicit Humean grounds that man cannot have the knowledge to work out such a philosophy: "for inferior Intelligences, like men, such Philosophies have always seemed to me uninstructive enough." Rather, "naked Facts, and Deductions drawn therefrom in quite another than that omniscient style, are my humbler and proper province."

Leaving aside the question of his paradoxical certainty of the reality of God despite God's unknowability, this manner of thinking had a curious result for Carlyle. It entailed a commitment to relativism, at least in the natural world, which, if followed out logically, would have led to a concern with the problems of "point of view." And *Sartor* certainly demonstrates an awareness of those problems in its total rejection of the omniscient stance. Carlyle was not willing, of course, to settle for all the logical implications of his view: he would not surrender God or the absolute, asserting always that whether man knew it or not, the Infinite was *there*, beyond the limits of his knowledge. But *Sartor* undeniably has the surface ambiguity that the absence of an omniscient narrator creates. Indeed, what gives *Sartor* its peculiar status in the hierarchy of Carlyle's works is the extraordinary doubleness of vision it embodies. Carlyle's self-awareness, as dramatized in the Editor and Teufelsdröckh, extends not only to the recognition of his dual impulses (toward self-consciousness, self-righteousness, and self-assertion, for example, as well as toward work, humility, and self-denial); of the extravagancies and inadequacies of his style; but also, of the ultimate limitations of the whole work. Carlyle knew that there were likely to be better ways to promulgate his doctrine. He complained to his brother in October 1833, at about the time *Sartor* had begun to appear in *Fraser's*, "Alas, the *thing* I want to do is precisely the thing I cannot do. My mind would so fain deliver itself adequately of that 'Divine Idea of the World'; and only in quite *in*adequate approximation is such deliverance possible."

The last chapter of *Sartor* reveals how Carlyle's self-awareness operated at this stage of his career toward wider tolerance and flexibility. Without undercutting the elaborate notions worked out in the rest of the book, it makes, rhetorically, concessions which later would be for him impossible. Perhaps were it not for his need for fictional spokesmen it would have been impossible for him then; but the effect, whatever the cause, is a softening of the hard moralizing impact of the book. The Editor apologizes again for Teufelsdröckh's style (and for his own) and regrets that such a brilliant man found it necessary to express his important ideas by "rummaging among lumber-rooms; nay too often [by] scraping in kennels." He then suggests what even the most unsympathetic reader should find attractive about Teufelsdröckh: "His attitude, we will hope and believe, is that of a man who had said to Cant, Begone; and to Dilettantism, Here thou canst not be; and to Truth, Be thou in place of all to me: a man who had manfully defied the 'Time-prince,' or Devil, to his face; nay perhaps, Hannibal-like, was mysteriously consecrated from birth to that warfare, and now stood minded to wage the same, by all weapons, in all places, at all times." Carlyle did not, then, attempt to conclude his work by showing the Editor wholeheartedly asserting the truth of all Teufelsdröckh's views. There is no retraction, but there seems to be a willingness to settle for the cardinal virtue—sincerity—and let the rest take care of itself if need be. This acknowledgment that only Teufelsdröckh's seriousness and not his mystifications need be taken seriously is part of what gives the book its undogmatic flexibility. His last words in *Sartor* typically emphasize the urgency of the battle: " 'It is the Night of the World, and still long till it be Day: we wander amid the glimmer of smoking ruins, and the Sun and the Stars of Heaven are as if blotted out for a season; and two immeasurable Phantoms, HYPOCRISY and ATHEISM, with the Gowl, SENSUALITY, stalk abroad over the Earth, and call it theirs: well at ease are the Sleepers for whom Existence is a shallow Dream.' " Atypically, these remarks are prefaced by the gentlest solution proposed in the Carlyle canon—Love. "A man, be the Heavens ever praised, is sufficient for himself; yet were ten men, united in Love, capable of being and of doing what ten thousand singly would fail in. Infinite is the help man can yield to man."

As has already been shown, no one knew better than Carlyle that beyond the universal limitations of man, he suffered from peculiar limitations as an artist. His apologies for and explanations of his mode of writing punctuate the book. "Perhaps," the Editor says, "Necessity as well as Choice was concerned" in Teufelsdröckh's writing as he did. "Seems it not conceivable that, is a Life like our Professor's, where so much bountifully given by Nature had in Practice failed and misgone, Literature also would never rightly prosper: that striving with his characteristic vehemence to paint this and the other Picture, and ever without success, he at last desperately dashes his sponge, full of all colours, against the canvas, to try whether it will paint Foam?" The "foam" might, of course, be *Sartor* itself. Such a passage as this is, perhaps, one of those in which Carlyle tries to turn "an inherent defect into a virtue," but it is important to see how thoroughly it succeeds. The explanation does not, of course, exempt the book from criticism of its wildness, but when seen in relation to the autobiographical passages, it does tend to put its whole structure "in character." It is part of the strategy by which we are made to test the validity of the ideas by examining character.

If Teufelsdröckh is partly excused from the chaos of his manner by "Necessity," the Editor is largely excused by the constantly repeated idea that he is forced to wrestle with Teufelsdröckh's intractable material in order to win from it some shape and coherent meaning. This wrestling is responsible for a good part of the book's drama, since it is analogous to the readers', and upon the Editor's success everything depends. Thus, the second chapter, "Editorial Difficulties," is given over to discussing how what is essential and valuable for the English reader might be distilled from the "boundless, almost formless contents" of *Die Kleider*. Without biographical documents the Editor finds the difficulties compounded, and he has therefore for "some months" "read and again read" the book until it has become "in several points" "lucid and lucent."

The wrestling grows more violent and even affects the Editor's health when Heuschrecke ships him material for a biography in six totally disorganized paper bags marked by the signs of the Zodiac. His difficulties here are deliberately paralleled to those with the book itself: "Daily and nightly does the Editor sit (with green spectacles) deciphering these unimaginable Documents from their perplexed *cursiv-schrift*; collating them with the almost equally unimaginable Volume, which stands in legible print. Over such a universal medley of high and low, of hot, cold, moist and dry, is he here struggling (by union of like with like, which is Method) to build a firm Bridge for British travellers." The struggle in the second part is more fruitful, but apologies for and reminders of the disorder are nevertheless profuse; it is even hinted that there is a latent insanity in Teufelsdröckh.

These reminders and apologies, however, are not all that go to justify the chaos. It is interesting that the very chaos out of which the Editor is attempting to bring meaning becomes in *Sartor* a symbol of one of its central ideas, just as the whole fictional structure becomes representative of the book's ideas in fairly precise ways. The idea of the physical world as apparent chaos which really bodies forth a single ultimate spiritual truth is an aspect of Teufelsdröckh's doctrine that all things are related ("There is not a red Indian, hunting by Lake Winnipic, can quarrel with his squaw, but the whole world must smart for it: will not the price of beaver rise?"). From his point of view the apparent incoherence of his six bags would be immaterial. All the facts and ideas ultimately connect and move toward the oneness of the infinite. The disorder of his works, moreover, parallels the notion that he (a representative of every man) is a whole bundle of transcendental-descendental oppositions. His works juxtapose the most extravagantly inappropriate facts and feelings because he is their living embodiment. The fiction then becomes a justification for the peculiar disorder of the symbol.

Grace Calder's discovery that Carlyle freely switched around chapters and paragraphs of *Past and Present* tends to confirm the view that much of the material in the first and third books of *Sartor* is interchangeable. Although the book is not quite as chaotic as the Editor keeps insisting, from the point of view of logic much of it is mere repetition. The notions of wonder, of the infinite, of *Palingenesie*, of descendentalism and transcendentalism, are worked at from many different directions, with many different examples. Teufelsdröckh's magnificent vision of Weissnichtwo from his windows effectively introduces the reader to his peculiar modes of seeing, but it would have come equally appropriately in the chapter on "Organic Filaments," or "Natural Supernaturalism." Almost everything Carlyle wants to say about man, nature, society, space, and time is announced in that passage. Teufelsdröckh's inscrutability, his "calmness and fixedness" of expression, are part of the fiction, operating to allow him to drive them home more and more forcefully. For the same reason, the Editor asserts his confusion about notions that are actually clear. He omits presenting much of *Die Kleider* on the grounds of unintelligibility, and in his first "pause" states that everything is still largely obscure to the reader except for a few flashes of meaning: "The Philosophy of Clothes is now to all readers, as we predicted it would do, unfolding itself into new boundless expansions, of a cloudcapt, almost chimerical aspect, yet not without azure loomings in the far distance, and streaks as of an Elysian brightness; the highly questionable purport and promise of which it is becoming more and more important for us to ascertain."

What must be noted is that the Editor's mystifying activities correspond also to key ideas of the book: first, to Carlyle's insistence on wonder, on the translation of the ordinary into the miraculous; this is, of course, effectively achieved by forcing the reader to puzzle even over things which ought not to produce uncertainty. Second, to Carlyle's rejection of system as inadequate to account for the complexity and wonder of existence. The Editor's troubles allow Carlyle to avoid setting down his ideas in a few clear axioms, as many of his commentators (for example, Sterling and Holloway) have been able to do quite easily. His ideas, he felt, should not have been amenable to systematic codification. "Our Professor's method," the Editor says, in a passage which might apply equally to the method of *Sartor*, "is not, in any case, that of common school Logic, where the truths all stand in a row, each holding by the skirts of the other; but at best that of practical Reason, proceeding by large Intuition over whole systematic groups and kingdoms; whereby, we might say, a noble complexity, almost like that of Nature, reigns in his Philosophy, or spiritual Picture of Nature: a mighty maze, yet, as faith whispers, not without a plan." Thus it is part of Carlyle's quite conscious and—given the nature of his ideas—justifiable plan that the details are not inevitably right in their placing within the whole work.

Such a justification, however, might seem a lapse into what Yvor Winters has called the fallacy of imitative form; it is true that the justification needs more substance. The structure of *Sartor* is emotional, not logical. And the best justification comes from a recognition that the large movement of the book, like the smaller movements of particular passages, is directed to some emotionally satisfying rather than to a logically unarguable conclusion. Morse Peckham sees such a movement in a regular slow progression in the direction of increased comprehension on the part of the Editor—a development by "psychological continuity." The writing of the book corresponds in rough chronology to the Editor's receiving the volume on clothes and hearing from Heuschrecke that biographical information about Teufelsdröckh is available (Book I); and "reopening the great *Clothes-Volume*" (Book III). In fact, however, at the start of the book the Editor is already in awe of Teufelsdröckh and fully impressed with the value of his ideas. In characteristic Carlylean double-negative fashion, he says at first mention of *Die Kleider* that it "has not remained without effect" for him. The Editor's first problem, it will be remembered, is not in comprehension but in determining "How might this acquired good be imparted to others, perhaps in equal need thereof." He is already convinced, and the tension between the Editor and Teufelsdröckh through the rest of the book is no further resolved. (The "resolution," if the book may be said to have one, is extra-literary—the 1830 revolution in Paris and the expected upheaval in England.)

In this as in all things, Carlyle's method is essentially static. As he is

not capable of developing character, of moving beyond the anecdote to the
narrative, or of using the violence of his prose centrifugally rather than
centripetally, so he is not capable of constructing his book according to the
principle of "psychological continuity," which implies real movement out
from the center to a new position. The meaning of the clothes philosophy
itself has no development: the center stands unchanged as the social garments
are tattered and destroyed. From start to finish the relation of most of the
characters to each other and to the audience remains the same. Teufelsdröckh
remains the mysterious sage, Heuschrecke the model of what hero-worship
ought not to be, and the Editor the model of what it should be. Heuschrecke
is the fool who, like Sancho Panza, incredibly says intelligent things on
occasion but who follows his master unquestioningly despite obvious dif-
ferences in outlook (it should be remembered that he is a Malthusian). The
Editor is awed by the great man, inferior to him, but unwilling to follow
him in utter blindness. He remains certain also that most of his readers not
only have failed to follow him but are actively antagonistic.

The peculiarly static quality, once again corresponding to a central
notion of the whole book, does not in fact diminish the dramatic tension. If
the pattern is different from what one conventionally expects to find in fiction,
it is still capable of producing its own kind of satisfaction. The book has an
emotional structure—a set of repeated patterns—and the literal surface of
the book increasingly subserves these patterns. Each Book begins at its most
neutral and prosaic point and moves to a climax of faith and affirmation,
each climax more powerful than the preceding. Thus the first chapter begins
with a survey of the subjects of science and philosophy, preparing the way
for the clothes philosophy. Chapter Ten, the climax of Book One, closes
with the most distinctively violent Carlylean rhetoric thus far, affirming the
universality of wonder and mystery and unequivocally preaching, mocking,
reprimanding:

> —*Armer Teufel!* Doth not thy cow calve, doth not thy bull gender?
> Thou thyself, wert thou not born, wilt thou not die? "Explain"
> me all this, or do one of two things: Retire into private places
> with thy foolish cackle; or, what were better, give it up, and
> weep, not that the reign of wonder is done, and God's world all
> disembellished and prosaic, but that thou hitherto art a Dilettante
> and sandblind Pedant.

To complete the pattern, the first Book ends with a retrospective and "Prospective" view, paralleling chapters at the end of Book Two ("Pause") and
Book Three ("Circumspective" and "Farewell"). The second Book begins

with the gentlest passages in *Sartor*, especially in the second chapter ("Idyl-lic"), but climaxes in the penultimate chapter with Carlyle's most famous personal expression of faith, "The Everlasting Yea." The third Book is per-haps the least logically constructed of all, but the rhetorical pattern is the same, beginning as it does with examples from "Incidents in Modern His-tory" and reaching its climax in the chapter which at least in terms of doctrine is the real climax of the whole work, "Natural Supernaturalism." Here the notion of the power and pervasiveness of Spirit is most forcefully set down:

> Thus, like a God-created, fire-breathing Spirit-host, we emerge from the Inane. Earth's mountains are levelled, and her seas filled up, in our passage: can the Earth, which is but dead and a vision, resist Spirits which have reality and are alive? On the hardest adamant some footprint of us is stamped-in; the last Rear of the host will read traces of the earliest Van. But whence?—O Heaven, whither? Sense knows not; Faith knows not; only that it is through Mystery to Mystery, from God and to God.

The spiritual intensity of this passage reminds us that it is possible to see the structure of *Sartor* in another way, as akin to that of the traditional sermon. In terms of its own fiction it is, of course, a book review, much like, as G. B. Tennyson has shown, the book reviews Carlyle had been doing through the best part of his writing career. But the natural direction of Carlyle's reviews was toward some sort of spiritual revelation. And *Sartor's* three parts fit the overall pattern of the mediaeval sermon. *Sartor* begins with the announcement of a text (that is, *Die Kleider*) and with some genuine if obfuscating exposition of the text; it moves on, in Teufelsdröckh's biography, to a kind of exemplum (certainly the second section is more intelligible read this way than as a piece of novelistic fiction); and then, in a complicated way—after a clearer restatement of themes—the third section concludes with a peroration and application. Teufelsdröckh's ideas are loose in the world; there is a revolution in Paris; great changes are coming in England; and Teufelsdröckh himself is where the old clothes of society are being torn away. But just as the traditional pattern of the sermon is continuous expan-sion of a single idea, a set of variations on a text, so *Sartor*, even when read in this way, remains a giant elaboration of a basic insight into the spiritual nature of the material universe.

Thus no matter how one attempts to explain it, the whole structure of the book parallels the style. It is a series of elaborate reflections circling about a central position. These reflections never move far beyond their first state-ment, but become increasingly violent and emotionally intense, increasingly rich in exemplification, but always fundamentally simple. Each of the complicated fictions serves as a defense of this highly illogical structure against criticism, as a defense of Carlyle himself, and as another mode of expression of the central ideas.

We should be in a better position now to see how *Sartor* reflects both an idiosyncrasy and that broad general mood which tended to make fiction the dominating art form of the period. It marks the transition from the Romantics to the Victorians because it adds one quality to the Romantic vision which had not yet become dominant—desperation. Carlyle lived through the Romantics' period of greatness (having been born the same year as Keats) without ever having been of it, and he watched as the great Romantic ideals were shattered by history. Instead of a universe integrated by love and a nature harmonious with man, instead of the artist as legislator or hero, instead of great social reformations and a new reign of justice, of man dignified, unique, and honest, he found a mechanical world governed by outmoded laws, by mere respectability ("Dilettantism"), by political economies and rational systems which seemed to attempt to justify the dehumanization of man he thought he saw all about him. He found himself instinctively at odds with the conservatism of a continent in rebound from the French Revolution and hypocritically, as he saw it, committed to a success morality dressed in the old clothes of Christianity. Despite his occasional fits of pantheism in *Sartor*, he found it difficult to perceive the harmony between man and nature which was indispensable to the Romantic affirmation. Through Teufelsdröckh, he tells us "what it was like to have arrived at the dead-end of the eighteenth-century, to inhabit the mechanical universe of the Newtonian world-view, a universe without so much meaning as would render it even hostile." He had for himself to work through the experience that would once again infuse meaning into life.

At the time of writing *Sartor* that experience—a kind of triumph—was fresh to him, but he could not, as we have seen, unabashedly recount it with Wordsworth's solemn and epic confidence. He could not establish himself as a sage in *Sartor* because, though like the Romantics in having won through to a deeply personal affirmation and discovery of his identity, he was not able to see the experience as anything but personal in a world obviously inimical. If he had the temperament of the Romantic glorying in his own uniqueness, he saw that salvation was possible only by submerging that uniqueness. The historical moment for the possibility of Great Expectations had passed with the French Revolution, and though Carlyle grabbed desperately at every hint that history might confirm the tentative optimism of *Sartor* (note his response to the revolutions of 1830 and 1848, even to the repeal of the Corn Laws), the only good of which he was certain lay hidden behind history and himself. Thus every aspect of his thought which deals with man's temporal existence was negative: *Entsagen*, the worship of sorrow, silence, hero-worship. His theoretical position was that of the popular notion of Job: man cannot by his nature genuinely know; he must therefore renounce happiness, assume that Divine Justice is somehow in operation, and work.

With the Romantic unwillingness to remain suspended in doubt, this kind of desperate affirmation is all that saved Carlyle; but only at a point of balance in which the desperation does not hold the upper hand could he achieve that openness to experience and breadth of tolerance which is the distinctive characteristic of the great novelists of the century. Though even in *Sartor* Carlyle had Teufelsdröckh preach a doctrine fundamentally opposed to the Romantic notion of experience, the preaching is, as we have seen, muffled by the fiction, which shows how a man wins through by experience to affirmation and which therefore artistically justifies the preaching. But Carlyle was already attempting, out of desperation, to erect his subjective experience into dogma, though even this he had to do through the devices of fiction. It is the fiction which keeps Carlyle from a direct attempt to impose on his readers an affirmation without requiring of them equally that they undergo their own experience in order to achieve it. Langbaum, who has discussed this point at length in a slightly different context, has argued that in his later works Carlyle was unfaithful to the "morality of Romanticism," best summarized in a speech by Faust:

> Yes! to this thought I hold with firm persistence;
> The last result of wisdom stamps it true:
> He only earns his freedom and existence,
> Who daily conquers them anew.

This becomes the morality of the Browningesque monologue, and of the novel itself. But it is lost with the triumph of desperation.

Carlyle's faith in experience is expressed in *Sartor* by his willingness, already noted, to keep both Teufelsdröckh and the Editor between him and the points he wants to make. In later works, he usually used a single fictional commentator—much more closely identifiable with Carlyle—whose views he himself would "place." As Grace Calder points out, "when Carlyle uses the dramatic method of creating personages and allowing them to speak in the first person . . . he can scarcely restrain himself from interpreting the actors' speeches directly to the audience." To a certain extent, the Editor does the same thing with Teufelsdröckh's speeches, but in this case the interpreter is not always meant to be right. The effect, then, though perhaps ultimately unambiguous, is genuinely dramatic. Had Carlyle's talents and religious background made it possible, this not altogether full commitment to experience would almost certainly have led to the creation of the kind of fiction which we regard as characteristically Victorian—full of authorial intrusions, omniscient treatment of character, complex plot lines, and a profound sense of human limitations. But as the balance shifted late in the century and experience itself became all that remained of the values passed on by the Romantics, the need for intrusion and omniscience diminished.

Whatever the time, faith in experience is one of the conditions of good fiction. George Eliot and Dickens go wrong precisely where they lose their faith in it and force themselves to believe in things which everything else in their created worlds seems to contradict, as for example, the loving reunion of Maggie and Tom at the end of *The Mill on the Floss*, or the incorruptible moral beauty of Esther Summerson in *Bleak House*. Usually, however, these writers, even when they become most intrusive, do not interfere with the independence of the experience rendered. *Sartor Resartus* comes as close to this kind of freedom as any of Carlyle's works, and his turn to history and the primacy of "fact" shortly after this was probably not so much an expression of willingness to trust experience as an escape from the need to trust it. Although he was too scrupulously honest a man to have been able to distort his sources consciously, he never wrote a history in which the facts had not already led him to his desired conclusions and in which they were not immediately turned into symbols. At best the turn to history was an expression of willed faith in the notion that the world and experience are under some supernatural moral control. Usually it represented a quest for an ideal of behavior and heroism essential to the salvation of contemporary England.

But with all the qualifications necessary, Carlyle insisted on fidelity to the facts, and was always impressive when attempting to capture the sense of what it really means to say that something exists or existed. This is, of course, most powerfully evident in the narrative of Jocelin's chronicle in *Past and Present*, but it is also evident in the constant evocation of wonder in *Sartor*. Carlyle had a rare ability to intensify experience by placing things in the largest possible context so that any "Drawing-room is simply a section of Infinite-Space, where so many God-created Souls do for the time meet together." Although he was not capable of rendering the wonder of existence with the slow and unglamorous fictional precision of such writers as George Eliot, the allusive and anecdotal quality of his prose—the mad chaos of its surface—suggests, at least in *Sartor*, that he was not ready to reduce the complexity of appearances even while he was ready to assert that any particular manifestation is "simply" an aspect of the "Infinite."

What draws him considerably closer to the area of fiction, and particularly of the traditional novel, is the supreme value he attached to biography. "History," he said, "is the essence of innumerable Biographies" (*Essays*), and as Harrold points out, Teufelsdröckh's slightly garbled Pope-like quotation from *Wilhelm Meister*, "Man is properly the *only* object that interests man," became "one of the two or three master-thoughts of Carlyle." Thus the last chapter of *Sartor* concludes not with another assertion of the doctrines but with a biographical fact—Teufelsdröckh has disappeared. The impulse to biography, it appears, becomes an impulse to drama since it led Carlyle to turn exposition into a battle among characters representing different positions, making one's relation to an idea depend on one's relation to a character: if he be sincere and admirable so must be the idea. Everyone who comes into contact with Teufelsdröckh, despite his eccentricities, loves him—from the bumbling Heuschrecke, to Blumine, to Lieschen, to his fellow drinkers at the Grüne Gans, to the Editor himself. Carlyle had to show that it is difficult to get through to the idea (and thus the reader must work hard himself); and those who don't work at it must, of course, receive their proper epitaphs, as does Count Zähdarm literally, or the women at the "aesthetic tea." He needed, in other words, by whatever means he could control, to turn meaning into experience.

The relevance of the biographical and autobiographical impulses to the achievements of Victorian literature is too well known to need rehearsing. But a comment by Northrop Frye suggests how closely the arts of autobiography and fiction are connected. "Most autobiographies," he says, "are inspired by a creative, and therefore fictional, impulse to select only those events and experiences in the writer's life that go to build up an integrated pattern." This is clearly true of Teufelsdröckh's story, but it is not difficult to see how directly it applies to other famous Victorian autobiographies: Mill's, for instance, which Gertrude Himmelfarb has shown to have minimized the split between father and son and to have omitted an even worse breakdown than the one recorded in the chapter on his "Mental Crisis"; or Newman's *Apologia*. And if, as Fry notes, "There is no literary reason why the subject of a confession should always be the author himself," the notion operates over the whole field of Victorian fiction.

Carlyle's emphasis on "sincerity" is also related to the emphasis on biography (since what matters most is, as we have seen, Teufelsdröckh's good character rather than his ideas), and in another way to the fictional impulse. A fiction such as *Sartor* inevitably shifts attention away, at least in part, from the substance to the point of view from which it is being related. We need to attend to the quality of the character talking since, as we have seen, in Carlyle's view no man is capable of knowing the whole truth. We move here perilously close to relativism, as in the poetry of Browning, and stay clear of it largely in the same way as Browning: by belief in what can't be known, and by trusting in some fundamental values (like sincerity) to lead the reader out of the wilderness of conflicting and incomplete views. The obvious connection of elements of this vision with the later work of James and Conrad—indeed, with much of the modern novel—needs no emphasis. What is striking is that Carlyle was one of the first of the Victorians to attempt to find some means for expression of this vision, and in so doing he anticipated many developments of the novel.

Another important connection between Carlyle's vision and method and the novel in general can be discerned in *Sartor*. The fiction serves to help Carlyle express his views satisfactorily because "the prophet's sense of things is more readily expressed concretely and not abstractly." All the sages "insist on how acquiring wisdom is somehow an opening of the eyes, making us see in our experience what we failed to see before," and their problem then, as the Editor seems aware, is to quicken "the reader to a new capacity for experience" (Holloway). This applies to Carlyle in several ways: in the general fictional framework which dramatizes the ideas; in the violence of his rhetoric, intended to shock the reader into a new kind of attention, and, hopefully, into a receptivity to a new kind of experience; and in the way his unsystematic mind persists in breaking out into anecdote and allusions.

Finally, *Sartor* suggests another crucial way in which the temper of the times moved inevitably toward fiction. Like many Victorian sages, Carlyle began with a view that made the position of sage logically impossible but emotionally inevitable. The desperation already noted made it imperative that someone speak out against the forces leading to what seemed inevitable destruction. But he had important doubts about his own powers which only force of will in his later years seemed to overcome on the surface of his consciousness. I have attempted to show that this nervousness about self was one of the conditions of valuable art for Carlyle, committed to what the Editor calls "proselytizing"; and it clearly led Carlyle, as it led those who followed him, in the direction of fiction.

Fiction—and, in the Victorian period with its emphasis on the "real," the "true," and the "ordinary," the novel—is the supreme form for creating disguises which keep the author from the kind of exposure that Carlyle feared. He was afraid of being discovered inadequate to the heroic task he had undertaken, and of leaving his personal and artistic inadequacies open to ridicule. Even before the uncertainty about absolutes became so complete that omniscience almost completely disappeared for a while from fiction, Victorian novelists had created a form which reduced the necessity for the author to speak out absolutely, which allowed experience itself to speak, and which reduced moral commentary to what credibly might be spoken by any intelligent and morally committed person (Thackeray's god-like stance in *Vanity Fair* is not at all typical). Autobiography emerges disguised in a way not dissimilar from that in *Sartor*. The author like Carlyle could in such fiction assert his identity, demand sympathy for it, evoke moral meaning from it, and preserve without fear of exposure his sense of limitations and uncertainty.

Only through fiction could the serious artist, committed to some kind of radical moral reorganization of society, speak to an audience about whose values he could not be sure. He needed both to protect himself and to discover a mode that would somehow attract everyone. Disguise and a reliance on widely available experience were the answer. Partly for this reason, Carlyle was committed to demonstrating the miraculous nature of the ordinary, and in this respect he was totally in accord with the whole "humanist" movement of the time, and especially with a writer like George Eliot, who also turned from her Byron to her Goethe. Much of the effect of Victorian fiction depended on the likelihood that readers would be fascinated by the details of comparatively ordinary life. Although *Sartor* seems altogether fantastic and outside the experience of that life, its doctrine entails reverence for ordinary life, and the whole book is engaged in attempting to domesticate an experience which, Carlyle believed, the British people have only mistakenly thought foreign. Thus the Editor *is* English and loyal to England (protesting too much his qualities of "Diligence and feeble thinking"); thus mad Teufelsdröckh, despite his mysterious god-born origins, had a rather pleasant and ordinary youth, climaxing, as usual, with a painful love affair. In fact, what is new in *Sartor* is not the substance, but the new way of seeing that substance. . . . It is no accident that *Sartor*, like Tennyson's *In Memoriam*, became for people like Froude the work that saved them from moral and spiritual disintegration.

It is possibly not true that all or even most of nineteenth-century fiction had its source, like Carlyle's, in the need for self-defense and for the expression of a fundamental duality of vision. But these qualities in combination with a profound sense of the urgency of moral reform seem inevitably to find richest expression in fiction. Moreover, whether temperamentally or intellectually (though likely, as in Carlyle, a combination of both), the fiction writer usually finds assumption of a mask particularly comforting. It allows him a flexibility and openness to experience which formal suasion in his own person would tend to discourage, especially because it allows for the exploration of unconventional positions without explicit commitment. Carlyle's nervousness and uncertainty and the peculiar balance of his thoughts and feelings at the moment led him directly to fiction. That is not the only route to it, but like Carlyle's work, the Victorian novel and much of the work of the great essayists tend to weaken when the nervousness is disregarded and the will insists on finding meaning everywhere and confidence where there can only be hesitation.

The bitterness of much of Carlyle's later work seems to have been a function of his desperation. He looked everywhere and instead of people found heroes and villains—Robert Peel, Governor Eyre, and Frederick the Great; St. Ignatius Loyola and the "Nigger" (Jew also). As he came to realize that people would never take him seriously enough to reform themselves, he grew increasingly heedless of the dangers of self-exposure. His wounds were already too deep to be lacerated much more, and he became the victim of his own exaggerated rhetoric. Although he never entirely gave up the device of using spokesmen, the fictions became increasingly transparent. They were never again treated with the flexibility and richness one finds in *Sartor*. Driven by need, Carlyle began to mistake Teufelsdröckh and Sauerteig for himself, and the gentleness of much of his personal character was transformed in his prose into dogmatic abuse and violent denunciation. He willed the certitude of his fictions to be his own and was no longer, as he was in *Sartor*, his own best critic. F. R. Leavis has usefully suggested that George Eliot's fiction begins to weaken as soon as she blurs the distinction between herself and her characters. Analogously, Carlyle's art never again achieved the quality of *Sartor* because he never knew so clearly how different he was from his own creations.

The complex (not always conscious) deception that grew out of need for self-protection was one of the main forces in the nineteenth century leading to the dominance of fiction as an art form. The even more complex self-deception that grows out of need for certainty and the absolute, out of the *Sehnsucht nach der Unendlichkeit*, was one of the main forces that led to the baffling intermixture of pap and nonsense in the great works of the time. Sheer (even if disguised) force of will carried Carlyle away from fiction, but the lesson of *Sartor* might well be that all Victorian art aspired to the condition of fiction, not music, and where it swerved from this condition it tended to fail.

BRIAN JOHN

The Fictive World:
Past and Present

Past and Present (1843) is a suitable example of that marriage of history, vision, and art which Carlyle upheld as his alternative to the myopic present. The work is divided into four parts, entitled "Proem," "The Ancient Monk," "The Modern Worker," and "Horoscope." Clearly Carlyle's eye is upon past, present, and future, the numerous ways in which time past and time present interact, and the subsequent or future enlargement of man's experience and self. This is to be no cold objective eye cast upon the historically accurate fact; Carlyle's history is vivid, alive, essentially subjective but equally essentially epic in grandeur and scope. Indeed, he was perpetually writing his nineteenth-century epic, despite his calling it history or biography, literary or social criticism. In *Past and Present* he even clarifies "our Epic" as no longer being Virgil's "Arms and the Man" nor the Dandy's "Shirtfrills and the Man," but as having now become " 'Tools and the Man'." Some twelve years earlier, in a notebook entry of February 1831, he had asked himself, "Are the true Heroic Poems of these times to be written with the *ink of Science*? Were a correct philosophic Biography of a Man (meaning by philosophic *all* that the name can include) the only method of celebrating him? The true History (had we any such, or even generally any dream of such) the true Epic Poem?—I partly begin to surmise so." More recently, in *On Heroes and Hero-Worship*, he had described Luther as a quasi-poet: "He had to *work* an Epic Poem, not write one."

This is history seen against a background of Divine Force, Eternal Melodies, and Infinities of Time and Space; history as part of the Creation,

From *Supreme Fictions: Studies in the Work of William Blake, Thomas Carlyle, W. B. Yeats, and D. H. Lawrence.* © 1974 by McGill-Queen's University Press. Originally entitled "The Fictive World of Thomas Carlyle."

Fall, and Redemption; history in the epic, biblical, and Miltonic sense, involving divine as well as temporal participants, but brought up to date and given Romantic and Victorian bearings. We may see this plainly enough by comparing Carlyle's history of the French Revolution with Blake's poem on the same subject: in both works there is the same concentration upon the Revolution as a transcendental fact; the rising-up of the organic self no longer willing to submit to the static dead world of the *ancien régime*; the same vitalism with its apocalyptic imagery of thunder and fire, and its elemental imagery of earth, air, fire, and water; the same involvement of heaven and earth in violent catastrophe; the same concentration upon the heroic; even the same booming rhetoric and imagery of darkness, night, and sickness. What is so markedly different is Carlyle's especially Victorian fear that the release of dynamic energy will lead to anarchy in the Chartist England of the late thirties and Hungry Forties. Carlyle, as we have seen, was more of a conservative than Blake could ever be.

Just as this is history in an extraordinary sense, so too the writing goes beyond that mode we associate with history. For Carlyle's arguments consist of a succession of principles, images, and examples which intermingle and persistently attack the reader whenever opportunity arises, and which eventually work in conjunction to bowl him over and convert him to Carlyle's position. Needless to say, the arguments are not noted for their logic, their reliance upon rationality, or their moderation. Indeed, to read Carlyle for logic is to misread him. Rather, like D. H. Lawrence in our century, Carlyle appeals to our intuitive sense, to that divine spark in all men which enables them to transcend the limitations of a rational intelligence and grasp the eternal truth.

On turning to *Past and Present*, then, we are confronted with those targets we find elsewhere in Carlyle—those evils we may call plastic and which are conducive only to darkness. [John identifies as *plastic* those elements which lead to undesirable, and as *esemplastic* those elements which lead to desirable consequences, which follow from the fictile nature of the world—ed.] In shuttling back and fore in time, from present to past, Carlyle became only too aware of the spiritual decline of the modern world. And at the heart of darkness is the quack, sham, flunkey, valet, or phantasm: Carlyle uses a variety of terms to pinpoint that evil in all its protean shapes. The quack is synonymous with the cowardly and insincere, antithetical not only to the heroic but to the eternal nature of things upon which the heroic depends and with which it coincides.

> For Nature and Fact, not Redtape and Semblance, are to this
> hour the basis of man's life; and on those, through never such

strata of these, man and his life and all his interests do, sooner
or later, infallibly come to rest,—and to be supported or be swal-
lowed according as they agree with those. The question is asked
of them, not, How do you agree with Downing Street and ac-
credited Semblance? but, How do you agree with God's Universe
and the actual Reality of things? This Universe *has* its Laws. If
we walk according to the Law, the Law-Maker will befriend us;
if not, not. Alas, by no Reform Bill, Ballot-box, Five-point
Charter, by no boxes or bills or charters, can you perform this
alchemy: "Given a world of Knaves, to produce an Honesty from
their united action!" It is a distillation, once for all, not possible.
You pass it through alembic after alembic, it comes out still a
Dishonesty, with a new dress on it, a new colour to it. "While
we ourselves continue valets, how *can* any hero come to govern
us?" We are governed, very infallibly, by the "sham-hero,"—
whose name is Quack, whose work and governance is Plausibility,
and also is Falsity and Fatuity; to which Nature says, and must
say when it comes to *her* to speak, eternally No!

The appeals to Nature and Fact, as opposed to artifice and Semblance, are
inevitable and central to Carlyle's thinking. But here also is that continuing
dialogue carried on in his prose between himself and imaginary voices,
personae whose purpose is solely to state the contemporary alternatives in
all their weak stupidity, insensitivity, and absurdity. Here also is that same
use of clothes imagery which proved so successful to his satire in *Sartor
Resartus*. For what is a valet but a servant, a flunkey, no true hero, and whose
prime duties involve the laying out of clothes and the dressing of his gentleman? The valet goes hand in hand with the Dandy whom Carlyle ridiculed
and whose prominence in early nineteenth-century society he viewed with
alarm. Given Carlyle's propensity to satire, he shares the satirist's awareness
of the discrepancy between reality and appearance, between man as he is
and man as he should be. And what better example of such discrepancy is
there than the Dandy? Carlyle's logic was irrefutable: "A heroic people
chooses heroes, and is happy; a valet or flunky people chooses sham-heroes,
what are called quacks, thinking them heroes, and is not happy."

So that when Carlyle transports us back to the feudal and medieval, he
asserts roundly, "Coeur-de-Lion was not a theatrical popinjay with greaves
and steel-cap on it, but a man living upon victuals,—*not* imported by Peel's
Tariff." The assertion moves from the theatricality of the Dandy to the
economics of Peel's Corn Laws. The injustices and economic sufferings
associated with the Corn Laws are thus unheroic and seen as part of that

larger denial of the heroic which includes the theatrical. Similarly, when Carlyle escorts us to St. Edmundsbury, where his heroic monk, Samson, and a host of other medieval worthies are to be found, we are given certain directives which will enable us to perceive more clearly. For Carlyle's vision of history is not that of his contemporary pedant, Dryasdust, a persona borrowed from Scott, nor that of the dilettante. He is struck by the present ruins of the abbey, a suitable comment upon our times, but is not prevented from imaginatively reconstructing that ruined world and seeing the essential life and vitality it represented and still instructs us with.

> O dilettante friend, let us know always that it *was* a world, and not a void infinite of gray haze with fantasms swimming in it. These old St. Edmundsbury walls, I say, were not peopled with fantasms; but with men of flesh and blood, made altogether as we are. Had thou and I then been, who knows but we ourselves had taken refuge from an evil Time, and fled to dwell here, and meditate on an Eternity, in such fashion as we could? Alas, how like an old osseous fragment, a broken blackened shin-bone of the old dead Ages, this black ruin looks out, not yet covered by the soil; still indicating what a once gigantic Life lies buried there! It is dead now, and dumb; but was alive once, and spake. For twenty generations, here was the earthly arena where painful living men worked out their life-wrestle,—looked at by Earth, by Heaven and Hell. Bells tolled to prayers; and men, of many humours, various thoughts, chanted vespers, matins;—and round the little islet of their life rolled forever (as round ours still rolls, though we are blind and deaf) the illimitable Ocean, tinting all things with *its* eternal hues and reflexes; making strange prophetic music! How silent now; all departed, clean gone. The World-Dramaturgist has written: *Exeunt.*

The imagery is precisely appropriate, persuasive in its concreteness: the shin-bone, decayed as it may be, still evincing greater truth than the phantasms we choose to see; the arena reflecting that struggle all men either endure nobly or relinquish weakly; the abbey seen as an island in the midst of the eternal ocean, thus commenting upon man's smallness and his relationship to the Divine. And his last image, of God as "The World-Dramaturgist," points to the cosmic character of Carlyle's conception of history, but also, what is equally relevant, to his concentration upon the significance of individual players in this Divine Comedy. Like Blake and Yeats, among others, Carlyle saw history as a procession of great men, rather than an interplay of social, economic, or political forces. The latter phenomena occur only because of the emergence or disappearance of the heroic man. To quote Novalis, admired not only by Carlyle but by Hardy later, "Character is Fate."

When we turn to those images Carlyle uses to point out scornfully the inadequacy of the present, we find only death, mechanism, and hollow appearance of the real. There are two rightly famous examples to which he returns frequently in *Past and Present*: that of the dummy Pope in a Corpus Christi Day procession and that of a London hatter's advertisement. With obvious satirical relish and irreverence and that dramatic invention he uses continually, Carlyle describes the papal plight:

> The old Pope of Rome, finding it laborious to kneel so long while they cart him through the streets to bless the people on *Corpus-Christi* Day, complains of rheumatism; whereupon his Cardinals consult;—construct him, after some study, a stuffed cloaked figure, of iron and wood, with wool or baked hair; and place it in a kneeling posture. Stuffed figure, or rump of a figure; to this stuffed rump he, sitting at his ease on a lower level, joins, by the aid of cloaks and drapery, his living head and outspread hands: the rump with its cloaks kneels, the Pope looks, and holds his hands spread; and so the two in concert bless the Roman population on *Corpus-Christi* Day, as well as they can.
>
> I have considered this amphibious Pope, with the wool-and-iron back, with the flesh head and hands; and endeavoured to calculate his horoscope. I reckon him the remarkablest Pontiff that has darkened God's daylight, or painted himself in the human retina, for these several thousand years. Nay, since Chaos first shivered, and "sneezed," as the Arabs say, with the first shaft of sunlight shot through it, what stranger product was there of Nature and Art working together? Here is a Supreme Priest who believes God to be—What, in the name of God, *does* he believe God to be?—and discerns that all worship of God is a scenic phantasmagory of wax-candles, organ-blasts, Gregorian Chants, mass-brayings, purple monsignori, wool-and-iron rumps, artistically spread out,—to save the ignorant from worse.

In the same way that the Augustan poet's effect depends upon the subtle balancing of paradox within the couplet or the suspension of a line, so too does Carlyle's satirical tone depend upon the movement of his sentences; upon the fearful piling up of unfavourable evidence; the precise placement

of a word to obtain the greatest ironic effect (as in the absurd clerical par-
aphernalia listed here and finally modified by the adverb "artistically"); upon
the scornful editorial interjection ("What, in the name of God, *does* he believe
God to be?"); and upon the sudden deflation of the conclusion ("to save the
ignorant from worse"). However, as Levine has argued, Carlyle's mature
prose is distinguished from his early, more eighteenth-century style by its
"drama" and "passion," relying for its effect upon a dramatic, rather than
an intellectual, presentation and appeal.

But we need not go abroad for phantasms, as Carlyle quickly points
out. Another image is seized upon to give vent to his *saeva indignatio*:

> The Hatter in the Strand of London, instead of making better
> felt-hats than another, mounts a huge lath-and-plaster Hat, seven-
> feet high, upon wheels; sends a man to drive it through the streets;
> hoping to be saved *thereby*. He has not attempted to *make* better
> hats, as he was appointed by the Universe to do, and as with this
> ingenuity of his he could very probably have done; but his whole
> industry is turned to *persuade* us that he has made such! He too
> knows that the Quack has become God. Laugh not at him, O
> reader; or do not laugh only. He has ceased to be comic; he is
> fast becoming tragic.

The tragedy is more easily recognizable when we attend to other imagery
Carlyle uses to define the present: images of sickness and disease, paralysis
and disability. So that we find the condition of England, for example, imaged
as a "chronic gangrene" at the heart of which is the fact that man has lost
his soul, lost all awareness of soul, abandoned the eternal principle of soul
which should be the foundation of self and society. "This is verily the plague-
spot; centre of the universal Social Gangrene, threatening all modern things
with frightful death."

Appropriately enough, Carlyle inherits the Romantic image of the upas
tree, a mythical tree poisoning all things around it. And with that dialectic
which for Carlyle runs through all things, the upas has its antithesis in another
favourite Carlylean image, the Tree Igdrasil. The dialectic then is defined
by way of a host of images, of sickness and evil as opposed to vitality, health,
and goodness. The life-giving organic Force is in the present perverted into
the inorganic stasis which is the death of the universe and self. The tree,
like that of Matthew Arnold's Scholar-Gypsy and many another Romantic
tree, evidences the eternal, is a suitable image for the eternal permeating the
temporal—the only testimony of permanence, stability, and continuity in a
world rapidly resembling a darkling plain. "I am for permanence in all

things," Carlyle asserted. And since "the Life-tree Igdrasil, in all its new developments, is the selfsame world-old Life-tree," it is this which enables Carlyle to write his history, to focus his eyes and ours upon that which is permanent in a shifting world. For it is his business as editor of "these confused Paper-Masses now intrusted to him"

> to select a thing or two; and from the Past, in a circuitous way, illustrate the Present and the Future. The Past is a dim indubitable fact: the Future too is one, only dimmer; nay properly it is the *same* fact in new dress and development. For the Present holds in it both the whole Past and the whole Future;—as the LIFE-TREE IGDRASIL, wide-waving, many-toned, has its roots down deep in the Death-kingdoms, among the oldest dead dust of men, and with its boughs reaches always beyond the stars; and in all times and places is one and the same Life-tree!

Carlyle's sentences are correspondingly all-embracing, reaching out in all directions, and thrilling with the same expression of force and vitality. For a similar rhetorical effect we turn again to D. H. Lawrence, who shares the same panache, the same charismatic appeal, and whose sentences depend equally for their persuasiveness upon such a piling-up of phrases and biblical alliteration. Paul West has gone further, seeing in *Sartor Resartus* "the nearest thing to the verbal debauchery" of Joyce's *Ulysses*. And certainly Carlyle is more conscious and precise than his blurring of vision and sound makes him appear. His is a calculated, if cantankerous, imprecision; a style in a state of flux, or Becoming. V. S. Pritchett has said Carlyle "used language as a forceps," and indeed it is birth pangs we associate with his creative style. Like an Old Testament Jehovah, he seeks to refashion the world after his own image, creating it anew and capturing its essence in the very concreteness of his style. At best such a stylistic achievement can only approximate that solidity he ascribed to action alone. Moreover, the prophetic voice has no time for the unwilling reader; we either embrace Carlyle or reject him violently. He answers affirmatively, as did Blake, to the question posed in *The Marriage of Heaven and Hell*, "does a firm perswasion that a thing is so, make it so?" For, like Blake, he believed "firm perswasion" entailed the rising up of the self in all its fullness and grasping the transcendent Fact.

Devices like the dummy Pope and the hatter's advertisement serve to dramatize and make concrete Carlyle's satire and are reiterated frequently. Once established, they both hold the strands of his arguments together and convince us of his veracity. Having received the image once, and having had it hammered at us thereafter, we come finally to recognize the reference and with the recognition—a *déja connu*—comes eventual acceptance. For just as he has particular images and concrete instances which describe and define the abstract principle to be upheld or denied, so too Carlyle plies us with a long line of such images, instances, and personae which dramatize them. He populates a whole world, in fact, in the manner of the satirist, a world which careers along a course he wishes us to reject absolutely.

The fictile nature of the world is such, therefore, as to give rise either to good or evil: good government, order, peace, and heroic aristocratic life; or bad government, order, peace, and heroic aristocratic life; or bad government, disorder, war, and unheroic democratic life. The potentialities within existence, as within man, are infinite. For we have it in us to pursue light or darkness, follow the gleam or the sham. If the present world offers us only the wrong choices, we may reject them, to work for the more desirable and, in the end, only alternative, founded upon hero-worship. For the antithesis of the sham, the dandy, the external man, is the right inner-true man, the hero. What characterized the medieval past for Carlyle was precisely this willingness, on a mass scale, to recognize the eternal realities and choose the heroic man to govern. The present depends upon certain machinery— a suitably industrial and nonvital image—machinery of the ballot box, extended suffrage, the Workers' Charter; and the result is the chaos of the nineteenth century. Rid ourselves of reliance upon mechanical devices by which to choose our heroes and the essentially benevolent, interpenetrating organic Force will correct the balance. The true man will organically evolve, as Carlyle shows in the election of Samson as the new abbot of St. Edmundsbury. And he will prove the "very singular man and landlord" that the original Edmund, later canonized, was seen to be. Of the latter, St. Edmund, Carlyle wrote:

> For his tenants, it would appear, did not in the least complain of him; his labourers did not think of burning his wheat-stacks, breaking into his game-preserves; very far the reverse of all that. Clear evidence, satisfactory even to my friend Dryasdust, exists that, on the contrary, they honoured, loved, admired this ancient Landlord to a quite astonishing degree,—and indeed at last to an immeasurable and inexpressible degree; for, finding no limits or utterable words for their sense of his worth, they took to beatifying and adoring him! . . . His life has become a poetic, nay a religious *Mythus*; though, undeniably enough, it was once a prose Fact, as our poor lives are; and even a very rugged unmanageable one.

"No man," Carlyle adds, "becomes a Saint in his sleep."

Medieval society, founding its pattern of life upon the feudal system, was essentially one of relationship, of bonds of love and affection, loyalty, fidelity, and obedience. "The Feudal Baron had a Man's Soul in him," lived a "fruitful enlarged existence," had "men round him who in heart loved him; whose life he watched over with rigour yet with love; who were prepared to give their life for him, if need came. It was beautiful; it was human! Man lives not otherwise, nor can live contented, anywhere or anywhen. Isolation is the sum-total of wretchedness to man. To be cut off, to be left solitary: to have a world alien, not your world. . . . It is the frightfulest enchantment; too truly a work of the Evil One." So far has plasticity led us, when we fail to organize or render organic that which lacks proper shape and order. Blake labelled this condition "Single vision & Newtons sleep," at the opposite pole to which was the reorganized self. And precisely this isolation, alienation, and enchantment Carlyle saw in the St. Ives Workhouse in Huntingdonshire, an experience which affected him so deeply that, with another visit, to St. Edmundsbury in Suffolk, it gave rise to *Past and Present*. To echo the particular persona he uses at the beginning of the work, the picturesque tourist, "There was something that reminded me of Dante's Hell in the look of all this; and I rode swiftly away."

It was indeed a Dantean Hell which Carlyle had stumbled upon: the hopeless, degrading state to which England's poor were doomed, in the name of progress, efficiency, laws of economics, and charity. He rightly called them "Workhouse Bastilles" or "Poor-law Prisons." Feudal society with its practice of the principle of relationship overcame such economic and spiritual alienation by recognizing that men could make legitimate demands upon their lords and their lords on them. Society was thus organized and unified, its plasticity rendered esemplastic: man one with man, with Nature, and with God. Latter-day society distorted that relationship into one of cash payment and substituted "nomadism" for permanence and reduced men to the level of things. Despite his tirades against "rose-pink Sentimentalism" and misplaced philanthropy, Carlyle remains vitally concerned with man as man.

In order to dramatize the mammonism of the present, Carlyle relies primarily upon three recurrent images, three dramatic and concrete instances that serve as metaphors for the cash-payment condition of contemporary society: that of the Workhouse Bastille; of the Stockport assize case he called also the Ugolino Hunger-tower, or -cellar; and, lastly, of the typhoid Irish widow. The Workhouse Bastille imposes a state of enchantment upon its inhabitants and upon England as a whole, a dreadful enchanted sleep from

which Carlyle attempts to rouse us to an awareness of the unreality and hell
of the present and the glorious eternal existence surrounding us. The parallel
with Blake's sleeping figures is obvious. The Ugolino Hunger-tower, taken
from Dante's *Inferno*, is seen in its present form as revealed by the case at
the Stockport assizes:

> A Mother and a Father are arraigned and found guilty of poi-
> soning three of their children, to defraud a "burial-society" of
> some 3£.8s. due on the death of each child: they are arraigned,
> found guilty; and the official authorities, it is whispered, hint
> that perhaps the case is not solitary, that perhaps you had better
> not probe farther into that department of things.

He concludes in sombre incredulity: "This is in the autumn of 1841." Or
the third instance, of the typhoid Irish widow, again a historical fact which
he read of in a contemporary account:

> A poor Irish Widow, her husband having died in one of the Lanes
> of Edinburgh, went forth with her three children, bare of all
> resource, to solicit help from the Charitable Establishments of
> that City. At this Charitable Establishment and then at that she
> was refused; referred from one to the other, helped by none;—
> till she had exhausted them all; till her strength and heart failed
> her: she sank down in typhus-fever; died, and infected her Lane
> with fever, so that "seventeen other persons" died of fever there
> in consequence. The humane Physician asks thereupon, as with
> a heart too full for speaking, Would it not have been *economy* to
> help this poor Widow? She took typhus-fever, and killed sev-
> enteen of you!—Very curious. The forlorn Irish Widow applies
> to her fellow-creatures, as if saying "Behold I am sinking, bare
> of help: ye must help me! I am your sister, bone of your bone;
> one God made us: ye must help me!" They answer, "No; im-
> possible; thou art no sister of ours." But she proves her sisterhood;
> her typhus-fever kills *them*: they actually were her brothers,
> though denying it! Had human creature ever to go lower for a
> proof?

The irony here is clear and effective; and its effect upon the reader is heightened by Carlyle's refusal to give the facts in a purely historical way. The
facts must be dramatized, people made to come to life, persona conflicting
with persona, in order that we be moved out of our nineteenth-century
indifference and misguidedness.

Once more the instance is played off against the medieval and feudal, in the figure (taken from Scott's *Ivanhoe*) of "Gurth, born thrall of Cedric the Saxon, . . . greatly pitied by Dryasdust and others." Carlyle admits that "Gurth, with the brass collar round his neck, tending Cedric's pigs in the glades of the wood, is not what I call an exemplar of human felicity." Though he may idealize the medieval past, Carlyle is not entirely blind to its limitations. Indeed, in "Horoscope," the last section of *Past and Present*, he turns from "the hard, organic, but limited Feudal Ages," to "glance timidly [*sic*] into the immense Industrial Ages, as yet all inorganic, and in a quite pulpy condition, requiring desperately to harden themselves into some organism!" But in weighing the condition of Gurth's thralldom with that of the Irish typhoid widow, in comparing the extent to which Gurth's relationship with his master is one founded on obedience, yet the present is still found wanting. "Gurth to me seems happy, in comparison with many a Lancashire and Buckinghamshire man of these days, not born thrall of anybody!" And he concludes scornfully: "Gurth is now 'emancipated' long since; has what we call 'Liberty.' Liberty, I am told, is a divine thing. Liberty when it becomes the 'Liberty to die by starvation' is not so divine!" The same tragic absurdity of the situation we find in the shirtless millions in an age of cheap cotton, or in the Irish *Sans-potato* in "Chartism."

Now it matters little to Carlyle that we might accuse him of a gross idealization of the past, of focusing strangely unhistorical eyes, of sharing, with Scott, Tennyson, Morris, or the early Yeats, that same impulse to retreat into a romantic past. For although he may proclaim that "this is not playhouse poetry; it is sober fact," Carlyle is neither sober nor in the usual sense factual. Indeed, his method of arriving at Fact bears considerable resemblance to the Romantic imaginative process. What constitutes a Fact for Carlyle is that which is recognized by the whole man rising up in a creative oneness of self, to an intuition, in an essentially fictive moment, of the eternal realities. The moment is one in which past, present, and future fuse into a transcendent moment, in and out of time; a numinous moment when the self is confronted in its vortex vision with the transcendent Fact. Such a transcendence is possible in the first place because Carlyle's universe is essentially optimistic, a place where good will inevitably triumph over evil; and, in the second, only if the self is constituted in such a way as to correspond in its esemplastic unity to similar, though larger, unities which are Nature and God. This epiphany is perhaps clearest in Carlyle's several classifications of the hero in *Heroes and Hero-Worship*: of the hero as divine, as prophet, as possessing transcendental wisdom; in short, as the supremely good and supremely wise man. Its most concrete expression is in the quasi-mystical experience Teufelsdröckh undergoes in *Sartor Resartus*. Consequently, history is transformed into transcendental Fact and involves the working out of the redemptive process in the universe and in individual men. Those who are heroic in Carlyle's eyes have the greatest propensity to grasp such a Fact. All men, in essence, possess this ability; it is more completely possessed and practised by some to whom we should turn for leadership. For they glance from heaven to earth, follow the gleam, struggle to know it and communicate it to society at large. Again Carlyle's logic is (to him) irrefutable: to his critics he answered simply, in the manner of Blake and any other prophet, that they were unable to perceive as completely and transcendentally as he.

In attempting to enlarge upon the imaginative process by which men are to find themselves and the only true reality, again we find Carlyle depending not only upon certain Romantic principles and arguments but upon recurrent Romantic and traditional imagery. The most obvious and inevitable images are those of light, darkness, and fire. The darkness is that of the myopic present, the satanic principle pulling all things down to one common level of mechanism and death: "dead and dark,—all cold, eyeless, deaf," a "thick Egyptian darkness" of materialism and the Flesh. The fire is both phoenixlike and apocalyptic, and prepares for the light. As such, the fire corresponds to Carlyle's elevation of war and violence, an elevation which seems to accompany almost inevitably a philosophy of Force. The light is that which all men necessarily prefer and should strive to attain, the light of the transcendent Fact. And one dominant image in the section of *Past and Present* dealing with the medieval past is that of the light burning in St. Edmund's shrine. The imagery of light is extended further to include the heightened perceptions, particularly the superior eyesight, of Carlyle's medieval heroes: "these clear eyes of neighbour Jocelin," "daily in the very eyesight, palpable to the very fingers of our Jocelin"; Samson with "those clear eyes." Or again, in that more sacramental tone he reveals on occasion, Carlyle pronounces, with obvious relevance to his own art, "It is not known that the Tongue of Man is a sacred organ; that Man himself is definable in Philosophy as an 'Incarnate *Word*.' "

We should not be misled by Carlyle's transcendentalism to believe that he thus depreciated the physical and sensory. His transcendentalism goes hand in hand with a sacramentalism. Quoting Novalis, for example, to comment upon the dead St. Edmund, Carlyle clarifies the need for obedience: " 'Bending before men,' says Novalis, 'is a reverence done to this Revelation in the Flesh. We touch Heaven when we lay our hand on a human Body.' " For, like Blake, Carlyle could conceive the Divine Image as the Human Form

Divine—"Go or stand, in what time, in what place we will, are there not immensities, Eternities over us, around us, in us"—though he is never as thoroughgoing as Blake and considerably more élitist. Yet his concluding chapter to *Past and Present* is strongly reminiscent of Blake in its apocalyptic vision and tone:

> Gradually, assaulted from beneath and from above, the Stygian mud-deluge of Laissez-faire, Supply-and-demand, Cash-payment the one Duty, will abate on all hands; and the everlasting mountain-tops, and secure rock-foundations that reach to the centre of the world, and rest on Nature's self, will again emerge, to found on, and to build on. When Mammon-worshippers here and there begin to be God-worshippers, and bipeds-of-prey become men, and there is a Soul felt once more in the huge-pulsing elephantine mechanic Animalism of this Earth, it will be again a blessed Earth.

The hero is characterized not only by his superior eyesight but by his silence, his denial of cant and noise, and his struggling to articulate the inarticulate. Samson is the silent strong man, whose "*in*eloquence" is "his great invaluable 'talent of silence'!" Carlyle prefers "silent practice" to "talking theory," a practical sense he saw in the Romans, English, and Russians as opposed to the "ever-talking, ever-gesticulating French." For the capacity for silence involves also the recognition of the Eternal Silence.

Hence the modern man of letters, as distinguished from Carlyle's literary hero, is a "twangling, jangling, vain, acrid, scrannel-piping man," whose sole purpose is to soothe the reader's soul "with visions of new, still wider Eldorados, Houri Paradises, richer Lands of Cockaigne." The literary hero, on the other hand, offers poetry which is *"musical Thought,"* work which is discernible from a mere "Daub of Artifice" by its relevation of the Infinite. One sees "Eternity looking through Time; the Godlike rendered visible." Carlyle's objections to fiction, then, in *Past and Present*, are directed against the ultra-sentimental novels of the Minerva Presses and not against fiction per se. The imagination proper, with its insight into the *natura naturans*, by way of symbols, remains the best means to truth. Nor is it restricted to the aesthetic mode but extended to include the metaphysical and practical modes also. Carlyle in fact is not far from the orthodox Romantic position as evidenced in Coleridge's distinctions between Imagination and Fancy, Reason and Understanding. Indeed, Carlyle described Shakespeare and Goethe in an early essay, "Goethe's Works" (1832), as melting down reality to create it anew—the esemplastic action of the secondary imagination. Carlyle's term was *"fusible"*: "For Goethe, as for Shakespeare, the world lies all translucent, all *fusible* we might call it, encircled with WONDER." A similar task in the practical world he envisaged for the industrial hero in his later works.

Carlyle is indeed as much concerned with the integration of the personality as the major Romantics; in the final analysis, this is his overall concern. Despite his attacks upon the Byronic self-consciousness, which he saw, with utilitarianism, as responsible for modern egotism, subjectivism, and sentimentalism, Carlyle is no less preoccupied with the self and its potential fullness of experience. More, in certain respects we can see him working with characteristically Romantic principles, though perhaps using them in an individual way. Above all, he does so in a way we may term "literary." Not always is he as persistently fictive, as in *Sartor Resartus*, but he demands critical literary attention. With all his disregard for literature, his faulty ear, his limited critical opinions, Carlyle remains the self-conscious, creative artist, using an armoury of satirical techniques which we do not always credit him with being capable of using.

There remain still other fictive elements in Carlyle's style. The great weight of his truth, for example, is achieved partly by his own attempts at conversion and partly by persistent reference to and dependence upon a large number of sources or authorities. My list is not meant to be complete, but amongst those cited in *Past and Present* [are] not only Jocelin of Brakelond but also Homer, Virgil, Horace, Seneca, Ovid, the Bible, Dante, Shakespeare, Ben Jonson, Milton, Cromwell, Dryden, Addison, Dr. Johnson, Sterne, Goldsmith, Voltaire, Novalis, Richter, Maria Edgeworth, Burns, Scott, Tennyson (it helped his reputation), and, for good measure, Carlyle himself. We might note the number of epic poets included; indeed, Carlyle's authorities are almost exclusively literary. He is not engaged in name-dropping nor literary snobbery, attempting to display the nature and extent of his reading. The many literary and topical allusions with which his work abounds derive in part from the editorial role he was fond of playing, a role which was in varying degrees a defence against personal ridicule. Like Eliot in *The Waste Land*, he is also attempting to suggest the eternal nature of the problems facing mankind and to indicate the inadequacy of the present in confronting these problems and providing the kinds of answers men have always had to rely upon. In other way, too, he shows by his extensive cross-references that kind of enlightenment which awareness of the past, in literature as well as history, can provide us with. In this respect for the past and man's particular attempts at answering the riddles of the universe, he shows himself the historian but also, and eminently, the artist.

But Carlyle does not stop here. *Past and Present* is not only laced with the authority of those who are truly great but populated with a whole dra-

matis personae, either of Carlyle's own invention or taken from contemporary
society or from his reading. So that the work comes alive in a more dynamic
way yet again, with a glorious gallery of personae worthy of Thomas Love
Peacock or Byron in *Don Juan*. Another contemporary parallel, as Levine
has noted, is Browning, who, like Carlyle, is preoccupied with the revelation
of personality in all its complexities in a transcendent and numinous moment.
However, Carlyle's insights are limited by his satirical intent: his personae
remain two-dimensional in a way Browning's almost never do. Indeed, Carlyle fails to recapture that "solidity" he recognized in action—"Narrative is
linear, Action is *solid*"—and his personae remain pale, inadequate versions
of the real. Whatever solidity or fuller expression of the real which Carlyle's
prose communicates is achieved not by his personae but by that kind of
saturation of "plethora" Paul West has described. The style blurs and absorbs
rather than makes more precise, for Carlyle seeks to convulse as well as
convert.

Apart from the obvious characters in Carlyle's epic—St. Edmund, Abbot Hugo, Samson, and Bozzy Jocelin—we find a world of lesser fictitious
ones who appear and disappear when the occasion demands, representing
the scales of virtues and vices, somewhat in the manner of Dante's *Inferno*:
"Bobus Higgins, Sausage-maker on the great scale, . . . raising such a clamour for this Aristocracy of Talent" in the *Houndsditch Indicator* (a fictitious
paper, incidentally) and whose arguments run "in a vicious circle, rounder
than one of [his] own sausages"; Dryasdust, the pedantic historian; Sauerteig,
one of Carlyle's imaginary philosophers; Blusterowski and Colacorde, "editorial prophets of the Continental-Democratic Movement"; Teufelsdröckh,
carried over from *Sartor*; those arch-enemies, Sir Jabesh Windbag, Mr. Fac-
ing-both-ways, Viscount Mealymouth, Earl of Windlestraw, all antithetical
to the real aristocracy of talent; "the indomitable Plugson too, of the respected
Firm of Plugson, Hunks and Company, in St. Dolly Undershot"; or a
Voltairean Prussian, "his Excellenz the Titular-Herr Ritter Kauderwälsch
von Pferdefuss–Quacksalber" ["Sir Gibberish Clovenfoot–Quack Doctor"];
and so on. It may be Carlyle lacks the verve and gusto of Byron, but they
both have their roots in eighteenth-century satire. We remember also that
among his contemporaries Carlyle's laugh was notorious. In *Past and Present*
he is willing to allow even the near-scatological joke when he quotes Jocelin's
description of my Lord of Clare: "The Earl, crowded round (*constipatus*) with
many barons and men-at-arms." "I love honest laughter," Carlyle writes,
"as I do sunlight, but not dishonest." And it is the tragic absurdity of the
modern world his laughter makes us constantly aware of: in a society characterized by its overproduction and unfed, unclothed masses, he sees only

"millions of shirts, and empty pairs of breeches, [which] hang there in judgment against you." His vision is sharper, his language and tone more satirical,
than Thomas Hood's in "The Song of the Shirt," and his sympathy may be
correspondingly more effective and convincing.

The social commitment in all this is in part the inevitable consequence
of Carlyle's satirical intent and in part the result of his uneasiness with his
own profession of writing. Consequently, "Literature . . . is a quarrel, and
internecine duel, with the whole World of Darkness that lies without one
and within one." This much we have seen. Yet the social commitment did
not entail the abandonment of literary techniques nor mean that Carlyle was
unable to practise them effectively. Certainly he became more desperate in
later life, more aware of society's unwillingness to seek spiritual health, and
certainly his later fictions become increasingly transparent, his personae real
people (Governor Eyre, Sir Robert Peel, Hudson, the railway tycoon). We
cannot conclude that his creative vision is abandoned, that the greater prac-
ticality of the *Latter-Day Pamphlets* or "Shooting Niagara" clashes with the
use of fictive techniques. To do so would be to misread these works much
as did his contemporaries. Fitzgerald himself wrote to a correspondent: "Do
you see Carlyle's Latter-Day Pamphlets? They make the world laugh, and
his friends rather sorry for him. But that is because people will still look for
practical measures from him. One must be content with him as a great satirist
who can make us feel when we are wrong, though he cannot set us right.
There is a bottom of truth in Carlyle's wildest rhapsodies." We in turn
overlook Carlyle's comic genius and, even in those works denouncing literature as lying, his reliance upon fictive and, more particularly, satirical
techniques.

The structural image, for example, of "Shooting Niagara: and After?"
is that of Niagara Falls, that disastrous state to which England, by way of
the 1867 Reform Act, is being drawn like a drowning man. The image is
surprisingly undeveloped, but there remain other supporting images: of the
whirlpool; the Pit of Hell; the swarmery of bees denoting the contemporary
muddle; the "malodorous quagmires and ignominious pools" of the pestilential present; the inevitable imagery of light, fire, darkness, and sleep; and
that animal imagery Carlyle was so fond of that his world seems full of rabid
dogs and dumb cattle, or more fearful creatures (the chimera, boa constric-
tors, rattlesnakes, and apes). The concrete and dramatic sense is still here,
though the tone is more abrasive and authoritarian, the irony more inclined
to heavy sarcasm.

Most important of all is Carlyle's distinction between the Speculative
and the Industrial hero, a distinction which clarifies his final position and

recurrent faith in the creative vision. While he may spend more time with the practical or Industrial hero, yet he is also insistent that both types belong to the "Aristocracy of Nature" as distinguished from the hereditary aristocracy. Though their functions are different—the Speculative hero fulfills himself in speech, the Industrial in silent action—

> these are of brother quality; but they go very different roads: "men of *genius*" they all emphatically are, the "inspired Gift of God" lodged in each of them. They do infinitely concern the world and us; especially that first or speaking class,—provided God *have* "touched their lips with his hallowed fire"! Supreme is the importance of these. They are our inspired speakers and seers, the light of the world; who are to deliver the world from its swarmeries, its superstitions (*political* or other);—priceless and indispensable to us that first Class!

Carlyle does not fail to estimate either the worth of the Speculative hero or the "visionary" nature of the task, for it is a role he took upon himself. What needs noting, however, is the all-important qualification: the Speculative hero's worth depends upon the extent to which he is *truly* inspired—"provided God *have* 'touched their lips with his hallowed fire'!" Likewise, while he might proceed to reject scornfully "Art, Poetry and the like" as "that inane region," "a refined Swarmery," and warn the Aristocrat against "Fiction" with its "alarming cousinship . . . to *Lying*," he does so to distinguish "real 'Art' . . . as Fact." Hence, the Bible is "the *truest* of all Books," and "Homer's *Iliad*, too, that great Bundle of old Greek Ballads, is nothing of a *Fiction*." In Shakespeare he admires "not the Fiction" but "the fact"; "the traces he [Shakespeare] shows of a talent that could have turned the *History of England* into a kind of *Iliad*, almost perhaps into a kind of *Bible*." This is indeed the great work in hand for Victorian England, and we have seen the extent to which Carlyle's own work, with its elevation of heroes, its personae, imagery, dramatic and concrete sense, above all its attempts at epic grandeur and revelation of the cosmic Divine Fact, approximates to the task.

While only halfway in his career Carlyle was described by Elizabeth Barrett in an enthusiastic letter to Robert Browning (27 February 1845) as "the great teacher of the age." She proceeded in more explicit fashion to comment upon Carlyle's dual position as artist-sage, seeing the two roles as by no means antithetical:

> He fills the office of a poet—does he not?—by analysing humanity back into its elements, to the destruction of the conventions of

the hour. That is—strictly speaking—the office of the poet, is it not?—and he discharges it fully, and with a wider intelligibility perhaps as far as the contemporary period is concerned, than if he did forthwith "burst into a song."

Whether we accept this view of the poet is irrelevant, though it is a view by no means foreign to either Yeats or Lawrence in their conceptions of the artist. In the case of Carlyle, his fictive world is certainly nothing like the sober fact he would have us believe, and his achievement lies in literature rather than in history or philosophy. For his creative vision leads him to enunciate in Victorian terms the familiar Romantic aesthetic principles—of energy, creativity, imagination, transcendence, symbol—and to express that creative vision through essentially literary means. His two roles—of historian and literary hero—are always together influencing his vision to make the Carlylean Fact indeed a *fictive* one.

PHILIP ROSENBERG

A Whole World of Heroes

THE HERO IN CARLYLEAN HISTORY

Behind Carlyle's critique of democracy as an inadequate way of meeting the needs of the people—that is, as an inadequate method of organizing England for political and social regeneration—lay a positive sense of the direction English political life must take. The so-called hero theory served Carlyle as a focal point around which he could arrange all that he wanted to affirm about contemporary political reality. For him the hero theory was both a historical and a moral principle, and his claim that it "lay most legible" in all that he had written is not far from the truth.

There is nothing in the least complex or intricate about Carlyle's conception of heroes, their role in history, and the role he would have them play in society as he wants it to be, although the amount of polemical ink spilled on the subject can lead one to imagine that Carlyle's thinking about heroes and the heroic is a mass of subtleties which requires considerable critical unraveling. The hero theory is neither more nor less than the claim that, in the final analysis, the process we call history is a web of individual actions.

Carlyle begins his one book devoted specifically to the subject of heroes with the statement that "Universal History, the history of what man has accomplished in this world, is at bottom the History of the Great Men who have worked here." It is an unfortunate opening, in that it has provided so convenient—though inaccurate—an encapsulation of his hero theory that practically all of the critical literature on the subject has amounted to little more than an extended gloss on this single text. For example, in Sidney

From *The Seventh Hero: Thomas Carlyle and the Theory of Radical Activism.* © 1974 by the President and Fellows of Harvard College. Harvard University Press, 1974.

Hook's *The Hero in History* we find that scornful attention is directed at "the Carlylean fantasy that the great man was responsible for the very conditions of his emergence and effectiveness," a conclusion which Hook apparently derives from Carlyle's statement that great men are at the "bottom" of the historical process. Hook then goes on to contrast Carlyle's excesses in this department with the more reasonable ideas of other thinkers who limited the latitude of history's great men to the area marked out by routinely present possibilities: "The reaction to the exaggerated 'heroism' of Carlyle in the nineteenth century did not deny the existence, and even the necessity, of the hero and heroic action in history. What it maintained was that the events to which such action led were determined by historical laws or by the needs of the period in which the hero appeared. . . . These social forces would summon up when necessary from the deeps of mankind some hero whose 'mission' it was to fulfill the historic tasks of the moment. The measure of his greatness consisted in his degree of awareness of what he was called upon to do."

Surely Hook is right to call the idea of an omnipotent hero capable of turning the course of history an excess, but the fantasy is Hook's rather than Carlyle's. Indeed, one does not even know where to begin refuting such an interpretation—and it has been so influential, so commonly received as true, that its pernicious effects on Carlyle's reputation are beyond computation—for it is so totally unrelated to anything Carlyle wrote as to be beyond contradiction. Were it not for the fact that this sort of mangling of Carlyle by Hook and others has been so influential, one would of course ignore these parodies of Carlyle's thought. As it is, one must deal with them, and perhaps one may even be thankful to these distortions for providing an occasion for clarifying just how much Carlyle's hero theory means to imply about the role of the hero in history.

If one begins by applying a little common sense to the matter, one recognizes at once that the statement that history is fundamentally the history of great men makes no outlandish claims at all. It is, on the contrary, almost a truism. By opening any history book at random one can see immediately that there are far more capital letters than the number of sentences in the book might lead one to expect. Indexes are compiled for history books on the basis of the perception that the most salient moving forces of history are entities with proper names. Great men are, obviously, what most historical writing is concerned with, and it is therefore reasonable to assume that they are crucial to history itself.

Nowhere does Carlyle imply that these great men have an absolute power over the historical milieu in which they work. On the contrary, he

was acutely aware of the importance of the character of an age in determining
the range of achievement possible in that age; before one could determine
what actions were possible at a given moment it was necessary to read the
"signs of the times," as Carlyle indicated by inaugurating his career as a
social commentator with an essay under that title. Thus Carlyle would not
have written, as Albert Mathiez did in describing the political situation on
the eve of the French Revolution, that "What was wanted at the head of the
monarchy, to dominate the crisis which threatened, was a king. But there
was nobody but Louis XVI." Carlyle never permitted himself to forget that
forces far larger than those which any man could have at his disposal already
had dictated that "the French Kingship had not, by course of Nature, long
to live." In such a context, Louis' incompetence could only "accelerate Nature," and, conversely, a heroic king could have done no more than retard
it. Although Carlyle does, indeed, exhort the king to take bold and forthright
action, he generally does so with an ironic awareness that such action could
be no more than a dignified, lovely, but nonetheless vain gesture. Thus
Louis' attempt to flee in June 1791, which resulted in his ignominious capture
at the Varennes archway by a grocer and a handful of villagers, earns from
Carlyle this apostrophe: "Phlegmatic Louis, art thou but lazy, semi-animate
phlegm, then, to the centre of thee? King, Captain-General, Sovereign Frank!
if they heart ever formed, since it began beating under the name of heart,
any resolution at all, be it now then, or never in this world. . . . Alas, it
was not *in* the poor phlegmatic man. Had it been in him, French History
had never come under this Varennes Archway to decide itself," Carlyle
concludes, offering the tantalizing suggestion that a hero in Louis' place
indeed could have turned the course of history.

Yet if one looks beyond this single sentence, offered at a moment of
intense crisis as a way of characterizing the pusillanimous king, one cannot
fail to observe that Carlyle knew that action of even the most heroic stamp
could have done nothing to stop the course of the Revolution. Even as the
king first contemplates flight, Carlyle asks, "Grant that poor Louis were safe
with [General] Bouillé, what, on the whole, could he look for there? Exasperated Tickets of Entry [i.e., émigrés] answer: Much, all. But cold Reason
answers: Little, almost nothing." The frequent apostrophes in his *History of
the French Revolution* should not be taken to mean that Carlyle imagined that
bold and heroic action could deflect the larger forces of history; it was, rather,
a question of meeting those forces with dignity. Thus Carlyle often calls
upon a hero or would-be hero to act, to give some existential gesture asserting
defiance of an unacceptable and unalterable state of affairs. Even after Louis
is sentenced to death, Carlyle continues to urge him to action, not because

he believes any possible action could stay his execution, but precisely because it cannot. "The silliest hunted deer dies not so," Carlyle reminds the king.

So far is Carlyle from holding the doctrines of historical indeterminacy that Hook attributes to him that he is at great pains to point out, in connection with each of the heroes he discusses, the extent to which the hero's actions were shaped and conditioned by the world around him. The hero must be, he insists time and time again, in touch with "reality": "A man is right and invincible, virtuous and on the road towards sure conquest," Carlyle announces, "precisely while he joins himself to the great deep Law of the World, in spite of all superficial laws, temporary appearances, profit-and-loss calculations; he is victorious while he cooperates with that great central Law, not victorious otherwise. . . ." Just as Hegel writes that "World-historical men—the Heroes of an epoch—must . . . be recognized as its clear-sighted ones," so Carlyle expresses his awareness of the historical limits within which the hero must operate by placing a high valuation on insight and clarity of vision as the most important qualities in a heroic actor. Muhammad is a hero to Carlyle because "The great Fact of Existence is great to him," because "He has actually an eye for the world," because reality "glared-in upon him"; great poets are Carlylean heroes because of their "sincerity and depth of vision," and Shakespeare is held to be the supreme poet because there is not to be found "such a power of vision . . . in any other man"; Luther is placed in Carlyle's pantheon because of his unrelenting awareness of "the awful realities of things": "It is the property of every Hero, in every time, in every place and situation, that he come back to reality; that he stand upon things, and not shows of things"; John Knox, Carlyle says, is a man who "cannot live but by fact: he clings to reality as the shipwrecked sailor to the cliff." Mirabeau, Carlyle claims, "has become a world-compeller, and ruler over men," not because he controls historical forces and can direct them at his will, but because he sees and understands the historical forces with which he must work: "the characteristic of Mirabeau . . . is veracity and sense, power of true *insight*, superiority of vision." In the same way Danton, the "Mirabeau of Sansculottes," derives his power from his ability to comprehend the true state of things: "it is on the Earth and on Realities that he rests"; "like Mirabeau, [he] has a natural *eye*. . . ." Even "Cassandra" Marat, with his infallibly accurate diagnoses of the situation around him, and Robespierre, "his feline eyes excellent in the twilight," take on heroic dimensions in proportion as they are able to "control" the Revolution by guiding it over a course whose direction is dictated by forces which they do not control.

In all of these cases the greatness of the hero derives from his ability to recognize an as yet unrealized truth and to assist as midwife at its birth. Luther, Carlyle points out, did not bring the Reformation, for "the Reformation simply could not help coming." The Carlylean hero is never a man who fashions history out of his own will, but is at all points a man willing, Carlyle says, to submit to the "great deep Law of the World," just as Hegel says that his world-historical man is one "whose own particular aims involve those large issues which are the will of the World-Spirit." Thus a hero like Cromwell is impotent to act until historical developments have prepared the way for his mission: "Long years he had looked upon it [the godlessness of the king's government], in silence, in prayer; seeing no remedy on Earth; trusting well that a remedy in Heaven's goodness would come,—that such a course was false, unjust, and could not last for ever. And now behold the dawn of it; after twelve years silent waiting, all England stirs itself; there is to be once more a Parliament, the Right will get a voice for itself: inexpressible well-grounded hope has come again into the Earth. Was not such a Parliament worth being a member of? Cromwell threw down his ploughs, and hastened thither."

Just as Cromwell is, Carlyle makes clear, in an important sense a product of the movement he led, so it is true of all of Carlyle's heroes that they act in response to the social needs of the cultures which produced them. "Before the Prophet can arise who, seeing through it [the false idol worshipped by the people], knows it to be mere wood, many men must have begun dimly to doubt that it was little more." In this fact lies the open secret of Carlyle's theory of heroes and hero-worship, for on page after page Carlyle tirelessly reiterates that the hero is the virtual delegate of his followers, led on and incited by them, reflecting their desires back to them in the form of leadership. As Luther approached the Diet of Worms in 1521, "The people . . . crowded the windows and housetops, some of them calling out to him, in solemn words, not to recant: 'Whosoever denieth me before men!' they cried to him,—as in a kind of solemn petition and adjuration. Was it not in reality our petition too, the petition of the whole world . . . : 'Free us; it rests with thee; desert us not!' "

It is always the case with the hero, Carlyle writes, that "What he says, all men were not far from saying, were longing to say." Because this is the inevitable condition of herohood, it follows that the necessary preconditions for heroism lie in the people themselves: "Not a Hero only is needed, but a world fit for him; a world not of *Valets*;—the Hero comes almost in vain to it otherwise!"

In thus acknowledging that the hero's career is shaped by the society in which he finds himself, Carlyle made sure that his hero theory was at all points compatible with his awareness of the role the masses of anonymous men play in history. "Social Life is the aggregate of all the individual men's Lives who constitute society; History is the essence of innumerable Biographies," he had written years earlier, and there is no contradiction between this statement and the one with which he opens *On Heroes and Hero-Worship*. For Carlyle the idea that history should be the biography of great men and the idea that it should be the essence of the biographies "of all the individual men . . . who constitute society" were alternative forms of the same truth. A hero was a great man precisely because he was able to speak articulately "what all men were longing to say."

"BUT I SAY UNTO YOU . . ."

Carlyle's hero theory is Hegelian and Weberian rather than Nietzschean. For Nietzsche the context in which the hero can realize himself is a society of mass men, of "herd animals": "Whoever has preserved, and bred in himself, a strong will, together with an ample spirit, has more favorable opportunities than ever," Nietzsche wrote. "For the trainability of men has become very great in this democratic Europe; men who learn easily and adapt themselves easily are the rule: the herd animal, even highly intelligent, has been prepared. Whoever can command finds those who *must* obey. . . ." The willfulness of the hero and the will-lessness—that is, the willing submission—of his followers are the key variables in the etiology of power as Nietzsche traces it.

Carlyle, however, speaks of submission in connection with the hero theory only rarely, and when he does it is significantly the hero rather than the hero-worshipper who must submit. The hero's role in "this great God's-World," Carlyle writes, is "to conform to the Law of the Whole, and in devout silence follow that; not questioning it, obeying it as unquestionable." In stark contrast to the Nietzschean idealization of will, Carlyle asserts that "Great souls are always loyally submissive, reverent to what is over them; only small mean souls are otherwise." Nowhere is the hero-worshipper called upon for anything like the total surrender of self that characterizes the hero. On the contrary, the role of hero-worshipper is entered into by exercising discretionary choice in "electing" the hero as one's leader and oneself as his follower. In both *Past and Present* and *On Heroes and Hero-Worship* Carlyle lays great emphasis on the importance to a society of selecting the leaders it will follow. Thus Carlyle, who, as we have seen, satirized political elections, nevertheless maintained that an election "is a most important social act; nay, at bottom, the one important social act." The contradiction between these starkly opposite evaluations of the worth of elections is, I think, on the surface merely. The elections which Carlyle speaks of as among the most important social acts are not at all like the routinely administered ballotings by which one chooses between candidates for institutional office; indeed, as we shall see shortly, the decision to follow a hero is invariably a repudiation of the routinely offered choices. Electing a leader in Carlyle's sense is a matter of great moment and takes on some of the characteristics associated with a religious conversion, for it constitutes no less than a decision as to what one's own calling is to be; to be truly meaningful, an election must be not so much a choice *between* potential leaders as a choice *of* a leader. What is more, insofar as it is a true election it is in a very real sense an election of oneself into the role of charismatic followership as much as it is an election of the hero. Such an "election" is the beginning of action for the individual making the decision, for in casting one's lot with a hero one commits oneself to an active role in the cause the hero leads; in contrast, the political election is an end of action, for in casting a ballot one votes for a candidate to whom, if he is successful, one will delegate one's potential for action.

Carlyle's belief that the hero is called upon to submit to superior powers whereas his followers are permitted to exercise discretion in choosing or not choosing to follow him is a logical corollary of his understanding of herohood as primarily a matter of insight into the true state of social or even cosmic affairs. In this respect the distinction between the hero and the hero-worshipper exclusively depends upon the fact that the former has his insight directly, via an intuitive apprehension of reality or an explicit communication from god, whereas the follower gains insight only indirectly, from the mouth of the hero himself. Followership, therefore, is essentially a voluntaristic, noncoercive relationship to the hero, for the follower "obeys those whom he esteems better than himself, wiser, braver; and will forever obey such; and even be ready and delighted to do it."

In recognizing that submission is relevant to hero-worship primarily with regard to the hero's relationship to *his* source of authority rather than with regard to the follower's relationship to the hero, Carlyle anticipated what was to become, in the writings of Max Weber, one of the most important and paradoxical aspects of the theory of charismatic power. Thus Weber notes on the one hand that the charismatic leader "does not derive his 'right' from their [his followers'] will, in the manner of an election. Rather, the reverse holds: it is the *duty* of those to whom he addresses his mission to recognize him as their charismatically qualified leader." But on the other hand it is also the case that "The genuinely charismatic ruler is responsible precisely to those whom he rules," for although he invariably does not "regard

. . . his quality [of charisma] as dependent on the attitudes of the masses toward him," the fact remains that "It is recognition on the part of those subject to authority which is decisive for the validity of charisma." In other words, although the hero is self-appointed—that is, he sees himself as appointed by god or by necessary forces in world history—and tends to see his followers as duty-bound to acquiesce in his charismatic authority (just as he himself is duty-bound to acquiesce in the dictates of his authority source), it is nevertheless the case that the followers have no duty to the hero except insofar as they accept the validity of his charisma and acknowledge that his path is the true one for them.

Carlyle drew two conclusions from this understanding of the nature of duty in a charismatic relationship. In the first place, he maintained that hero-worship is in no way incompatible with the traditional Protestant emphasis on "private judgment." The notion that Protestantism stands for freedom of private judgment as against the institutionally coerced judgments of Roman Catholicism is, Carlyle argues, deeply mistaken. The Catholic Church may indeed define for its votaries various forms of belief, but it can do so only because its votaries are convinced that Roman Catholicism is on the whole valid. "The sorriest sophistical Bellarmine, preaching sightless faith and passive obedience, must first, by some kind of *conviction*, have abdicated his right to be convinced. His 'private judgment' indicated that, as the advisablest step *he* could take."

At first glance this argument itself seems somewhat sophistical, and we may well wonder at the validity of contending that the abdication of the right to judgment constitutes a legitimate exercise of judgment. In this connection, however, we should note that the case here is not really comparable to the seemingly analogous case, discussed by John Stuart Mill, involving the question of whether the concept of freedom entails the right to sell oneself into slavery. The difference between the two—and it is enough of a difference to render them incommensurable—is that the situation Carlyle is dealing with involves an ongoing process whereas Mill is concerned with what obviously must be a single irreversible event. The person who accepts the role of followership and thereby exercises his option to renounce his private judgment does so for as long as and insofar as he continues to be convinced of the validity of the charismatic claims of the leader.

The second conclusion Carlyle derived from his understanding of the role of submission with respect to charismatic authority led him to minimize the distinction between hero and hero-worshipper. As he saw it, both parties in the relationship submit to what they take to be the true and just mandate of god and/or history and are, through this submission, acting out of their own convictions. Unlike Nietzsche, for whom hero and hero-worshipper are diametrically opposed concepts, Carlyle argues that the difference between them is merely one of degree, for the hero is a man with enough power of vision to see the truth of the world as it stands before him, whereas the follower has power of vision sufficient only for seeing the truth when it is shown to him. It is for this reason that Carlyle was able to say that hero-worship itself is a form of heroism. "The Valet does not know a Hero when he sees him!" Carlyle told his audience at the lectures on heroes and hero-worship, echoing the point made by both Goethe and Hegel. "Alas, no: it requires a kind of *Hero* to do that . . . ," he explained, just as, in *Past and Present*, he reminded his readers that hero-worship was possible only "by being ourselves of heroic mind."

There is nothing fanciful in Carlyle's notion that only a heroic mind can choose to follow a hero, for the hero and his followers are always a band of rebels, compacted together in a daring and invariably dangerous mission. The charismatic leader and his followers are inevitably a revolutionary force inasmuch as their mission is based on a sense of duty unconnected to the institutional sources which legitimate authority in the sociopolitical world. From the point of view of legitimate institutions, therefore, charismatic authority at best can stand as merely an alternative to them, but in most cases it will directly threaten them. "Charismatic domination," Weber writes, "means a rejection of all ties to any external order. . . . Hence, its attitude is revolutionary and transvalues everything; it makes a sovereign break with all traditional or rational norms. . . ." "From a substantive point of view, every charismatic authority would have to subscribe to the proposition, 'It is written . . . , but I say unto you . . .' "

Because charisma is by definition a counterlegitimate force, the charismatic leader requires of his followers the courage to renounce all normal ties to society and to turn their backs on what they have been taught to see as a legitimate order. The type of "passive obedience," Ernst Cassirer accuses Carlyle of preaching can have no place in the camp of the hero. It was not docility of temperament that induced "thirteen followers" to take up Muhammad's mission and go with him into the desert; if those who followed Cromwell can be accused of passive obedience, then legitimate authority is in more trouble than it realizes. "I am come to set a man at variance against his father," Jesus warned his disciples as a way of reminding them that charismatic followerhood demands the courage to say no to all normal bonds of loyalty. "He that loveth father or mother more than me is not worthy of me," he declared, making clear that it is precisely passive obedience that must be renounced if one is to join in the active obedience of charismatic followership.

Although critics of theories such as Carlyle's often contend that submission to a charismatic leader readily degenerates into a permanent system of subordination, in fact this danger is effectively minimized by the principled nature of Carlyle's support of charismatic leadership. Charisma is, as Weber explains, an extremely unstable political base. It tends either to collapse when faced with temporary defeats or to routinize itself into an institutional structure which is by its nature no longer charismatic. Although this latter possibility has led to the charge that Carlyle's hero theory is inherently totalitarian, such a criticism could be valid only if Carlyle's ideas about heroes were considerably less self-conscious than they are, if they had been developed as political propaganda rather than as political theory. As propaganda, a defense of the prerogatives of any particular leader on the grounds of his charismatic election indeed could be transformed readily into support of the leader even after he had used his charismatic mandate to build a system of dictatorial institutions.

As theory, however, the defense of the charismatic hero retains its integrity despite practical disappointments. It is in the nature of political theory to be self-conscious and critical, to stand aside from the pragmatic vicissitudes of politics and to measure them by its own unchanging yardstick. The hero, being human and fallible, may attempt to cash in his charisma, to erect a dictatorial apparatus, but it is precisely at this point that those who, like Carlyle, are committed on principle to nonbureaucratic and non-statist types of leadership will turn from him as from a traitor. Moreover, it is not inconceivable that a charismatic leader himself, if he is in principle committed to maintaining the charismatic and revolutionary nature of his own rule, would resist attempts to institutionalize his leadership. Indeed, Richard H. Solomon, in his provocative study of Maoist China, suggests that the Cultural Revolution of the late 1960s sprang from just such an impulse on the part of Mao Tse-tung: "it has been Mao himself . . . ," Solomon writes, "who has resisted the trend toward reconsolidation of domestic political order out of his fears that the momentum of social change would die. The Cultural Revolution is not a manifestation of the failure of Party rule; quite the contrary, it is a result of Mao's objection to the Party's success."

Perhaps Carlyle was being naive in his belief that charismatic leaders and their followers could remain true to their principles, but I can find nothing inherently unreasonable in his faith that there is no better training

for resistance to the imposition of power than the combination of self-assertion and self-discipline required for membership in a band of rebel followers.
And when these traits are combined with a conscious, theoretical commitment to charismatic rebellion itself, the dangers of a lapse into totalitarianism
are, at the very most, no greater than they inevitably must be so long as the
means of massive coercion exist.

Carlyle's call for a rebirth of the spirit of hero-worship is, we should
now be able to see, a call for resistance rather than for submission. When
Carlyle criticized contemporary culture on the grounds that the mass of men
no longer seemed able or willing to find and follow heroes, he distinguished
between two contrasting types of non-hero-worshippers. On the one hand
there are the "Vallets," a term taken, via Hegel or, more likely, Goethe,
from the aphorism that no man is a hero to his valet and applied to all those
who are constitutionally or on principle opposed to acknowledging the existence of men superior to themselves. The second type of non-hero-wor-
shipper is the "Flunkey," the very antithesis of the Valet. Just as the Valet
is the man temperamentally indisposed to perceiving heroism where it exists,
so the Flunkey is a man temperamentally disposed to perceiving it where it
does not exist. It is Flunkeyism, Carlyle warns, that will be the undoing of
democracy in England, for the very deference which Bagehot was to celebrate
a few decades later as the magical mortar that held the British sociopolitical
system together meant to Carlyle that, for the most part, the *demos* of England
was fatally disposed to defer to its social superiors rather than to its true
betters. Never much worried that the masses, under democracy, would
become self-willed and disinclined to accept the leadership of wiser men,
Carlyle greatly feared that, through an excess of deference, they would
submit themselves to the leadership of respectable quacks. "Seek only deceitful Speciosity, money with gilt-carriages, 'fame' with newspaper-para-
graphs, whatever name it bear, you will find only deceitful Speciosity;
godlike Reality will be forever far from you," he warned.

Time and again, therefore, Carlyle uses the hero theory to remind his
readers of the dangers of excessive willingness to defer to self-proclaimed or
socially acknowledged superiors. In this sense, the first task of the man who
would worship heroes is a revolutionary task—the withholding of deference
from all those not worthy of it and the ejection of them from government.
When the spirit of hero-worship is fully developed, Carlyle prophesies, "we
shall . . . know quacks when we see them; cant, when we hear it, shall be
horrible to us! We will say, with the poor Frenchman at the Bar of the
Convention . . . : *'Je demande l'arrestation des coquins et des lâches.'* 'Arrestment
of the knaves and dastards': ah, we know what a work that is; how long it

will be before *they* are all or mostly got 'arrested':—but here is one; arrest him, in God's name; it is one fewer! We will, in all practicable ways, by word and silence, by act and refusal to act, energetically demand that arrestment,—'*je demande cette arrestation-là!*'— and by degrees infallibly attain it."

Most commentators on Carlyle's hero theory have emphasized the hero-worshipper's loyalty to his leader, and in doing so they have forgotten that loyalty in this context must be preceded by a courageous act of disloyalty to the established order, which is the habitat of the "knaves and dastards" whose arrestment is the first order of business in a heroic world. In general, the literary critics who have had their innings with Carlyle have followed Freud in assuming that the relationship between a follower and a charismatic leader is modeled on and therefore stands as a continuation of normal patrilineal authority. The family, according to Freud, is the prototype of all authority relationships: "What began in relation to the father," Freud wrote, "is completed in relation to the group," for "The leader of the group is still the dreaded primal father. . . ." Such an analysis of group leadership is valid only if one is aware—as Freud himself was but as literary Freudians tend not to be—that an identification of this nature is a two-edged weapon, for to whatever extent the leader of the group "is still" the primal father, he is also precisely *not* the father. To say that the charismatic leader replaces the father is to indicate some of the tensions inherent in the situation of the follower, who can perceive himself as loyal insofar as he sees the hero as the father, and can perceive himself as criminal insofar as he sees the hero as taking the place of the father. Undoubtedly, no relationship of charismatic leader and follower is totally free of this ambivalence, and there is probably no point at all in taking either of the polarized halves of it to be the essential feature of the relationship as a whole. It is simultaneously true that the charismatic figure continues "what began in relation to the father" and that, as Max Weber observed, charisma "is contrary to all patriarchal domination." The charismatic hero takes on the roles of father, priest, and king, but in doing so he is a stranger in the father's place, an iconoclast in the priest's, and a regicide in the king's.

THE SEVENTH HERO

"I am for permanence in all things," Carlyle wrote, knowing full well that there could be no permanence in the historical world. All clothes grow old, he had recognized from the start, and require to be cast off; new clothes must be made to replace them. With each moment that passes, some bold and heroic insight ossifies itself into an institutional form, routinizes itself, and thus becomes no longer capable of generating true political action. It becomes, in Karl Mannheim's terminology, an occasion for administrative and reproductive functioning rather than for political creativity. With each moment, therefore, one hopes that a hero will arise to call upon all those who are willing to become "sansculottes"—to go with him outside of the institutional sphere, and there establish a new order, a new culottism, which is in turn fated to be overthrown by the next sansculottes.

"[I]n this Time-World of ours there is properly nothing else but revolution and mutation," Carlyle had acknowledged in his *History of the French Revolution*, and it therefore followed that the only permanence possible to man was the permanence of revolutionary change itself. In his attempt to build a political system on the basis of revolutionary charisma, Carlyle had finally arrived at the only possible completion for the system of his thought. From whichever angle one approaches it, all of Carlyle's thought points to this one overriding conclusion. In terms of his lifelong search for a mode of self-realization, a way out of the enervating solipsism of the world of self-centered egoism, which would at the same time avoid the alienation or annihilation of self that resulted from simple work in the routinely present world of organized social categories, Carlyle had long known that creative action in the time-world of history was the possibility that must be explored. Yet the hero-actor must be a revolutionary because all true action is inherently revolutionary, a repudiation of the world of formula and a commitment to the creation of new modes of social interrelationship. As a political ideology which takes as its highest ideal a continuous openness to historical action, Carlyle's theory of political action is a doctrine of permanent revolution.

Moreover, revolution entails by definition the universalization of herohood, as Carlyle had shown by laying bare the way the French Revolution had abrogated the monopoly of political action formerly enjoyed by kings, courtiers, and legislators, and had moved the historical arena out onto the streets. "The most indubitable feature of a revolution," Leon Trotsky has written, in a statement which accurately reflects Carlyle's sense of the matter, "is the direct interference of the masses in historic events. In ordinary times the state, be it monarchical or democratic, elevates itself above the nation, and history is made by specialists in that line of business—kings, ministers, bureaucrats, parliamentarians, journalists. . . . The history of a revolution is for us first of all a history of the forcible entrance of the masses into the realm of rulership over their own destiny."

Carlyle's hero is preeminently the man who forces his way into the realm of rulership over his own destiny, and his followers are those who make it possible for him to do so by their readiness to enter the world of creative action with him. This asymmetrical dependency in the relationship of leader and follower is at the heart of the radical meaning of Carlyle's hero theory, for the presence of a heroic disposition among those from whom the hero is to draw his followers is, as we have seen, a vital prerequisite for the hero's own career. Conversely, the heroic readiness of the masses makes the existence of the hero, as authoritative leader of others, in an important sense irrelevant. The very process which makes the hero possible, the coming into being of a mass of people prepared and willing to act resolutely on what they believe to be the true nature of things, necessarily creates a revolutionary situation in which the people will refuse to tolerate sham, quackery, and the imposition upon themselves of government by those unfit to govern.

For this reason Carlyle, who preached of the duty to find and follow a hero, never felt the personal necessity of subordinating himself to a leader, never found a contemporary hero to worship. More than a few students of Carlyle have noted this fact as a discrepancy in his teachings on hero-worship, maintaining that secretly Carlyle always had himself in mind when he spoke of heroes. Far from being a discrepancy, however, this is as it should be. *On Heroes and Hero-Worship* deals with six types of heroism, but it points inexorably toward a seventh hero—the hero as oneself. Precisely because true hero-worship is to Carlyle a form of heroism, the coming of the hero is not a matter of crucial moment to the man ready for action. "[W]e will strive and incessantly make ready, each of us, to be worthy to serve and second such a First-Lord!" Carlyle writes of the hero. "We shall then be as good as sure of his arriving; sure of many things, let him arrive or not."

With his hopes centered on the formation of a world permanently open to political action—a permanently revolutionary world—Carlyle felt, as he reflected on the centuries of revolution that had commenced with the Protestant Reformation, much reason for optimism. "In all this wild revolutionary work, from Protestantism downwards, I see the blessedest result preparing itself. . . . If Hero mean *sincere man*, why may not every one of us be a Hero?" he asked in 1840. Why not, indeed, he answered three years later: " 'Hero-worship,' if you will,—yes, friends; but, first of all, by being ourselves of heroic mind. A whole world of Heroes . . . that is what we aim at!"

JOHN P. FARRELL

Transcendental Despair:
The French Revolution

There are two much-quoted descriptions of *The French Revolution*. Mill began his review of it by saying that "this is not so much a history, as an epic poem." Froude, a long while later, responded: "It is rather an Aeschylean drama composed of facts literally true, in which the Furies are seen once more walking on this prosaic earth and shaking their serpent hair." Froude is more accurate. The French Revolution did not achieve epic harmony as a political event, and it does not do so in Carlyle's symbolic retelling either. The work is addressed to Carlyle's own world and it attempts to discover a new social order. The discovery, indeed, is made; but how forbidding it is we shall see. As a history, the book rests on the negative content of revolution; its essential purpose is to redefine, radically, the meaning of hope in a transitional age. This theme is made quite explicit.

> Hope deferred maketh the heart sick. And yet, as we said, Hope is but deferred; not abolished, not abolishable. It is very notable, and touching, how this same Hope does still light onwards the French Nation through all its wild destinies. For we shall find Hope shining, be it for fond invitation, be it for anger and menace; as a mild heavenly light it shone; as a red conflagration it shines: burning sulphurous-blue, through darkest regions of Terror, it still shines; and goes not out at all, since Desperation itself is a kind of Hope. Thus is our Era still to be named of Hope, though in the saddest sense,—when there is nothing left but Hope.

From *Revolution as Tragedy: The Dilemma of the Moderate from Scott to Arnold.* © 1980 by Cornell University. Cornell University Press, 1980. Originally entitled "Carlyle: The True Man's Tragedy."

The book insists on this point and on the tragic action it specifies. It is through the idea of tragedy that Carlyle explains the strange metamorphosis of hope upon which his analysis of the revolution depends. Strikingly, we are given a development that first envisions a tragedy based on the revolution's positive content, moves, after a fashion, toward a tragic action that responds to its latent content, and at last wrests hope from despair by siphoning energy from the revolution's negative content. These phases are shaped by the central, governing feature of the book's design. Carlyle's history is divided into three parts: "The Bastille," "The Constitution," and "The Guillotine." At the exact midpoint of the book—that is, halfway through "The Constitution"—occurs the death of Mirabeau. Carlyle sees Mirabeau as a political figure, but he also sees him as a man inspired by a poetic consciousness. In Mirabeau's death we witness the loss of imagination in the revolution. It is the great crisis of the whole book, and it organizes the events preceding it and following it. For before Mirabeau's death we have been shown that the *philosophes* cannot make their revolution through reason work. And after Mirabeau's death, the irrational force of the Jacobins is unleashed. Representing Nature's savage assertion against a life founded on lies, the Jacobins emerge to establish the primitive rights of "Reality." ("The Guillotine" is the climax of this process.) Thus the book's three principal stages come to this: the galling of the *philosophes*; the death of Mirabeau; the violence of the sansculottes. Each is represented as, in its own way, a tragic event, though clearly Carlyle looks constantly to the last stage, which he calls "transcendental despair." Transcendental despair brings a ferocious kind of catharsis where hope is reborn not so much out of pity and fear as out of blind terror.

There is nothing implausible in finding that Carlyle uses a narrative design that matches the general scheme of revolutionary content discussed earlier in this study. Carlyle was imbued with the idea of revolution; his art was its mirror. But it is important, of course, to see that his understanding of tragedy in *The French Revolution* is stamped by his own characteristic emphases. As a visionary historian, he comes bearing the tragic knowledge that reform is grievous—even for orators in the National Assembly. As a poet, he sees a tragic situation when the creative man is strangled by innumerable "packthreads." And, as a political thinker, he stresses that the greatest catastrophe lies in the fact that men have been forced to rebel by the fiats of history and by the dictates of their own alienated nature. There is, as well, a certain degree of resemblance between the phases of the Revolution as Carlyle discerns them and the stages of modern history defined in his essay on Scott. The world of the *ancien régime* is historically analogous to the void in which Scott worked, where several things had to be carried to their ultimatum and crisis. "The Constitution" is a version of the labyrinth in which seekers of the new world wander without discovery and can only curse the present. "The Guillotine" is the hell of radical action.

"The Bastille" begins with a survey of the void, the decadent age in which no ideal could grow or prosper. Belief and loyalty had passed away. "All Solemnity has become Pageantry; and the Creed of persons in authority has become one of two things: an Imbecility or a Macchiavelism" (sic). The leaders of France try to support their false position by loans and *lettres de cachet*, but they cannot overcome their nullity. The historic meeting of the Estates General becomes an occasion for Carlyle to review the injustice of the traditional arrangements in French society. Later, when the Third Estate summarily converts itself into the National Assembly, the journey out of the void has begun.

The crisis of July 14 is now predictable. Carlyle, in this part of the book, engages our sympathy for men who have taken upon themselves the grief of revolution. "O poor mortals, how ye make this Earth bitter for each other; this fearful and wonderful Life fearful and horrible; and Satan has his place in all hearts? Such agonies and ragings and wailings ye have, and have had, in all times:—to be buried all, in so deep silence; and the salt sea is not swoln with your tears. The tone that one hears in this passage has been carefully built up over two chapters (Book Five, Chapters iv and v). These chapters take us to the night of July 13. "Under all roofs of this distracted City is the nodus of a drama, not untragical, crowding towards solution. The bustlings and preparings, the tremors and menaces; the tears that fell from old eyes! This day, my sons, ye shall quit you like men."

The fall of the Bastille is the solution, however, of only an intermediate drama. A larger drama begins, or rather, the issues in the larger drama suddenly emerge. What is happening is "surely a great Phenomenon: nay it is a *transcendental* one, overstepping all rules and experience; the crowning Phenomenon of our Modern Time." The taking of the Bastille proved that the "age of Conventionalities" was over, that mere formulas would not do. For long years it had seemed "as if no Reality any longer existed . . . and men were buckram masks that went about becking and grimacing." Then, "on a sudden, the Earth yawns asunder, and amid Tartarean smoke, and glare of fierce brightness, rises Sansculottism, many-headed, fire-breathing, and asks: What think ye of *me*? Well may the buckram masks start together terror-struck. . . . *Wo also to many a one who is not wholly buckram, but partly real and human*" (italics, added). Carlyle has brought before us, not Teufelsdröckh but the sansculotte with blood on his hands, and he has named him the singular reality of the modern world. This is the sort of "fact" that matters to the visionary historian. It is in itself a tragic fact, and it points toward other, not less tragic facts. One such fact, guardedly hinted at, is the woe in store for those who are partly real and human (mainly, the moderates).

The way in which Carlyle will finally judge these facts (particularly in "The Guillotine") is unobtrusively decided in the very next paragraph. "Truth of any kind breeds ever new and better truth; thus hard granite rock will crumble down into soil, under the blessed skyey influences; and cover itself with verdure, with fruitage and umbrage. But as for Falsehood . . . what can it, or what should it do but . . . decompose itself, gently or even violently, and return to the Father of it,—too probably in flames of fire." This is the bedrock of moral consciousness in *The French Revolution*, which one may dismiss as grotesquely expedient or accept as a tragic vision. For it is clearly the function of tragedy in this book to hallow "truth of any kind," making it palatable until some sweeter truth can be raised by the blessed skyey influences.

At this point in "The Bastille" the awesome difficulty of climbing completely out of the void is stressed. Hannah Arendt's analysis of the revolutionary's dilemma is apposite: "If foundation was the aim and end of revolution, then the revolutionary spirit was not merely the spirit of beginning something new but of starting something permanent and enduring. . . . From which it seems to follow that nothing threatens the very achievements of revolution more dangerously and acutely than the spirit which brought them about." This is precisely what Carlyle calls "the question of questions . . . for rebellers and abolishers." In "The Bastille" this question illuminates the inevitable collapse of the moderate party that tried to lead the revolution. For the moderates were the prisoners of the freedom they celebrated. Carlyle carefully builds up the tensions that began to debilitate the philosophical seekers of freedom, once they called revolution to their assistance. They became figures in the dramatic dialectical dance.

> The Revolution is finished, then? Mayor Bailly and all respectable friends of Freedom would fain think so . . . ? Which last, however, is precisely the doubtful thing, or even the not doubtful. Unhappy Friends of Freedom; consolidating a Revolution! They must sit at work there, their pavilion spread on very Chaos; between two hostile worlds, the Upper Court-world, the nether Sansculottic one; and beaten on by both, toil, painfully, perilously,—doing, in sad literal earnest, "the impossible."

"The Bastille" concludes with the insurrection of the "maenad-led" mob in early October and the retrieval of Louis from Versailles. These events show the impossibility of consolidating the revolution. The king and the people had scores to settle.

"The Constitution" summarizes the fruitless labor of rationalizing the revolution to which the friends of freedom were condemned. All the while, Carlyle reminds us, sansculottism was maturing. "Thus if the sceptre is departing from Louis, it is only that, in other forms, other sceptres, were it even pike-sceptres, may bear sway." No one yet takes the sansculottes seriously, except Mirabeau, who begins "to discern clearly whither all this is tending." The passive point of view is that of the moderate patriots who believe the Constitution will march—once it gets legs to stand on. The active point of view, however, is the visionary's who knows that "dark is the way of the Eternal as mirrored in this world of Time: God's way is in the sea, and his path in the great deep."

So the National Assembly plays at making miracles while Louis commences his forty-one months of ever increasing danger in the Tuileries and the sansculottes grow from kittens into tigers. The miracle sought by the National Assembly would have been wrought "successfully, had there been any heaven-scaling Prometheus among them; not successfully, since there was none." The problems are massive. A civil constitution for the clergy must be worked out, the provinces of France must be united, royalists must be watched, traitors arrested, food found, and the angry kings of Europe kept in their place. "Such things has an august National Assembly to hear of, as it goes on regenerating France. Sad and stern: but what remedy"? As always, the remedy is Hope. "O blessed Hope, sole boon of man: whereby, on his strait prisonwalls, are painted beautiful far-stretching landscapes; and into the night of very Death is shed holiest dawn."

Carlyle, at this point, drops even the narrowest account of the political maneuvering the debate in Paris, and grandly mines a once familiar political vocabulary for its special metaphorical meanings. Whole chapters are developed around such terms as "symbolic representation" and "federation" as Carlyle suggests the profound social and spiritual implications of what the world stares at in perplexity. These implications plainly resolve themselves into a single significance: the enormity of attempting to replace the religious *Thou shalt* with the secular *I will*. This is a leap toward anarchy made in the guise of government. "With noise and glare, or noiselessly and unnoted, a whole Old System of things is vanishing piecemeal: the morrow thou shalt look, and it is not."

As the relative ineffectuality of the unvisionary legislators becomes apparent, the strength of the clubs grows. Jacobins, Cordeliers, the Feuillants breed and multiply. The clubs are actually cells shaping a new organic structure to replace the old one that has vanished and the theoretical one that arrived stillborn. Although there are many clubs, only one carries the right genetic code. "All clubs . . . fail, one after another. . . . Jacobinism alone has gone down to the deep subterranean lake of waters."

By the end of 1790 France had reached a state of "clangour and clamour, debate, repentance,—evaporation. Things ripen towards downright incompatibility." Only one man could have saved France from the agony of inconclusiveness. But Mirabeau died in the spring of 1791. From the beginning, Mirabeau is made a hero. Carlyle gives little space in *The French Revolution* to Mirabeau's bizarre career prior to 1789, and, although he alludes to his "questionable" nature on several occasions, we are given few details of his disreputable background. He is introduced mysteriously: "Count Mirabeau, who has got his matrimonial and other Lawsuits huddled up, better or worse; and works now in the dimmest element in Berlin . . . scents or descries richer quarry from afar. He, like an eagle or vulture, or mixture of both, preens his wings for flight homewards."

But Mirabeau found that the nobles would not have him as one of theirs, and so he "stalks forth into the third Estate." In order to ingratiate himself with his prospective constituency (at least as rumor would have it), he opened a cloth shop in Marseilles, and "became a furnishing tailor." Carlyle remarks that "even the fable that he did so, is to us always among the pleasant memorabilities of this era."

Once established, Mirabeau is no longer eagle or vulture: Carlyle begins to see him as a Lion. It is occasionally assumed that Carlyle made so much of Mirabeau only because there was no other great man to admire. There is no question that he is less than a perfect hero for Carlyle, but that Carlyle genuinely esteemed him is clear both from the history and from passages in his other works. In the "Six Lectures on Revolutions in Modern Europe" (1839, unpublished but reported in *The Examiner*), Carlyle was emphatic in his estimate:

> The "strongest man" of the eighteenth century was Mirabeau, "a very lion for strength,—unsubdueable—who could not be beaten down by difficulty or disaster, but would always rise again: *an instinctive man*,—better than a premeditative; your professional benefactor of mankind being always a questionable person." Mirabeau would have been the Cromwell of the French Revolution, had he lived. "A gigantic heathen was he, who had swallowed all formulas; a man whom we must not love, whom we cannot hate, and can only lament over, and wonder at."

This is the Mirabeau who commands Carlyle's allegiance in *The French Revolution*, the Mirabeau who says, "The National Assembly? *C'est moi.*"

Carlyle sees Mirabeau's death as climactic because without him France could not easily escape from the labyrinth of its own making. The alternatives facing it were "slow-pining chronic dissolution and new organisation; or a swift decisive one; the agonies spread over years, or concentrated into an hour. With a Mirabeau for Minister of Governor, the latter had been the choice; with no Mirabeau for Governor, it will naturally be the former." Mirabeau was composed of a rare union, "the glorious faculty of self-help" combined miraculously with "the glorious natural gift of *fellowship*." This makes him "a born king of men. . . . A man not with *logic-spectacles*; but with an *eye*." As the miasma of constitution making spreads over France, Mirabeau tries to effect a compromise with Louis (for which he will later be vilified) and to reconcile all of the conflicting parties by the force of his indomitable will. Carlyle makes a brilliant portrait of Mirabeau commanding France to stand back from the abyss.

> What can murmurs and clamours, from Left or from Right, do to this man; like Teneriffe or Atlas unremoved? With clear thought; with strong bass voice, though at first low, uncertain, he claims audience, sways the storm of men: anon the sound of him waxes, softens: he rises into far-sounding melody of strength, triumphant, which subdues all hearts; his rude seamed face, desolate, fire-scathed, becomes fire-lit, and radiates: once again men feel, in these beggarly ages, what is the potency and omnipotency of man's word on the souls of men. "I will triumph, or be torn in fragments," he was once heard to say. "Silence," he cries now, in strong word of command, in imperial consciousness of strength, "Silence the thirty voices, *Silence aux trente voix*!"—and Robespierre and the Thirty Voices die into mutterings; and the Law is once more as Mirabeau would have it.

And yet it is ordained that as France "waxes ever more acrid, feversick: towards the final outburst of dissolution and delirium," Mirabeau is enfeebled by disease. The most significant aspect of Carlyle's treatment of Mirabeau is revealed in his portrait of the Lion's final days. We have seen that Carlyle put the moderate friends of freedom in a blind alley between court and mob, where they could, pathetically, do nothing. Mirabeau comes to be the Atlas, or the almost "heaven-scaling Prometheus," who could enter this symbolic space and break the politics of polarization. Death, however, overtakes him. Carlyle replaces the pathos of impossibility with the tragedy of defeated possibility.

To us, endeavouring to cast his horoscope, it of course remains
doubly vague. There is one Herculean Man; in internecine duel
with him, there is Monster after Monster. Emigrant Noblesse
return, sword on thigh, vaunting of their Loyalty never sullied;
descending from the air, like Harpy-swarms with ferocity, with
obscene greed. Earthward there is the Typhon of Anarchy, Political, Religious; sprawling hundred-headed, say with Twenty-
five million heads; wide as the area of France; strong in very
Hunger.

Whatever the future might have been, the terrible fact is that Mirabeau's
strength is at last exhausted, and "King Mirabeau is now the lost King":

Be it that his falls and follies are manifold,—as himself often
lamented even with tears. Alas, is not the Life of every such man
already a poetic Tragedy . . . full of the elements of Pity and
Fear? This brother man, if not Epic for us, is Tragic; if not great,
is large. . . . Here then the wild Gabriel Honoré drops from the
tissue of our History; not without a tragic farewell.

Mirabeau's death constitutes the major tragedy of *The French Revolution*.
His immense significance is that he represented a "Reality" in his personal
being. Translated into more conventional terms, this means that Mirabeau
was an insightful man, that he came to the truth of things by a process of
creative thought. His attributes made him that specially honored figure in
Carlyle: a tailor. There is a fundamentally important point here. A certain
kind of intellectual cultivation, learned in the established modes of civilized
life, and known to us as enlightenment, had proclaimed itself a power, but
shown itself to be effete. It could not make the constitution march because,
at bottom, its habits of thought had grown mechanistic. Mirabeau tran-
scended the mechanistic; he thought symbolically. However, he did not push
so far beyond the modes of civilized life as to become a person separated
from personality. He did not dwell in caverns measureless to man. Before
Mirabeau, thought was pale. After Mirabeau, thought became demonic and
its own scourge. Some of the later leaders of the revolution, according to
Carlyle's pregnant terms, had personality and meant something real. But
Mirabeau was different even from these. As Carlyle put it in his 1837 essay,
Mirabeau had a genius equal to Napoleon's, "*but a much humaner genius, almost
a poetic one*" (italics added). This quality is brought forth in *The French Revolution* as Mirabeau's capacity for "fellowship." Unlike the philosophes, his
genius was dynamic. Unlike the sansculottes, he was not estranged from the
moral tradition of civility.

This is why "one can say that, had Mirabeau lived, the History of France and of the World had been different." Carlyle's account uses every suggestive detail he can find to establish the idea that, given time to do his work, Mirabeau might have turned from monolithic political action and secured the New Era on the basis of new spiritual insight. With Mirabeau gone, personality and mind disappear, and the impersonal force of prerational Nature, working through the sansculottes, arises in a maelstrom of murder.

The second half of "The Constitution" traces the total disintegration of the constitutionalist movement. The death of the real king, Mirabeau, persuades the false king, Louis, to flee. After his capture at Varennes an empty constitution is accepted. The National Assembly gives way to the Legislative Assembly, and then, while France fights off the First Coalition, the empty constitution expires. The cataclysm of August 10 (1972) ends with the emergence of the Paris Commune and the Jacobin clubs as the effective source of government in France. The way is open for the September Massacres. As Carlyle points out, the history of the Legislative Assembly had been a "series of sputters and quarrels; true desire to do [its] function, fatal impossibility to do it." The testing of possibilities is over; there remains no way out of the labyrinth except through the self-consummation of anarchy. "So, then, the Constitution is over? Forever and a day! Gone is that wonder of the Universe; First biennial Parliament, water-logged, waits only till the Convention come; and then will sink to endless depths. One can guess the silent rage of Old-Constituents, Constitution-builders, extinct Feuillants, men who thought the Constitution would march." Appropriately, Carlyle concludes "The Constitution" with the flight of Lafayette to Holland. The Hero of Two Worlds, the paragon of reason and moderation, hurries into exile on his gleaming white horse as the black demons of the Terror take their seats.

"The Guillotine" opens with the deadly work of the Septemberers. They are distinguished by their "lucency" (Scott would have said lunacy). But theirs is "lucency of the Nether-fire sort; very different from that of our Bastille Heroes, who shone, disputable by no Friend of Freedom, as in Heavenly light-radiance: to such phasis of the business have we advanced since then." In their lucency, a truth is finally perceived: "The Nation is for the present, figuratively speaking, *naked*: it has no rule or vesture; but is naked,—a Sansculottic nation." "The Guillotine" is written in defense of nakedness and the rights of reality, even if it must be the reality of the netherworld. This section may be read as standing in every point opposed to Camus's criticism of revolution. It accepts, as the passage just quoted shows, the betrayal of the original spirit of rebellion; it refuses to acknowledge a limit to murder; and it implicitly takes comfort in the fact that revolution ends by reinforcing the power of the state [*The Rebel*]. "As no external force, Royal or other, now remains which could control this Movement, the Movement . . . must work and welter, not as a Regularity but as a Chaos; destructive and self-destructive; always till something that *has* order arise . . . Which something . . . will not be a Formula . . . but a Reality, probably with a sword in its hand."

The tragic experience of "The Guillotine" is a corollary of its moral paradoxes. Freedom *from* revolution must now be the end and aim of the revolutionaries. The guillotining of Prometheus becomes an act of liberation. The revolution must learn to eat its children. Carlyle accepts these paradoxes and contradictions as adjuncts of the eternal mystery that reconciles freedom and necessity. Under the guidance of that mystery, the visionary historian calmly comprehends what the world gapes at in horror. Between the mystery and the horror Carlyle interposes his sense of tragedy, his sense that men were only carrying out "one of the sorrowfullest tasks poor Humanity has."

This is by no means to suggest that "The Guillotine" is a lament. Carlyle continually reminds us that while we may shriek, the sansculottes acted. Nevertheless, Carlyle appeals to the tragic spirit as a way of mitigating the horror that he says we must condone:

> For a man, once committed headlong to republican or any other Transcendentalism . . . becomes as it were enveloped in an ambient atmosphere of Transcendentalism and Delirium; *his individual self is lost in something that is not himself* . . . He, the hapless incarnated Fanaticism, goes his road; no man can help him, he himself least of all. *It is a wonderful, tragical predicament;*—such as human language, unused to deal with these things, being contrived for the uses of common life, struggles to shadow out in figures [italics added].

Tragic experience of this kind is, to say the least, a very long way from the experience of a Mirabeau or the experience of any of Carlyle's messengers of truth in the age of shams. It is the tragedy of historical determinism that sanctions the loss of personal conscience in the interests of a renovated universe. It resolves for Carlyle the moral problem posed by Camus: "Revolution is an attempt to conquer a new existence, by action that recognizes no moral strictures. That is why it is condemned to live only for history and in a reign of terror" [*The Rebel*]. By converting the reign of terror into a tragedy that preempts the moral will, Carlyle legitimizes its violence and exculpates its cosmic indifference to "common life."

In effect, the visionary historian has discovered the tragedy of transcendental despair, and in doing so has found an exit from hell. This is what "The Guillotine" tries to "shadow out in figures." Ordinary human speech and reason are incapable of identifying the "grand product of Nature" that the revolution has at last made manifest. "Now surely not realisation, of Christianity or of aught earthly, do we discern in this Reign of Terror, in this French Revolution of which it is the consummating." For the grand product of Nature comes not to "range itself under old recorded Laws of Nature at all, but to disclose new ones." There has been an oath taken that hypocrisies and lies shall perish, and perish they must. This is the first of the new laws and the foundation of all others. The men of the revolution must remain dedicated to their oath or else no rehabilitation of the universe will take place.

> The fulfillment of this Oath; that is to say, the black desperate battle of Men against their whole Condition and Environment,— a battle, alas, withal against the Sin and Darkness that was in themselves as in others: this is the Reign of Terror. Transcendental despair was the purport of it, though not consciously so. False hopes, of Fraternity, Political Millennium, and what not, we have always seen: but the unseen heart of the whole, the transcendental despair, was not false; neither has it been of no effect. Despair, pushed far enough, completes the circle, so to speak; and becomes a kind of genuine productive hope again.

In the end, then, extremism, if not a virtue, is at least its own reward. Hope springs from the infernal. This is a climax beyond the drama of tragic possibilities. At a point outside the purview of conventional morality, the search for new order, consistently inspired by hope, abruptly ends, and is replaced by the dictatorship of despair. Transcendental despair is in the nature of an absolute, a compelling, imperious command to order. For Carlyle, a whiff of grapeshot clears the head. "The Revolution, then, is verily devouring its own children? All Anarchy, by the nature of it, is not only destructive but self-destructive."

The difference between *The French Revolution* and *Sartor Resartus* is that *The French Revolution* counts heavily, even programmatically, on the negative content of revolution. Both books declare that ash will fertilize. But in *Sartor*, this doctrine is leavened by the visionary's very reluctance to address the political world, by his extensive exploration of "natural supernaturalism," and, perhaps, most of all, by his use of the comic vision to distance himself from the certainty of his postulates. *The French Revolution*, while it firmly places political action in a secondary and intermediary role, relies on the self-consummation of democratic politics as the indispensable prelude to the rebirth of spiritual purpose in the Western world. Unnatural supernaturalism is its tautological gospel. Transcendental despair, figured as a tragic action, is its answer to two centuries of constitution writers who had tried to define the means by which the state might keep itself intact while giving some scope to the freedom of the individual. What the law fails to control, a dose of nihilism will.

And yet *The French Revolution* is not a brutal book. As a work of art it is surely the equal of *Sartor Resartus*, though it has until recently been extravagantly neglected. What commends *The French Revolution* to us is not its desperate remedies, but its brilliantly particularized study of man in the throes of incomprehensible struggle. Several times I have contrasted Carlyle and Camus. They may also be compared. In his essay "Create Dangerously" Camus writes: "The prophet, whether religious or political, can judge absolutely and, as is known, is not chary of doing so. But the artist cannot . . . The aim of art . . . is not to legislate or reign supreme, but rather to understand first of all . . . No work of genius has ever been based on hatred and contempt. This is why the artist . . . absolves instead of condemning. Instead of being a judge, he is a justifier. He is the perpetual advocate of the living creature, because it is alive." In *The French Revolution*, Carlyle the prophet judges absolutely, but Carlyle the artist advocates the living creature. Because his art is so deeply informed by the phenomenon of revolution and because he committed himself so decisively to a polemical purpose, prophecy and art cannot, in Carlyle, be easily separated. But they can be so far separated, in *The French Revolution*, as to make it perfectly obvious that there is a Carlyle whose heart is on the side of light, not lightning.

GEOFFREY H. HARTMAN

Enthusiastic Criticism

*What is lacking in England, and has always been lacking, that half-actor and
rhetorician knew well enough, the absurd muddle-head Carlyle, who sought to
conceal under passionate grimaces what he knew about himself: namely, what
was* lacking *in Carlyle—real* power *of intellect, real* depth *of intellectual
perception, in short, philosophy.*

—NIETZSCHE, *Beyond Good and Evil*

In England, the most sophisticated anti-Romanticism came from Matthew
Arnold. He claimed that while the English Romantics were writers with
great energy and creative force, they did not "know" enough, and so missed
the chance of becoming universal figures, like Goethe. They could not transcend their national and parochial base. T. S. Eliot, in an introduction to
his first collection of essays, *The Sacred Wood* (1920), quotes Arnold on the
Romantics and adds: "This judgment . . . has not, so far as I know, ever
been successfully controverted." In *The Use of Poetry and the Use of Criticism*
a dozen years later, he expands Arnold's list. "We should be right too, I
think, if we added that Carlyle, Ruskin, Tennyson, Browning, with plenty
of energy, plenty of creative force, had not enough wisdom. Their culture
was not always well-rounded; their knowledge of the human soul was often
partial and often shallow." Who, then, will escape whipping? If there is one
criterion that distinguishes the present movement in criticism from that
prevailing, more or less, since Eliot, it is a better understanding and higher
evaluation of the Romantic and nineteenth-century writers.

From *Criticism in the Wilderness: The Study of Literature Today.* © 1980 by Yale University. Yale University Press, 1980. Originally entitled "The Sacred Jungle: Carlyle,
Eliot, Bloom."

In Arnold's estimate of the Romantics, there is more irony than truth. For revisionist studies have shown that these same Romantics were clairvoyant rather than blind precursors of later movements that tended to disown them while simplifying the radical character of their art. The irony deepens when we recall that philosophical criticism in the German style was *almost* introduced to England via Coleridge's *Biographia Literaria*. But Coleridge broke off the attempt with the excuse that he wished to reserve such "Constructive Philosophy" for his never-written *Logosophia*. Chapter 13 of the *Biographia* is interrupted by what might be called a *letter* from Porlock (Locke? Poor Luck?); that is, from a very prudent, practical-minded friend advising Coleridge not to proceed further in his kind of hypostatic discourse. Philosophical criticism, therefore, which had attained a first flowering in the work of Schiller, Fichte, Schelling, and the Schlegels, was to develop chiefly within a German matrix. It became increasingly alien to the English mind. While the two countries remained, for a while, eager to learn from each other in matters of art, in matters of criticism a serious split—a real "two cultures" situation—soon emerged.

It manifests itself as early as Carlyle's *Sartor Resartus*, composed in 1830–31, only fifteen years after Coleridge's *Biographia*. Here, indeed, English is a "Babylonish dialect" made of Germanisms, Swiftian gusto, and a baroque simulacrum of the earthy, archaizing diction of northern England. The book's crazy, mockingbird style is meant to be a nauseous cure or asafetida for British empiricism. "Teufelsdröckh," the name of its hero-author, means devil-dirt, or possibly devil-print. "Diogenes," his first name, means divinely born.

Matthew Arnold, recognizing the un-English character of the style, issued the warning: "Flee Carlylese as you would the devil." The rough, Germanizing wit of *Sartor* shows not only that, as in medieval times, wit and mystery go together, but it inserts an English work into a tradition which remains almost exclusively Teutonic, and leads from Luther through Jean Paul Richter to Nietzsche and Thomas Mann (compare *Dr. Faustus*). Nietzsche, though always keeping his distance from Carlyle, may have owed to him part of his awareness that no previous age was as prepared "for a Carnival in the grand style, for laughter and a high-spirited revelry, for transcendental flights of sublime nonsense" (*Beyond Good and Evil*). In "The Function of Criticism" of 1923, Eliot quotes from the editorial columns of an unspecified newspaper which not only associates "humorous" with "nonconformist" qualities, but attributes this combination to "the unreclaimed Teutonic element" in the English character.

Carlyle's remarkable style is, I am suggesting, an aspect of his covert transfusion of Northern religious enthusiasm (directly described by Walter

Scott when dealing with the Covenanters in *Old Mortality*) into German nature-enthusiasm and its transcendental symbolics. Carlyle maintains, of course, a defensively humorous distance from Teufelsdröckh's exotica by pretending to be his editor. But the problem of distance is a complex one: it involves defining the genre of a book that is at once commentary and fiction.

The "Clothes Philosophy" of *Sartor* stresses mediation: it distances humanity from nakedness, nature, even from the textual source (Teufelsdröckh's German manuscript, supposedly discovered by the "editor"), which is presented in *Sartor* only in an excerpted or retailored ("resartus") form. "We never get Teufelsdröckh unmediated," says G. B. Tennyson. But no writer who goes through the detour of a text gets himself unmediated.

Carlyle's disgust, moreover, at this potentially infinite regress of mediation—even though it provides a saving distance from absolute inwardness or solipsism—is quite obvious. His solution is to foreground the mediatory process, to make the writer's distance from any source so palpable that the retailored text is endowed with a factitious presence of its own. The very feel of *Sartor* depends on the "fragments, the titles, the passages taken from here and there, the works unfinished or stopped in midpassage . . . double and single quotation marks for passages cited, and editorial interpolation in the midst of quotations" (G. B. Tennyson). It is as if something groundless were being foregrounded—which, taken out of metaphysics or German *Naturphilosophie* and articulated as a theory of language, could evoke Heidegger and Derrida.

The formal effect, in any case, is a fading of the distinction between original and commentary. Quotation is king, yet everything is quotation. In *Sartor* criticism has found its carnival colors. Carlylese, instead of being a metalanguage, merges with the idiom of its source: its originality is its impurity, the contamination of gloss and original. But since the source is invented, Carlylese is actually a self-educing prose, maintained by the fiction not of a source alone, but of a source that needs an editor-translator-interpreter. Here is feigning indeed, though in the service of criticism.

Yet equally—this is the Puritan joker—in the service of religion. For Carlyle's attitude toward Teufelsdröckhian metaphysics is exploitative as well as empathic. German metaphysics, he wrote, is "a disease expelling a disease." He thought of it as literally the *crisis* and providentially appointed cure in the long illness of unbelief or excessive self-consciousness. It would eventually consume itself. He too may have the disease, since it is contagious, part of the "Spirit of the Age"; but the fever of his style has its creative as well as suffering aspect.

Sartor, then, is the Age of Criticism producing—out of itself as it were—

a fiction. The Negative is converted into Being, to echo Hegel; and this holds for the verbal style and genre of the book as clearly as for its famous journey from "The Everlasting No" to "The Everlasting Yea." We are dealing not with a historical curiosity but with a creative historiographical act—a revision of the English language which succeeded more in America (if we think of Melville's prose) than in England. Carlylese is a richer and rougher English, one that pretends to be contaminated by German; yet the German source is simply a device that motivates a different critical idiom. An enthusiastic type of criticism replaces an English type which was, and continues to be despite Carlyle, a critique of enthusiasm.

The issue of enthusiasm is not separable from that of religion, and could draw us into a complex analysis of the relation of literary style to religion and politics. The relation of enthusiasm to political fanaticism is a fearful reality that hovers over English history and the establishment of *via media* institutions from the reign of Elizabeth on. Literary criticism like everything else became a *via media* institution. Though the fear of enthusiasm gradually receded into the *angustiae* of the Gothic novel it was given a temporary renewal by the French Revolution with its regicide, its Reign of Terror, and its atheistic religion of reason.

It seems hardly credible, therefore, that the future author of *The French Revolution* (1837), who began *Sartor* in the year of the July revolution (1830), and failed to place his book with a publisher, perhaps because of the Reform Bill agitation, should so neglect the French scene. But the Northern (Anglo-Saxon) and Calvinist axis was the essential one for him, in terms of the difficult relation of literature, religion, and enthusiasm. Eighteenth-century Paris had been a mere *hortus siccus*, the "most parched spot in Europe," and even French revolutionary turmoil served only to reveal the poetry in history, to heave up huge symbols of repressed religiosity that pointed to the real creative ferment of mankind—religious rather than secular, religion struggling with the secular, and criticism with belief.

That *Sartor* uses one culture to criticize or complete another is not the important thing, however daringly performed. Its recovery of the relation of criticism to enthusiasm—to the religious question—and its understanding of what is common to criticism and fiction are more crucial. In these matters Carlyle is a genuine precursor of the philosophical critics of today.

Criticism differs from fiction by making the experience of reading explicit: by intruding and maintaining the persona of editor, reviewer, reader, foreign reporter, and so forth. Our struggle to identify—or not to—with imaginative experience, usually in the form of a story, is what is worked through. Both paradigmatically and personally the critic shows how a reader's instincts, sympathies, defenses are now solicited and now compelled. The psychological drama of reading centers on that aroused merging: a possible loss of boundaries, a fear of absorption, the stimulation of a sympathetic faculty that may take over and produce self-alienation.

This is felt to be too threatening even now whenever a critic fudges the line between commentary and fiction—this *merging*, which most criticism methodically *prevents*, but which Carlyle *represents*. After Carlyle, the "explicit reader" enters certain American authors (Poe and Melville, for example) in the fictional guise of a narrator who has barely escaped a visionary merger, or else as a too palpable authorial presence. In a countertradition, that of Flaubert and James, the author disappears, or evokes what has been called an "implicit author." But the emphasis remains on the sympathetic imagination, or on an enthusiast always about to merge, out of idealism, with the destructive element.

Should we discount the psychic danger of merging—the anxiety it evokes even in such formal activities as reading—an obverse difficulty may appear. This is the tendency to distance oneself too much, to make of distance a defense by claiming that origins are fake or contaminated or (at best) motivating fictions. It can lead to something that parallels Gnosticism's separation of the pure origin or purer good from a world created by the usurpatory demiurge; so "Teufelsdröckh" and his "editor" find themselves in unexpected theological company. The issue such an analysis raises is, again, the relation of fiction, criticism, and theology.

How much is implied by Emerson's famous statement in "Self-Reliance" (1841) that in reading others our rejected thoughts return with a certain alienated majesty? Could it imply identity with the pure origin, and a falling away from it when we lack self-reliance? "By our own spirits we are deified," Woodsworth wrote of poets in their strength: it is an extreme form of Gnosticism from its optimistic, even manic side.

"But thereof come in the end despondency and madness," Wordsworth adds. There is a dark obverse to the quest for autonomy and originality. What Emerson says of our reading can also be said of our dreams. We eventually recognize them as our rejected thoughts coming back with a fearful or majestic luster. The question is whether we *can* acknowledge them as ours. To do so is to take responsibility for them; to take on, for good or bad, a certain sublimity. In his optimistic moments Emerson sees no problem in this. Yet the distortions of the dream-work itself, and the many anti-self-consciousness theories that spring up in the nineteenth century, indicate there is a problem. So Carlyle talks in *Characteristics* of the "ideal unconscious," a strange notion when we think of how Freud viewed the unconscious at the end of the century.

A. DWIGHT CULLER

Mill, Carlyle,
and the Spirit of the Age

The 'spirit of the age,' " wrote John Stuart Mill in 1831, "is in some measure a novel expression. I do not believe that it is to be met with in any work exceeding fifty years in antiquity. The idea of comparing one's own age with former ages, or with our notion of those which are yet to come, had occurred to philosophers; but it never before was itself the dominant idea of any age." Mill was misinformed on this point, for, as Friedrich Meinecke has made clear, the phrase *spirit of the age* and its companion *spirit of a nation* were commonly employed by continental writers in the seventeenth and eighteenth centuries, particularly by Montesquieu and Voltaire. Nonetheless, Mill was apparently right that the phrase was not naturalized in English until the early nineteenth century, for the first instance cited by the *OED* is Shelley's (1820): "It is the spirit of the age, and we are all infected with it." During the next dozen years it was used by Southey, Henry Crabb Robinson, Landor, Hazlitt, Macaulay, Newman, Carlyle, Mill, Bulwer, and an anonymous writer in *Blackwood's* (1830), by which time it was established in the language. Indeed, the writer in *Blackwood's* complains, "That which, in the slang of faction, is called the Spirit of the Age, absorbs, at present, the attention of the world."

Given this new awareness, it became, said Mill, "a very fit subject for philosophical inquiry, what the spirit of the age really is; and how or wherein it differs from the spirit of any other age." Fichte was the first to analyze it in his lectures, *Characteristics of the Present Age* (1806), and he was followed in England by Hazlitt's *Spirit of the Age* (1825), R. H. Horne's *New Spirit of the Age* (1844), and especially by Carlyle's "Signs of the Times" and "Char-

From *The Victorian Mirror of History.* © 1985 by Yale University. Yale University Press, 1985.

acteristics" and Mill's "Spirit of the Age," all published within three years
of one another in 1829–31. One should also mention Edward Lytton Bulwer's
"View of the Intellectual Spirit of the Time," published in *England and the
English* in 1833.

The "spirit of the age" differs from the eighteenth-century stages or
states of society in being a much more volatile concept. Whereas a state of
society might last for many centuries, the spirit of the age might change
within a generation—hence the appropriateness of Horne's *New Spirit of the
Age* only twenty years after Hazlitt's. The state of society was also an institutional and sociological concept, whereas the spirit of the age carried
idealist suggestions of an indwelling spirit which informed all aspects of
society and gave it its character. One would, indeed, assume it came to
England directly from German Idealism, for its equivalent, *Zeitgeist*, was
being used by Herder, Fichte, Goethe, Schiller, and others in the late eighteenth and early nineteenth centuries. Doubtless it was affected by that usage,
but the phrase *Zeitgeist*, or "Time-spirit," though used occasionally by Carlyle, did not become current in England until employed, almost ad nauseam,
by Arnold in *Literature and Dogma* in 1873. The form of the phrase *spirit of
the age* suggests it came to England from French sources (*esprit de l'âge, esprit
du temps, esprit du siècle*), and indeed it apparently did carry revolutionary or
at least liberal suggestions. To Carlyle it was tinged with rationalism, and
the conservative writer in *Blackwood's* complains that he is continually being
told he must surrender to revolutionary change simply because it is the spirit
of the age. Hence, for his first essay Carlyle selected a phrase whose ante-
cedents are not liberal and continental but Biblical and apocalyptic: "O ye
hypocrites, ye can discern the face of the sky; but can ye not discern the
signs of the times? A wicked and adulterous generation seeketh after a sign;
and there shall no sign be given unto it."

The spirit of the age, according to Mill, "is an idea essentially belonging
to an age of change." Men do not think deeply about the character of their
own age until they are aware that it differs from the past. Then they divide
into those who praise the wisdom of their ancestors and those who extol the
march of intellect. "The present times," says Mill, "possess this character.
. . . The conviction is already not far from being universal, that the times
are pregnant with change; and that the nineteenth century will be known to
posterity as the era of one of the greatest revolutions of which history has
preserved the remembrance. Carlyle agreed. "The repeal of the Test Acts,
and then of the Catholic disabilities, has struck many of their admirers with
an indescribable astonishment. Those things seemed fixed and immovable;
deep as the foundations of the world; and lo, in a moment they have vanished,

and their place knows them no more!" Then followed the July Revolution in France, the burning of ricks all over the south of England, the ominous gathering of the forces of reform, and the Bristol riots when the Reform Bill was not passed. As a result there was a rage of prophecy, and Carlyle recorded in his notebook "a common persuasion among serious ill-informed persons that the *end of the world* is at hand: Henry Drummond, E[dward] Irving, and all that class.—So was it at the beginning of the Christian era; say rather, at the *termination* of the Pagan one." Carlyle did not believe it was the end of the world, but he did believe it was the end of an epoch, and so too did Mill. Indeed, most thoughtful Englishmen during the period of the 1820s and 1830s had a sense, far keener than they had ever had before, that they were living in the stream of history, that they were being swept by some great, irresistible force out of the past and into the future. So powerful, indeed, was this sense of history that the Spirit of the Age became almost a Genius or Daemon, replacing the older conceptions of Providence or Destiny and moving events forward, not in the name of God or Natural Law but of History itself.

It was in this context, in the 1820s and early 1830s, that both Mill and Carlyle developed their philosophy of history. There could hardly have been two young men more diverse in their origin, for Carlyle was raised in the tradition of Scottish Calvinism by devoutly religious parents, whereas Mill, the son of an agnostic, was "one of the very few examples, in this country, of one who has, not thrown off religious belief, but never had it." In the 1820s, however, each experienced a spiritual or mental crisis which brought them together in a common view of society and especially in a view of history. It was not that their paths crossed but rather that they converged for a moment and then moved apart again, though not so widely as before.

Carlyle has given a mythical account of his spiritual crisis in the life story of Diogenes Teufelsdröckh. "Nothing in *Sartor* thereabouts is *fact*," he wrote, "(symbolical myth all) except that of the '*incident* in the Rue St. Thomas de l'Enfer,'—which happened quite literally to myself in Leith Walk, [Edinburgh]. . . . I remember it well and could go yet to about the place." As for the rest, one can trace out in Carlyle's letters and notebooks the entire course of his and Teufelsdröckh's conversion. He had gone up from his native village to Edinburgh at the age of fourteen and there, reading Gibbon and Hume at the University, had lost his faith. He was poor, lonely, in ill health, unable to find meaningful work or spiritual sustenance; and all these rebuffs to his proud and suffering spirit seemed like a cosmic or Everlasting No. "It was God that said Yes:" he wrote in his notebook; "it is the Devil that forever says No." The Everlasting No has two aspects, an objective and a subjective. Objectively, "To me the Universe was all void of Life, of Purpose, of Volition, even of Hostility: it was one huge, dead, immeasurable Steam-engine, rolling on, in its dead indifference, to grind me limb from limb." But subjectively, this produced in Teufelsdröckh a kind of whining Wertherism: "And yet, strangely enough, I lived in a continual, indefinite, pining fear; tremulous, pusillanimous, apprehensive of I knew not what." The distinction between the two aspects of the Everlasting No is important because the experience on Leith Walk freed Carlyle from the one but not the other. In that moment he rose up, in native God-created majesty, and "shook base Fear away from me forever." This act of Protests against the Everlasting No does not lead Teufelsdröckh to the Everlasting Yea but merely to the Center of Indifference, a kind of spiritual No-man's land in which he must wander for a time until he can develop a new faith to replace the old. The culmination of the Everlasting No had come when "Doubt had darkened into Unbelief"; but then Teufelsdröckh had exclaimed, "Alas, the fearful Unbelief is unbelief in yourself." In the Protest Teufelsdröckh had freed himself from this second unbelief, had reasserted his own spirituality and separated himself from the material world. He now has to turn outward to that world and study man in society until he can see it too as instinct with spirit—until he sees nature as "the living visible garment of God" and society as a fabric woven by the divine element in man. He then will have achieved the Clothes Philosophy, which is the basis for the Everlasting Yea. He will have seen that the "Man of Sorrows" transcends the "Sorrows of Werther," that blessedness is better than happiness, and that the truly supernatural is a Natural Supernaturalism.

Carlyle worked his way out of his crisis by two routes, philosophy and history. In the German writers and philosophers whom he was reading from 1819 to 1830 he found a mystical or transcendental view of the universe of which he was initially suspicious but which he finally accepted as answering to his deepest needs and to the truth. But he was simultaneously working out, and again partly by their help, a philosophy of history. In the midst of his deepest misery, in January 1824, he wrote, "I have got half a new idea to-day about history: it is more than I can say for any day the last six months." In all likelihood this was the idea about the multidimensionality of history which he confided to his notebook in 1827: "An Historian must write (so to speak) in *lines*; but every event is a *superficies*; nay if we search out its *causes*, a *solid*: hence a primary and almost incurable defect in the art of Narration; which only the very best can so much as approximately remedy.—N.B. I understand this *myself*. I have known it for years; and written it *now*, with the purpose perhaps of writing it at large elsewhere." Carlyle developed this idea more lucidly in his essay "On History" (1830), but he wrote it "at large" in *The French Revolution*, in which his view of "the infinite nature of History,"—of history as "an ever-living, ever-working Chaos of Being, wherein shape after shape bodies itself forth from innumerable elements"—is fully displayed.

There were three species of historian whom Carlyle contemned: first, the sentimental literary historian, or Picturesque Traveller, who constructs elegant narratives of the doings of kings and queens. We come, for example, to the Reformation.

> All Scotland is awakened to a second higher life: the Spirit of the Highest stirs in every bosom, agitates every bosom; Scotland is convulsed, fermenting, struggling to body itself forth anew. . . . We ask, with breathless eagerness; How was it; how went it on? Let us understand it, let us see it, and know it!—In reply, is handed us a really graceful and most dainty little Scandalous Chronicle (as for some Journal of Fashion) of two persons: Mary Stuart, a Beauty, but over-lightheaded; and Henry Darnley, a Booby who had fine legs. How these first courted, billed and cooed, according to nature; then pouted, fretted, grew utterly enraged, and blew one another up with gunpowder: this, and not the History of Scotland, is what we good-naturedly read.

The second species was Dryasdust, the antiquarian, a character whom Carlyle borrowed from Sir Walter Scott and whom he represented as a mole burrowing through vast quantities of rubbish without any idea that the past was alive. The third type was the Philosophic Historian, who took the complex reality—nay, the infinitude of history—and reduced it to some finite little formula such as Progress of the Species. To Carlyle, Voltaire did not invent a new mode of history but merely continued the old mode of "philosophy teaching by Experience" according to *his* philosophy rather than that of the monks. But both philosophies were inadequate. Neither saw that history, as Carlyle believed, was "the essence of innumerable biographies"— that is, the inward spiritual life of all the nameless people living in any era. It was the history of the Spirit of the Age, of the Idea realizing itself in the actual.

As a result, the only true historian, according to Carlyle, was the artist or the poet, for only he had the power to lean over the "dark backward and abysm of time" and, by an act of divinization, seize upon its essential character. Only he had the literary art, symbolic or otherwise, to body it forth in its infinite complexity. The *History of Scotland* which elicited the diatribe quoted above was Scott's little potboiler of 1830, but although Carlyle went through a period of considering Scott "the great Restaurateur of Europe" and always lamented that "he had no message," he came to see that his true conception of history was not in his histories but in his novels. "There is something in his deep recognition of the worth of the Past, perhaps better than anything he has *expressed* about it: into which I do not yet fully see." But he soon came to see it. "These Historical Novels have taught all men this truth, which looks like a truism, and yet was as good as unknown to writers of history and others, till so taught: that the bygone ages of the world were actually filled by living men, not by protocols, state-papers, controversies and abstractions of men. . . . History will henceforth have to take thought of it." On Scott's death in 1832 he said simply, "He understood what *history* meant; this was his chief intellectual merit."

To Carlyle the best eighteenth-century historian was not Voltaire, Gibbon, Robertson, or Hume, but Boswell in his *Life of Johnson*. "It is not speaking with exaggeration, but with strict measured sobriety, to say that this Book of Boswell's will give us more real insight into the *History of England* during those days than twenty other Books, falsely entitled 'Histories,' which take to themselves that special aim." "The thing I want to see is not Redbook Lists, and Court Calendars, and Parliamentary Registers, but the LIFE OF MAN in England: what men did, thought, suffered, enjoyed; the form, especially the spirit, of their terrestrial existence, its outward environment, its inward principle." For the earlier period Carlyle turned to Shakespeare, for he found "something of *epic* in the cycle of hasty Fragments" which make up the history plays, and he thought that if Shakespeare had done more in that vein, he "could have turned the *History of England* into a kind of *Iliad*, almost perhaps into a kind of *Bible*." The *Iliad* and the Bible were for Carlyle the two great histories of antiquity, for if the true historian was a poet, so the true poet was also a historian. More and more literature seemed to Carlyle to be shot through by unreality, and he cited that strange thesis of his alter ego Sauerteig: "That History, after all, is the true Poetry; that Reality, if rightly interpreted, is grander than Fiction; nay, that even in the right interpretation of Reality and History does genuine Poetry consist."

What, then, was the right interpretation of reality? What was the poem which God had written upon the fabric of time? In virtually all the new German writers and philosophers whom Carlyle was reading he found a version of history which was much more congenial to his views than the rectilinear Progress of the Species assumed by much French and English thought. It did not conceive, in the first place, that this was the best of all possible ages, and it marked off the past into a series of epochs which vacillated between faith and skepticism, criticism and creation. One of the most elaborate of these schemes was Fichte's in *Characteristics of the Present Age*, a "high priori" work which divided history into five epochs through which mankind must proceed to achieve its goal of Freedom in accordance with Reason. The present age was the third or central one, an age of "completed Sinfulness" which had thrown off the Reason as Instinct of the first age and Reason as external Authority of the second without putting on Reason as Science or Art of the fourth and fifth ages. It is obvious that Fichte's five epochs reduce themselves to the tripartite dialectic—creative/critical/creative—which always occurs when a series of polar opposites succeed upon one another, the second creative epoch transcending and somewhat synthesizing the first two. Herder, Schiller, Novalis, Friedrich Schlegel, and Schelling all had such formulations, but it was in Goethe that Carlyle found the passage that influenced him the most. It occurred in a note, "Israel in der Wüste," which Goethe appended to the *West-östlicher Divan* (1819). Carlyle may have known it as early as March 1826, and it is said that at least a dozen passages in his works show the imprint of it. He translated it twice, once in his Notebook and once in the essay "Diderot," where it is attributed simply to "the Thinker of our time":

> "The special, sole and deepest theme of the World's and Man's History whereto all other themes are subordinated, remains the Conflict of UNBELIEF and BELIEF. All epochs wherein Belief prevails, under what form it may, are splendid, heart-elevating, fruitful for contemporaries and posterity. All epochs, on the contrary, wherein Unbelief, under what form so ever, maintains its sorry victory, should they even for a moment glitter with a sham splendour, vanish from the eyes of posterity; because no one chooses to burden himself with study of the unfruitful."

Though Goethe here suggests that there are entire epochs which have no history and quite vanish from the annals of the world, the more usual historicist view is that even epochs of unbelief serve their purpose in destroying the old, outworn creeds and making way for the new. In Fichte's scheme it was impossible for mankind to achieve the state of Reason as Science or Art without going through the stage of completed Sinfulness. Thus even the miserable eighteenth century had a purpose. But the reason Carlyle was so deeply affected by this new conception of spiritual periodicity was not merely that it helped him understand his age but also that it helped him understand himself. "Has the mind its cycles and seasons like Nature," he asked, "varying from the fermentation of *werden* to the clearness of *seyn*; and this again and again; so that the history of a man is like the history of the world he lives in? In my own case, I have traced two or three such vicissitudes: at present if I mistake not, there is some such thing at hand for me. Feby 1829." The alternation of creative, critical, and newly creative epochs in world history exactly corresponds to the three periods in Teufelsdröckh's life: the period of childhood faith, the Everlasting No and Center of Indifference, and the new faith of the Everlasting Yea. Hence Carlyle applies this new philosophy of history to his own state at the "Rational University," where "the young vacant mind [was] furnished with much talk about Progress of the Species, Dark Ages, Prejudice, and the like" till all were either blown out into windy self-conceit or reduced to impotent skepticism. "But this too is portion of mankind's lot. If our era is the Era of Unbelief, why murmur under it; is there not a better coming, nay come? As in long-drawn systole and long-drawn diastole, must the period of Faith alternate with the period of Denial; must the vernal growth, the summer luxuriance of all Opinions, Spiritual Representations and Creations, be followed by, and again follow, the autumnal decay, the winter dissolution." Whether Carlyle adopted the new philosophy of history because it accorded to the shape of his own experience or whether he shaped his own experience to accord to the new philosophy of history, it is clear that they are one and the same. The history of Teufelsdröckh's conversion is the history of the conversion of his age.

That a better time is coming was first formally announced by Carlyle in "Signs of the Times" (1829). The title alludes, as we have already noted, to the doomsday outlook of his contemporaries; neither does Carlyle initially take a cheerful view. "The grand characteristic of our age," he writes, is that it is an Age of Machinery. "Nothing is now done directly, or by hand; all is by rule and calculated contrivance." "Thus we have machines for Education: Lancastrian machines; Hamiltonian machines; monitors, maps and emblems." "We have Religious machines, of all imaginable varieties; the Bible-Society . . ." Science no longer depends on a Newton but on a Royal Society, art no longer on a Raphael but on a Royal Academy, philosophy no longer on a Descartes but on a Philosophic Institute. As we read on, however, we are aware that the very process of Carlyle's writing about the age and delineating its essential character begins the process of its spiritualization. Initially, he had taken machinery in the literal, material sense, but as he proceeded he made it increasingly metaphoric and symbolic, until at last he exclaimed, "Thus does the Genius of Mechanism stand by to help us in all difficulties and emergencies." So mechanization itself is spiritualized by Carlyle, and his essay is itself one of the "signs infinitely cheering to us . . . that a new and brighter spiritual era is slowly evolving itself for all men."

John Stuart Mill, eleven years younger than Carlyle, was converging on the same point from the opposite direction. Educated by his father in a generally Benthamite atmosphere, he had never read the works of Bentham himself until the French redaction by Dumont, the *Traité de Législation*, was put into his hands in the winter of 1821–22. "The reading of this book," says Mill, "was an epoch in my life; one of the turning points in my mental history." What primarily impressed him was "the chapter in which Bentham passed judgment on the common modes of reasoning in morals and legislation, deduced from phrases like 'law of nature,' 'right reason,' 'the moral sense,' 'natural rectitude,' and the like, and characterized them as dogmatism in disguise, imposing its sentiments upon others under cover of sounding expressions which convey no reason for the sentiment, but set up the sentiment as its own reason. It had not struck me before, that Bentham's principle put an end to all this. The feeling rushed upon me, that all previous moralists were superseded, and that here indeed was the commencement of a new era in thought." As Mill continues to describe this experience, the dry prose of his *Autobiography* comes to life, and one feels that Mill looking into Dumont's Bentham was almost like Keats looking into Chapman's Homer. "I felt taken up to an eminence from which I could survey a vast mental domain, and see stretching out into the distance intellectual results beyond all computation." Indeed, it was almost a religious conversion. "When I laid down the last volume of the Traité, I had become a different being. The 'principle of utility' understood as Bentham understood it, . . . fell exactly into its place as the keystone which held together the detached and fragmentary component parts of my knowledge and beliefs. It gave unity to my conceptions of things. I now had opinions; a creed, a doctrine, a philosophy; in one among the best senses of the word, a religion."

This religion lasted for five years. "From the winter of 1821, when I first read Bentham, . . . I had what might truly be called an object in life; to be a reformer of the world. My conception of my own happiness was entirely identified with this object. . . . But the time came when I awakened from this as from a dream. It was in the autumn of 1826. I was in a dull state of nerves, such as everybody is occasionally liable to; unsusceptible to enjoyment or pleasurable excitement. . . . In this frame of mind it occurred to me to put the question directly to myself: 'Suppose that all your objects in life were realized; that all the changes in institutions and opinions which you are looking forward to, could be completely effected at this very instant: would this be a great joy and happiness to you?' and an irrepressible self-consciousness distinctly answered, 'No!' At this my heart sank within me: the whole foundation on which my life was constructed fell down. All my happiness was to have been found in the continual pursuit of this end. The end had ceased to charm, and how could there ever again be any interest in the means? I seemed to have nothing left to live for."

As Mill analyzed his crisis in later years, he thought it revealed a psychological defect in Utilitarian theory. According to the theory, the greatest happiness of the greatest number was the end of life, and it was the task of the educator or statesman to create, in the mind of the individual, favorable associations with that end so that his personal happiness would be identified with it. In the case of Mill, however, he was so well acquainted with the theory and so given to intellectual analysis that the indoctrination did not work. He was like the preacher's son who, being "behind the scenes" and seeing his father at work, himself becomes an atheist. His father and Bentham had thoroughly demystified the old absolutes with the result that, for their own disciple, they could not mystify the new. They lacked the psychological and histrionic art to endow the new values with the aura of mystery which centuries of religious tradition had given to the old. Beyond this, Mill felt that there had been a general atrophying of his emotional life, so that his belief in the "greatest happiness of the greatest number" was a mere speculative opinion and was not grounded in genuine benevolence. He knew, and he did not know, that happiness was the end of life.

Mill attempted to find his way back from this dilemma by reading for the first time, in 1828, the poems of Wordsworth, which seemed "the very culture of the feelings, which I was in quest of." But he also happened to take up the *Mémoires* of Marmontel, the sentimental French dramatist, and "came to the passage which relates his father's death, the distressed position of the family, and the sudden inspiration by which he, then a mere boy, felt and made them feel that he would be everything to them—would supply the place of all that they had lost. A vivid conception of the scene and its feelings came over me, and I was moved to tears. From this moment my burthen grew lighter. The oppression of the thought that all feeling was dead within me, was gone. I was no longer hopeless; I was not a stock or a stone." This passage is customarily interpreted as a suppressed death-wish on the part of Mill against his harsh and domineering father, but that is surely a shallow interpretation. Mill was clearly aware that he did not love his father and that his father did not love him, but he respected his father as a great and good man and was deeply saddened by his death in 1836. A more plausible interpretation of the episode is that it is a critique of hedonism—it shows the educative power of sorrow. Happiness may be the end of life, but it is tragedy that has the power to elicit the nobleness of men. The actual passage in Marmontel, in which the little boy is elevated to greatness, is so melodramatic that it is a wonder Mill was not moved to laughter rather than tears; but his nerves were ready for tears and it is no wonder that he was cured of his addiction to Benthamism by a death-bed scene. Indeed, the moral that Mill drew was specifically formulated by the wise physician whom Marmontel's mother called in to attend the boy in his shock. "The physician . . . told her, that this was an effect of great concentrated grief, and that mine might be attended with the most fatal consequences, if it were not removed by some diversion. 'A journey, absence, and that as soon as possible is,' said he, 'the best remedy that I can indicate to you. But do not propose it to him as a diversion; to that great grief is ever averse: it must be ignorant of the care employed to divert it, and must be deceived in order to be cured.' " "The physician," Marmontel adds, "was right: there are griefs yet more attaching than pleasure itself."

This is the very theory that Mill developed as he recovered from his crisis: namely, that happiness may be the end of life but it should not be proposed as the object of life. Just as Benjamin Franklin discovered that he could not pursue humility directly because, the nearer he came to achieving it, the prouder he became of his humility, so Mill discovered that one must make something other than happiness the object of life and one would then achieve happiness by the way. One must both know, and not know, that happiness was the end of life, and to this end one must adopt what Mill calls (though he says that he had never heard of it under that name at that time) the "anti-self-consciousness theory of Carlyle." Mill is presumably referring to Carlyle's essay "Characteristics," in which Carlyle makes Self-consciousness, rather than Machinery, the distinguishing characteristic of the age and clearly prefers the unconscious naiveté of the great ages of Belief. But neither Carlyle nor Mill gives any explanation of how one is to go about deliberately cultivating anti-self-consciousness—how one can cease to be conscious of something one previously has known. Nonetheless, "this theory now became the basis of my philosophy of life," and one may see Mill implementing it in the various compromises of these years: the attempt to combine Macaulay's theory of government with his father's, the attempt to meld quantitative with qualitative conceptions of pleasure, and above all the attempt to believe in free will along with necessity. He had long seen that "it would be a blessing if the doctrine of necessity could be believed by all *quoad* the characters of others, and disbelieved in regard to their own," and so now he made a distinction between necessity as applied to human actions and as applied to nonhuman actions which enabled him to achieve that desirable end. As a result, "I no longer suffered under the burthen, so heavy to one who aims at being a reformer in opinions, of thinking one doctrine true, and the contrary doctrine morally beneficial." He could both believe, and not believe, in both free will and necessity.

Under the influence, then, of the Romantic poets and of a whole new

stream of ideas and attitudes flowing in upon him from the continent, Mill
was carried as far in his reaction against Bentham as he was destined to go.
It was at this point that he met Carlyle. They were brought together by the
agency of a third party, the Saint-Simonians in France. Claude Henri de
Rouvroy, Comte de Saint-Simon, was a nobleman of the ancien régime who
had participated in the American and French revolutions and then, in the
Napoleonic and post-Napoleonic era, produced a series of brilliant, speculative pamphlets which urged the reorganization of society on the basis of
science and technology. His most seminal insight was into the philosophy
of history, which he saw as consisting of "organic" and "critical" periods
which alternated so as to produce three great epochs of human culture, of
which two were past and the third was just beginning. Organic periods were
those dominated by a single unified philosophy or religion, which manifested
itself in a coherent social system. Critical periods were those in which this
overarching authority was lacking, and hence society was a mere agglom-
eration of individuals motivated by egoism. It was fragmented, atomistic, at
war with itself. The transition between the two periods was not abrupt, for
the moment one organic period achieved its full development, the process
of its dissolution began, and even before that dissolution was complete the
elements of the new organic period began to form. The fabric of society was
thus never ruptured, but there was a movement back and forth between
unity and diversity, criticism and creation.

The first great organic period was that of Polytheism in ancient Greece
and Rome, with its attendant social system based on slavery. This period
lasted through the age of Pericles in Greece and of Augustus in Rome and
was brought to an end by the critical thought of Socrates. The first critical
period thus extended from the time of Socrates to the third or fourth century
A.D., culminating in the barbarian invasions. The second organic period, the
Theological, with its attendant social system of feudalism, began with the
promulgation of Christianity, reached its height in the eleventh and twelfth
centuries, and lingered on till the time of Leo X in the religious sphere and
Louis XIV in the political. The second critical period began with the Reformation and continued through the Enlightenment and the French Revolution right down to the Revolution of 1830. In Saint-Simon's view the world
was now in the second phase of the second critical period, that in which the
destruction of the old theological world had been completed but nothing
new had been introduced in its stead. It was his role to announce the coming
of this New Era, which was to be Scientific or Positive in its world-view
and Industrial in its social organization. Scientists, engineers, educators, and
technologists would organize the industrial resources of the world in behalf

of the poor. The motto of the new society would be, "From each according to his capacity, to each capacity according to his work." So organized, society would move forward without the oscillations which had characterized the past, for Saint-Simon was clear that this third stage of society would be the last. "The Golden Age," he said, "which the inspiration of poets has placed in the cradle of humanity, is not behind us but before: it lies in the perfection of society."

It is clear that Saint-Simon has adopted the broad periodization of the eighteenth-century philosophes but has simply reversed their values. Their Ages of Superstition are his Ages of Faith, and their Ages of Criticism are indeed "critical" periods but less favorably conceived. "Looking back at the ages of Pericles, Augustus, Leo X, and Louis XIV, and then at the nineteenth century," said Saint-Simon, "one cannot help but smile; no one would think of drawing a parallel between the periods." Yet these are exactly the ages which Voltaire did parallel with his own age, which he regarded as the acme, not the nadir, of civilization. In Saint-Simon's view both organic and critical periods are necessary to the historical process, and one is technically no "better" than the other. Still, there is a distinct feeling that the organic periods, and the great creative geniuses who bring them about, are superior. The critical periods are dark, violent, and unpleasant, and the duty of everyone is to make them as short and nondestructive as possible. One does this by understanding and facilitating the historical process, and thus the supreme moral imperative is to recognize what one's place is in the stream of history and in which direction it is flowing.

Under the banner of this doctrine Saint-Simon gathered about himself a dedicated group of disciples, including Auguste Comte, who, after their leader's death in 1825, organized his speculations into a creed and attempted to convert not only their fellow countrymen but also their neighbors across the Channel. The leaders of the movement were Saint-Armand Bazard and Barthélemy-Prosper Enfantin, whose brilliant course of lectures, *Doctrine de Saint-Simon; exposition; première année, 1829*, was one of the most important publications of the group. Another of their number was the young scion of a wealthy family, Gustave d'Eichthal, who had met Mill at a meeting of the London Debating Society in May 1828 and, after becoming a Saint-Simonian, sent him a supply of literature, including Comte's *Système de politique positive* (1824). Mill read these materials in the summer of 1829 and was deeply impressed. "I was greatly struck," he says in the *Autobiography*, "with the connected view which they for the first time presented to me, of the natural order of human progress; and especially with their division of all history into organic periods and critical periods. . . . These ideas, I knew,

were not peculiar to the St. Simonians; on the contrary, they were the general
property of Europe, or at least of Germany and France, but they had never,
to my knowledge, been so completely systematized as by these writers, nor
the distinguishing characteristics of a critical period so powerfully set forth;
for I was not then acquainted with Fichte's Lectures on 'the Characteristics
of the Present Age.' " In July 1830, during the days of revolution, Mill went
over to Paris to observe the state of society and met with Bazard and Enfantin
and other leaders of the movement. He was further indoctrinated and from
this time on read virtually everything they produced. Indeed, the whole
Revolution aroused his "utmost enthusiasm, and gave me, as it were, a new
existence."

On coming home, he attempted to embody all his new thoughts and
feelings in a series of articles entitled "The Spirit of the Age," which appeared
in the *Examiner* from January 6 to May 29, 1831. It was his most Saint-
Simonian production. Being less concerned with cultural change than with
the transfer of power, he spoke of "natural" and "transitional" periods rather
than organic and critical, natural periods being those in which power is
exercised by those most fitted to exercise it, and transitional periods being
those in which it is not. The present age, he writes, is a transitional period,
and the hope is that the people will take their opinions from the cultivated
portion of mankind so that Europe can move into a new natural period
without violence. "I think you will be pleased with two or three articles of
mine in the Examiner," Mill wrote to d'Eichthal. "Although I am not a St
Simonist nor at all likely to become one, *je tiens bureau de St Simonisme chez
moi.*" By November 30, however, he had been brought "much nearer to
many of your opinions than I was before; and I regard you as decidedly *á
la tête de la civilisation.*" Indeed, "if the hour were yet come for England . . . ,
I know not that I should not renounce every thing, and become, not one of
you, but as you." For Mill was now inclined to think that the Saint-Simonian
social organization would, under some modification or other, "be the final
and permanent condition of the human race." He just did not think it would
come as quickly as they did, but would "require many, or at least several,
ages."

Meanwhile, in Scotland, Carlyle was also being drawn within the orbit
of the Saint-Simonians. His "Signs of the Times," reprinted in the *Revue
britannique*, was reviewed sympathetically by the Saint-Simonians, who saw
it as the work of one spiritually already with them and only needing to be
told about their organization in order to become a convert. In July 1830
d'Eichthal sent Carlyle a copy of their review and also a number of their
publications, including the *Nouveau Christianisme*, a proposal for revitalizing

Christianity by freeing it of its superstitions and rededicating it to the service of the poor. "Received . . . a strange letter from some *Saint-Simoniens* at Paris," wrote Carlyle, "grounded on my little *Signs of the Times*. These people have strange notions, not without a large spicing of truth, and are themselves among the *Signs*. I shall feel curious to know what becomes of them." After discussing them with Edward Irving while on a visit to London, Carlyle replied to d'Eichthal that he found "little or nothing to dissent from" in their writings—indeed, was in "entire sympathy" with them. Later he mentioned them to Goethe and received from him the warning, "*Von der Société St Simonienne bitte Sich fern zu halten*"—"From the St. Simonian Society pray hold yourself aloof." But Carlyle did not hold himself aloof. On the contrary, he wrote to his brother in London asking for more Saint-Simonian books, and on December 19 announced that he had translated the *Nouveau Christianisme* and was seeking a publisher. In April 1831 he received another packet of literature from d'Eichthal and told Goethe that the group had "discovered and laid to heart this momentous and now almost forgotten truth, *Man is still a Man*," though they were "already beginning to make false applications of it."

About this same time, while Carlyle was still in Scotland, he also read Mill's "Spirit of the Age," and saying to himself (as he afterwards told Mill), "Here is a new Mystic," determined on going to London to look up this potential disciple. They met for the first time on September 3, and Carlyle wrote his wife that "we had almost four hours of the best talk I have mingled in for long." The talk was all the better because "the youth . . . seemed to profess almost as plainly as modesty would allow that he had been converted by the Head of the Mystic School" and wished to be his disciple. Two years later Mill would painfully explain to Carlyle that the latter had misinterpreted the degree of their proximity and that he had since been moving further away from him, but for the moment they were united in their admiration of the Saint-Simonians. Mill brought d'Eichthal to meet his new friend, and Carlyle was delighted with this "little, tight, cleanly pure lovable *Geschöpfchen*: a pure martyr and apostle. . . . Mill goes so far as to think there might and should be martyrs: this *is* one."

Mill was right, for the movement was nearing its unfortunate end. The Society was making increasingly bizarre claims to be a new Christianity, with Enfantin as a new Jesus, and it also espoused a freedom between the sexes which Mill could approve but Carlyle could not. Then in December it unwisely sent a mission to London to convert the English, and as the missionaries were handsome bearded youths who were most fantastically dressed in red berets, blue or white drill trousers, and tunics of bluebottle blue revealing white waistcoats embroidered in red, Englishmen naturally feared not only for their religion and their property but also for their wives, and the police had to be called out to prevent a riot. Shortly thereafter the French government began proceedings against the group on charges of unlawful assembly and teaching immorality, and the three main leaders were sentenced to a year in prison. The last Mill and Carlyle heard of them they were setting out to the East in search of a female Messiah whom they expected to find on the banks of the Bosphorus. It seemed to both men a pity that so good and pureminded a group should have ended in such a fiasco, but they felt the whole episode revealed the weakness as well as the strength of the French character.

To both Mill and Carlyle the most valuable and lasting contribution of the Saint-Simonians was their philosophy of history. Mill had read a great deal of history as a child. Not only had he read all the Greek and Latin historians simply as a part of his lessons, but he had also read all the major historians in English of both the modern and the ancient world. The fact that his father was "fond of putting into my hands books which exhibited men of energy and resource in unusual circumstances, struggling against difficulties and overcoming them," indicates that the approach taken to these works was that of "philosophy teaching by examples." When he was a little older it was the typical Enlightenment view of the warfare of Reason against Superstition and Tyranny. When he came to the American war, for example, "I took my part, like a child as I was (until set right by my father) on the wrong side, because it was called the English side." And when he came to Mitford's History of Greece, in which he delighted for its vivid narrative, "my father had put me on my guard against the Tory prejudices of this writer . . . with such effect that in reading Mitford my sympathies were always on the contrary side to those of the author." In his eleventh and twelfth year he even wrote "a history of the Roman Government, compiled (with the assistance of Hooke) from Livy and Dionysius, [which] . . . was, in fact, an account of the struggles between the patricians and plebeians. . . . Though quite ignorant of Niebuhr's researches, I, by such lights as my father had given me, vindicated the Agrarian Laws on the evidence of Livy, and upheld to the best of my ability the Roman democratic party." History for the young Mill and his father was simply a quarry for "ideas respecting civilization, government, morality, mental cultivation," and a narrative of the Progress of the Species, the March of Intellect.

It was only in the years following his mental crisis that Mill came to the historicist view. In his essay on Coleridge he says that Bentham asked of a thing, "Is it true?" whereas Coleridge asked, "What is the meaning of it?" Mill learned from the Saint-Simonians to ask that second question. He learned that an institution may be perfectly rational and yet not be suitable for a particular people at a particular time, or that it may be irrational and yet of great benefit at that stage of their development. It was one of the great merits of the Saint-Simonians, he told d'Eichthal, to have pointed this out with respect to the medieval church, and a second great merit was their insistence that if one wishes to reform society, one needs to know into what stage of civilization society is coming. Otherwise one may propose reforms, good in themselves, which are not adapted to society in that phase of its development.

Mill could hardly fail to see that his father was as much without a developmental child psychology as he was without a developmental conception of history, and that there were certain things in his own education, good in themselves, which were not suitable to the particular age in which they were administered. It was not good for him never to have had a childhood. In an age in which every Victorian lost his religion it was not even good that he never had a religion to lose. He was thereby deprived of one of the great agonizing experiences of his era. Indeed, as Mill examined his own life in the light of the Saint-Simonian philosophy he must have concluded that he was exactly out of phase with his age. For it is clear that his "organic" period—comparable to Teufelsdröckh's idyllic childhood—was the period when Dumont's Bentham united "the detached and fragmentary component parts of my knowledge" and gave "[me] a creed, a doctrine, a philosophy; in one among the best senses of the word, a religion." The trouble is that his organic period was everybody else's critical period, and when he fell into his critical period, under the influence of the Romantic poets, German philosophy, and the Saint-Simonians, that corresponded to the new organic period of the rest of the nation. His Everlasting No, from 1826 to the mid-1830s, was the beginning of Carlyle's Everlasting Yea. And Mill's Everlasting Yea consisted of the compromise or synthesis he attempted to make of these two. For "in this third period (as it may be termed) of my mental progress . . . I had now completely turned back from what there had been of excess in my reaction against Benthamism." Mill insists that although there was a time in which he undervalued Bentham and the eighteenth century, he never joined in the reaction against it, and he was never confused or unsettled in his views. He continually rewove the fabric of his opinions so as to incorporate the new with the old, and he emphasized the necessity of Goethe's "many-sidedness." Thus, though the onset of the Everlasting No was abrupt for Mill, the movement from the No into the Everlasting Yea was not abrupt but was a process. Indeed, it was a continual process, for Mill differs from the Saint-Simonians in not believing that the coming organic phase will be the final one, but that the process of adjusting half-truth with half-truth will go on for at least the foreseeable future.

Thus Mill's assertion in 1831 that the present age is "an age of transition," remained true for him till the end of his life. In his very last years, when he was writing the final section of his *Autobiography*, he noted that this was a "period of transition, when old notions and feelings have been unsettled, and no new doctrines have yet succeeded to their ascendancy." And it will be remembered that one of his motives for writing the *Autobiography* was that "in an age of transition in opinions, there may be somewhat both of interest and of benefit in noting the successive phases of any mind which was always pressing forward, equally ready to learn and to unlearn either from its own thoughts or from those of others." "The chief benefit which I derived . . . from the trains of thought suggested by the St. Simonians and by Comte, was, that I obtained a clearer conception than ever before of the peculiarities of an era of transition in opinion, and ceased to mistake the moral and intellectual characteristics of such an era, for the normal attributes of humanity. I looked forward, through the present age of loud disputes but generally weak convictions, to a future which shall unite the best qualities of the critical with the best qualities of the organic periods." Mill never reached an organic period in the sense of a period of settled convictions. He moved back from his reaction against Benthamism to a modified Utilitarian position in which he nonetheless took along with him the "many-sidedness" of Goethe. Thus, all his life, like the life of his entire age, was an age of transition. Newman closes his spiritual autobiography by saying, "From the time that I became a Catholic, of course, I have no further history of my religious opinions to narrate . . . no variations to record." Mill, on the other hand, opens the last chapter of his autobiography by saying, "From this time [forth] . . . I have no further mental changes to tell of, but only, as I hope, a continued mental progress."

After his mental crisis Mill continued to read history even more extensively than before and wrote long review-articles on the work of Michelet, Guizot, Grote, Carlyle, and Armand Carrell. The reason for his interest is that in French and German historiography a revolution was occurring of which Englishmen were hardly aware. In Mill's view there were three stages in historical inquiry. The first is that which attempts "to transport present feelings and notions back into the past, and refer all ages and forms of human life to the standard of that in which the writer himself lives." This school has no sense of the "otherness" of the past, but, firmly persuaded that human nature is in all ages the same and that history is "philosophy teaching by examples," attempts to apply present ideas directly to the past. Of course, this kind is better than that which fails to make history live at all (Carlyle's Dryasdust), "and Mitford, so far, is a better historian than Rollin."

The second stage of historical inquiry is that of the Romantic school which "attempts to regard former ages not with the eye of a modern, but, as far as possible, with that of a contemporary; to realize a true and living picture of the past time, clothed in its circumstances and peculiarities." The founder of this school was Sir Walter Scott. Mill writes:

> Scott's romances have been read by every educated person in Great Britain who has grown up to manhood or womanhood in the last twenty years; and, except the memory of much pleasure, . . . they have left no traces that we know of in the national mind. But it was otherwise in France. . . . Scott's romances, and especially 'Ivanhoe,' which in England were only the amusement of an idle hour, [gave] birth (or at least nourishment) to one of the principal intellectual products of our time, the modern French school of history. M. Thierry, whose "Letters on the History of France" gave the first impulse, proclaims the fact. Seeing, in these fictions, past events for the first time brought home to them as realities, not mere abstractions; startled by finding, what they had not dreamed of, Saxons and Normans in the reign of Richard the First; thinking men felt flash upon them for the first time the meaning of that philosophical history, that history of human life, and not of kings and battles, which Voltaire talked of, but, writing history for polemical purposes, could not succeed in realizing. Immediately the annals of France, England, and other countries, began to be systematically searched; the characteristic features of society and life at each period were gathered out, and exhibited in histories, and speculations on history, and historical fictions.

Niebuhr furnished an imperishable model of this school in Germany, and Carlyle (had Mill been writing a little later, he might have added Macaulay) in England.

The third and highest stage of historical investigation is that in which "the aim is not simply to compose histories, but to construct a science of history. In this view, the whole of the events which have befallen the human race, and the states through which it has passed, are regarded as a series of phenomena, produced by causes, and susceptible of explanation." This third stage, which necessarily depends upon the completion of the second, "is rather a possibility to be one day realized, than an enterprise in which any great progress has yet been made. But of the little yet done in this direction, by far the greater part has hitherto been done by French writers." It is clear that Mill has in mind the Saint-Simonians, Comte, and Guizot.

Comte had extended the Saint-Simonian philosophy of history by transforming the three historical epochs, the Polytheistic, the Theological, and the Scientific or Positive, into three stages through which every branch of human knowledge must pass on its way to perfection. These stages were the Theological, in which the causes of phenomena were sought in the direct volition of divine beings; the Metaphysical, in which they were attributed to realized abstractions; and the Positive, in which phenomena themselves and the relations between phenomena were the only object of knowledge. Mill first became acquainted with this scheme from Comte's early Saint-Simonian tract, the *Système de politique positive*, which he read in the summer of 1829. He had good reason to be impressed with its truth because the revolution in his own thinking, when he read Dumont's Bentham in 1821–22, had taken him from the metaphysical to the positive. Having never had a religion, Mill had never known the theological stage, but when Bentham tore the scales from his eyes and showed him that phrases like *Law of Nature*, *Right Reason*, and *Moral Sense* were not real entities but merely hypostatized fictions, he was catapulted into the positive. When in 1842 he read the fifth and sixth volumes of the *Cours de philosophie positive*, in which Comte's scheme of history is worked out in detail and used as a means of classifying the sciences, Mill was lost in admiration, and it is probable that Comte's law of the three stages exceeded in importance for Mill the three historical epochs of the Saint-Simonians. The only thing he could not tolerate was the monolithic intellectual tyranny which Comte erected in the third stage.

For his general view of a free and pluralistic society he rather turned to Guizot. Guizot observes, according to Mill, "that one of the points of difference by which modern civilization is most distinguished from ancient, is the complication, the multiplicity, which characterizes it. In all previous forms of society, Oriental, Greek, or Roman, there is a remarkable character of unity and simplicity. Some one idea seems to have presided over the construction of the social framework, and to have been carried out into all its consequences." In modern society, on the other hand, there are "a number of distinct forces—of separate and independent sources of power"—the power of knowledge and cultivated intelligence, the power of religion, the power of military skill and discipline, the power of wealth, the power of numbers and physical force, and several others. "We believe with M. Guizot, that modern Europe presents the only example in history, of the maintenance, through many ages, of this co-ordinate action among rival powers naturally tending in different directions. And, with him, we ascribe chiefly to this cause the spirit of improvement, which has never ceased to exist, and still makes progress, in the European nations." If at any time any one power had attained dominance, Europe might have achieved greater perfection in that particular respect, but the whole society "would either have stagnated, like the great stationary despotisms of the East, or have perished for lack of such other elements of civilization as could sufficiently unfold themselves only under some other patronage."

It will be observed that this review of European civilization is really a preview of Mill's essay *On Liberty*, for that essay is also historicist in its assumptions to a degree that Mill's father and Bentham would have found difficult to understand. In a historical introduction Mill shows how the problem of liberty has changed over the centuries. At one time it was thought merely that the people had to be protected against the tyranny of their rulers, and this was done, first by exacting from the rulers a recognition of certain immunities (a Magna Carta or Bill of Rights) and then by establishing constitutional checks. A time came, however, when it was thought that, rather than tinkering with the machine, one should set it right once and for all by making the people their own governors, so that there could be no conflict of interest and no infringement upon liberty. This was the Benthamite stage. But now the progress of democracy, particularly in America, has shown that the people are not their own governors, rather the majority is, and that the minority, particularly those rare spirits who are in advance of their time, need to be protected against the majority. Moreover, the real danger now is not political but intellectual and cultural oppression.

Thus, the problem becomes a cultural issue, and in the remainder of the essay Mill envisions a Darwinian world (the year is 1859) in which not merely the survival of truth but also its healthy condition depend upon struggle and conflict. There have been three great periods of intellectual ferment in the modern world, Mill says, one in "the condition of Europe immediately following the Reformation; another, though limited to the Continent and to a more cultivated class, in the speculative movement of the latter half of the eighteenth century; and a third, of still briefer duration, in the intellectual fermentation of Germany during the Goethean and Fichtean period. These periods differed widely in the particular opinions which they developed; but were alike in this, that during all three the yoke of authority was broken. In each, an old mental despotism had been thrown off, and no new one had yet taken its place." Mill does not use the term *critical*, but it is obvious that he is describing miniature critical periods within the great critical era of the post-Reformation years. This is particularly apparent in the chapter "Of Individuality, as one of the Elements of Well-being," where Mill declares that "the end of man . . . is the highest and most harmonious development of his powers to a complete and consistent whole." The fact that this quotation comes from Wilhelm von Humboldt (as does the epigraph to the work as a whole) suggests that it embodies for Mill the many-sidedness of the Goethean period of German culture. Its antithesis is then identified with Calvinism. The Calvinistic theory is that "human nature being radically corrupt, there is no redemption for any one until human nature is killed within him." In opposition to this view Mill then quotes Sterling, the Coleridgean under whose influence he had moved farthest from Bentham: " 'Pagan self-assertion' is one of the elements of human worth, as well as 'Christian self-denial.' There is a Greek ideal of self-development, which the Platonic and Christian ideal of self-government blends with, but does not supersede. It may be better to be a John Knox than an Alcibiades, but it is better to be a Pericles than either; nor would a Pericles, if we had one in these days, be without anything good which belonged to John Knox." The dialectic of history would have produced, in Goethe or von Humboldt, the synthesis of Greek and Christian, of Knox and Alcibiades, which involves self-development *and* self-government. It is clear that Mill's desire is for history no longer to alternate between organic and critical phases but rather to combine the two. It should move steadily forward in a continual process of self-criticism and self-creation.

Prior to encountering the Saint-Simonians, Carlyle's philosophy of history, insofar as he had one, was based on the familiar analogy between the life of the world and the life of the individual. There were three stages: Imagination, Understanding, and Reason. This schema, common in eighteenth-century literary histories, provided the framework for an unfinished "History of German Literature" which Carlyle was commissioned to write by some London booksellers and which he worked on during the winter and spring of 1829–30 until the publishing arrangements collapsed in July of that year. He then quarried his manuscript for three review articles, on the *Niebelungenlied*, "Early German Literature," and on William Taylor's *Historic Survey of German Poetry*, which were published in various periodicals in 1831. From these articles, the manuscript of Carlyle's History, and a letter to Goethe, one can see what Carlyle's plan was. He intended to treat the Swabian Era, the period of the Minnesingers in the twelfth century, as the first great period of German poetry, whose essence was youthful wonder, with chivalry as the appropriate instrument to translate this idealism into action. To this there succeeded a period of Inquiry or Didacticism, which continued through various fourteenth- and fifteenth-century authors until it rose to an almost poetic intensity in Luther and then declined again into theological disputations and superficial refinements. Carlyle saw Lessing as "standing between two Periods, an earnest Sceptic, struggling to work himself into the region of spiritual Truth," but this region was not attained until the era of Goethe and Schiller. "Under you and Schiller," Carlyle wrote to Goethe, "a Third grand Period had evolved itself, as yet fairly developed in no other Literature, but full of the richest prospects for all: Namely, a period of new Spirituality and Belief in the midst of old Doubt and Denial: . . . wherein Reverence is again rendered compatible with Knowledge, and Art and Religion are one." The three periods, then, are not merely those of Imagination, Understanding, and Reason but also of Art, Science, and Religion—periods which Carlyle identifies with the Middle Ages, which is the youth of the modern world; the Renaissance, Reformation, and Enlightenment, which is its manhood; and the late eighteenth and early nineteenth centuries, which, in a breakdown of the analogy, are not old age but a new youthfulness on a higher plane.

It is obvious that this scheme, which involves a kind of periodicity between poetry and didacticism, is easily reconcilable with the Saint-Simonian philosophy, with its organic-critical-organic periods. As Carlyle first learned about the Saint-Simonians from d'Eichthal in the very month (July 1830) in which the plan for the History of German Literature collapsed, he must have been delighted to find his tentative views supported by so systematic and well ordered a scheme. He immediately plunged into the writing of *Sartor Resartus*, and so it is no wonder that that work, particularly the biographical portion of it, is full of Saint-Simonian references. Though Carlyle's philosophy of history first came to him from English and German sources, it was given its final form by the Saint-Simonians, as the "organic filaments," the first gossamery threads of the new society, make clear. The Professor himself, who is deeply radical, quotes "without censure that strange aphorism of Saint Simon's," that the Golden Age is not behind us but before, and when, at the end of the book, he mysteriously disappears, the Editor opines that he has either been spirited away by the Saint-Simonians or gone to their headquarters to confront them.

Carlyle's brilliant contribution to this philosophy of history is the Clothes metaphor by which it is represented. The metaphor of Machinery, which he had adopted in "Signs of the Times," was not really successful because, despite his Genius of Mechanization, there was no smooth way in which Mechanism could modulate into Dynamism. Neither was the more profound analysis of the age in terms of Self-consciousness in "Characteristics" satisfactory, since to become unconscious would be simply to return to the original condition and it seemed psychologically difficult to be "anti-self-conscious." But the metaphor of clothes was the perfect vehicle to express both the transcendental and the descendental aspect of Teufelsdröckh's philosophy, for if clothes bodied forth the inner spiritual reality behind appearances, they also, where that reality was absent or a sham, served as a "clothes-screen" to conceal the sham. Moreover, they lent themselves to change. New garments could continually be a-weaving, and, on the other hand, the old were easily subject to destruction. By introducing, apparently from German sources, the Phoenix, who expires in a magnificent conflagration and then arises from her own ashes, Carlyle introduced an apocalyptic and catastrophic element which apparently satisfied his Scotch Calvinism but was hardly consistent with the gradualist implications of "organic filaments." He tries to reconcile the two by means of the serpent. " 'In the living subject,' says [Teufelsdröckh], 'change is wont to be gradual: thus, while the serpent sheds its old skin, the new is already formed beneath. Little knowest thou of the burning of a World-Phoenix, who fanciest that she must first burn-out, and lie as a dead cinereous heap; and therefrom the young one start-up by miracle, and fly heavenward. Far otherwise! In that Fire-whirlwind, Creation and Destruction proceed together; ever as the ashes of the Old are blown about, do organic filaments of the New mysteriously spin themselves; and amid the rushing and the waving of the Whirlwind-element come tones of a melodious Deathsong, which end not but in tones of a more melodious Birthsong.' " The World-Phoenix is apparently of a different species from the ordinary in that it may take two centuries to combust.

The Saint-Simonian philosophy of history seems to have satisfied Carlyle for at least a decade, for it is presupposed in *The French Revolution* and it provides the general structure of the *Lectures on the History of Literature* which Carlyle delivered in 1838. In these lectures, as with the Saint-Simonians, there are two great eras of belief, the Polytheism of the Greeks and Romans, and the Christianity of the Middle Ages, each followed by a period of unbelief. The novel element is that since this is a history of literature and Carlyle has by this time decided that literature *is* self-consciousness— that it is the nation being conscious of its own life rather than living it—he is committed to the theory that great literature does not occur in ages of belief but rather when these ages are beginning to break up. This is the reason for the great efflorescence of literature in the Elizabethan Age, the period when Catholicism and Feudalism were beginning to end. The theory obviously does not account for Dante and Homer, who would seem to be great unconscious geniuses in ages of belief, but Carlyle would say that

Dante belongs to religion rather than literature and Homer to history. Shakespeare apparently rises above his age. On the other hand, the theory may explain why Virgil is inferior to Homer. "There is that fatal consciousness, that knowledge that he is writing an epic," which vitiates everything, and "it is remarkable how soon afterwards Roman literature had quite degenerated" into self-consciousness and skepticism. Milton is to Shakespeare as Virgil is to Homer, for "no great man ever felt so great a consciousness as Milton." The theory obviously makes nonsense of literary history and is not consistent with itself, but Carlyle apparently held it as true, at least for purposes of the lecture platform.

A second novel element is his attempt to explain cultural change. In his earlier "History of German Literature" he had avoided doing this, having no faith in "cause-and-effect" philosophers and scornfully rejecting, as reductive, proposed social and material explanations. But in the 1838 lectures he feels the need to explain change, and he hesitates rather lamely between the subjective explanation that systems of belief simply ceased to satisfy after a period and the more objective and progressive view that they were approximations of the truth, good for their time but necessarily superseded when better arrived. Carlyle must have felt less happy with the Saint-Simonian theory when he came to apply it in detail than he did when its novelty first burst upon him. But he never repudiated it, and elements of the system may be found in later works right up to and including *Frederick the Great*. It is supplemented, however, by other schemes which deal more minutely with the period in which Carlyle was chiefly interested, the last two hundred years before his own day.

Indeed, as one reads Carlyle, one feels that his time-scale was considerably shorter than Saint-Simon's and that for him a complete cycle of organic and critical periods had played itself out in the four hundred years of modern history. It is true that he says in several places that Protestantism, Puritanism, and the French Revolution are the three waves of the critical movement that destroyed the Catholic-Feudal system. "Protestantism was a revolt against spiritual sovereignties, Popes and much else. Nay I will grant that English Puritanism, revolt against earthly sovereignties, was the second act of it; and that the enormous French Revolution itself was the third act, whereby all sovereignties earthly and spiritual were, as might seem, abolished or made sure of abolition. Protestantism is the grand root from which our whole subsequent European History branches out." Still, Protestantism and Puritanism, with their heroes, Luther, Knox, and Cromwell, are so much admired by Carlyle that one cannot but think that these periods, though critical with respect to the Catholic-Feudal system, have carried that criticism to a point of intensity that almost constitutes them organic. (One recalls that Carlyle employed the same paradox with respect to Luther in the "History of German Literature": in a Didactic age he carried didacticism to an almost poetic intensity.) Doubtless Carlyle was projecting his own personal experience upon the backdrop of history, but for him it is the eighteenth century that is critical par excellence.

For that poor, wretched, miserable century he has almost nothing good to say. It was a century of sham, of unreality, of atheism and materialism, of pure formalism and superficial refinement, given to persiflage and mockery, a century of quacks and imposters. By accident several good men were born into it, such as Robert Burns and Dr. Johnson, but its representative figures were Hume and Gibbon in England and Voltaire in France. Voltaire especially was "emphatically . . . the man of his century," the very incarnation of the Spirit of his Age. This being so, Carlyle should have admitted that he had done the work that he came into the world to do, and he does concede, "He gave the death-stab to modern Superstition!" But he cannot quite forgive him for not doing more. " 'Cease, my much-respected Herr von Voltaire,' thus apostrophizes the Professor: 'shut thy sweet voice; for the task appointed thee seems finished. Sufficiently hast thou demonstrated this proposition, considerable or otherwise; That the Mythus of the Christian Religion looks not in the eighteenth century as it did in the eighth. Alas, were thy six-and-thirty quartos . . . all needed to convince us of so little! But what next? Wilt thou help us to embody the divine Spirit of that Religion in a new Mythus, in a new vehicle and vesture, that our Souls, otherwise too like perishing, may live? What! thou hast no faculty in that kind? Only a torch for burning, no hammer for building? Take our thanks, then, and ————thyself away.' " Carlyle could never quite decide whether he wished his Heroes to be Representative Men, embodying all the characteristics of their age, or Great Men, rising above their age. Voltaire was a Representative Man.

The French Revolution to Carlyle was simply the most momentous event since the fall of the Roman Empire—"the crowning Phenomenon of our Modern Time." "Truly, without the French Revolution, one would not know what to make of an age like this at all." Coming at the end of the eighteenth century, it is the negation of a negation—the French people saying No to the Everlasting No. It is comparable to the Protest on the Rue de St. Thomas de l'Enfer (and this may be why Carlyle set that episode in Paris), when Teufelsdröckh stood up in native, God-created majesty and defied the shams with which he was encompassed. In *The French Revolution* Carlyle represents it in terms of titanic natural forces—volcano, earthquake, fire, and raging storm, which destroy the frail wood-and-paper universe of the ancien régime. The trouble was, it issued in nothing. Carlyle's theory, according to Mill in his review, was that "the men . . . who attempted at that period to regenerate France, failed in what it was impossible that any one should succeed in: namely, in attempting to found a government, to create a new order of society, a new set of institutions and habits, among a people having no convictions to base such order of things upon." Thus, the Revolution emerged, not into the New Era which its leaders had promised, but into the Center of Indifference, into a spiritual vacuum. Had there been some great leader with a vision of his own, he might, by inspiring faith in himself, have inspired faith in his vision, but there was not. Mirabeau was truly an Original Man, who moved through the Revolution like a substance and a force, not like the formula of one, but Mirabeau did not live. Thus, at the end there was only Napoleon, a mixture of greatness and quackery, and he was a man of the past, not the future, a Werther or Byron, who wrote his lamentations on the pages of history and with the blood of dying men.

The question is, what lies ahead? In his earlier works, "Signs of the Times," "Characteristics," and *Sartor Resartus*, Carlyle had always ended on a serene and hopeful note. However dark the present age might appear, "the darkest hour is ever nearest the dawn." "Indications we do see . . . , signs infinitely cheering to us . . . , that a new and brighter spiritual era is slowly evolving itself for all men." The ground of this faith was primarily the new literature that was arising in Germany, particularly the writings of Goethe. But Goethe had died in 1832, and although it was not to be expected that his influence be felt immediately—it was rather like a tide which rises in mid-ocean forty-eight hours before it is felt on the shore—still "David Hume is at this hour pontiff of the world, and rules most hearts, and guides most tongues." As a result, the term *New Era* takes on a rather bitter tinge in Carlyle's writings. "Ever the 'new era' was come, was coming, yet still it came not," he wrote in 1832, and in 1839: "One has heard so often of new eras, new and newest eras, that the word has grown rather empty of late." New eras will come, but will they be better than the old and will they come soon? *The French Revolution* was a dire apocalyptic warning that if England did not reform its ways and do justice it would be damned, but if it reformed them in the way that France had it would also be damned. For what issued from the French Revolution was pure democracy, and to Carlyle democracy was not a new order but a transition state. It was the state in which one authority had been destroyed and no new authority had been introduced in its stead. It was a political Center of Indifference. The universe, said Carlyle, is not a democracy but a hierarchy—a hierarchy of merit. Napoleon had seen this—it was his one new idea: *la carrière ouverte aux talens*—but he himself had lacked talent and had created a false order. Nonetheless, "All human things," said Carlyle, "maddest French Sansculottisms, do and must work towards Order. . . . Disorder is dissolution, death. No chaos but it seeks a *centre* to revolve round. While man is man, some Cromwell or Napoleon is the necessary finish of a Sansculottism." If not Napoleon, then it must be Cromwell.

Cromwell was the very first subject Carlyle seized on for a book. He wrote to his brother in April 1822: "My purpose . . . is to come out with a kind of Essay on the Civil Wars, the Commonwealth of England—not to write a history of them—but to exhibit if I can some features of the national character as it was then displayed." The first thirty pages of his notebook are filled with material relating to this project. Ironically, Cromwell was not then a hero to him, for he had been reading Clarendon's History and had accepted the Royalist estimate. "Cromwell and the rest look much like a pack of fanatical knaves—a compound of religious enthusiasm, and of barbarous selfishness; which made them stick at no means for gratifying both the one and the other. Cromwell is a *very* curious person. Has his character been rightly seized yet?" Apparently he suspected not, for a month later he queried, "*How* was it such noble minds were generated in those times? I know not but think it well worth inquiring into." Still, as late as 1826 he declared, "What a fine thing a *Life of Cromwell*, like the *Vie de Charles XII* [by Voltaire] would be! The wily fanatic himself, in his own most singular features, at once a hero and a blackguard pettifogging scrub; and the wild image of his Times reflected from his accompaniment! I would travel ten miles on foot to see his *soul* represented as I once saw his body in the Castle of Warwick." By the next year he was thinking of a biography of Luther. "Luther's character appears to me the most worth discussing of all modern men's. He is, to say it in a word, a great man in *every* sense; has the soul at once of a Conqueror and a Poet. . . . A picture of the public Thought in those days, and of this strong lofty mind overturning and new-moulding it, would be a fine affair in many senses. It would require immense research.— Alas! alas!—When are we to have another Luther? Such men are needed from century to century: there seldom has been more need of one than now." And a few days later: "Begin to think more seriously of discussing *Martin Luther*. The only Inspiration I know of is that of Genius: it was, is, and will always be of a divine character."

Throughout 1833–34 Carlyle hesitated between a history of John Knox and the Scottish Reformation and a history of the French Revolution—quite a hesitation! He ultimately settled on the latter, but when he finished it in 1837 he determined to return to Cromwell, whom he now saw as a much maligned man. Luther, Knox, and Cromwell all figure as heroes in *Heroes and Hero-worship* (1841), but Carlyle thought Cromwell deserved a book to himself. He had trouble getting on with it, however, because his mind was distracted by the desperate plight of the poor. Then, in September 1842, as he was pursuing his researches in the East Anglian region associated with the Lord Protector, he came upon two places, quite unrelated to Cromwell, which deeply impressed his imagination—the ruined abbey of Bury St. Edmunds and the modern workhouse at St. Ives. These two institutions, the one symbolizing a harmonious society suffused with religion, the other a bankrupt modern world united only by the cash-nexus, represented for Carlyle the Past and the Present. On returning to London he began reading about the monastery and found in the Latin *Chronicle* of Jocelin of Brakelond an account of the ministry of Abbot Samson so inspiring that he was momentarily diverted from Cromwell and seventeenth-century Puritanism into an account of medieval Catholicism.

Carlyle's influence on Ruskin and Morris was so great that he has always been accounted a major figure in the Victorian revival of Medievalism, but in truth he knew little about the Middle Ages and was not deeply committed to it. He wholeheartedly accepted the nineteenth-century reversal of the values of the Enlightenment, accounting the Roman Augustan Age a period of sensualism and skepticism and the Middle Ages a period of faith and youthful wonder. In his unfinished "History of German Literature" he had described the Swabian Era as an era of great poetry, and in his *Lectures on the History of Literature* he had said bluntly: "The Middle Ages used to be called Ages of Darkness, Rudeness, and Barbarity. . . . But it is universally apparent now that these ages are not to be so called." Even the barbarian invasions were "a great and fertile period," accomplishing for the Roman Empire the same favorable destructive purpose as was accomplished for the ancien régime by the French Revolution. William the Conqueror was not a bloody tyrant but one who performed needful surgery upon the English nation. Feudalism, which even the Saint-Simonians had seen as only less oppressive than the slave-owners of antiquity, Carlyle saw as a system of mutual responsibility and interdependence. Summoning the dubious argument of etymology, he declared that in those days a Lord really was a *Law-ward* or guardian of the law, a Lady really was a *Hlaf-dig* or giver of the loaf, a Duke really was a *Dux* or leader, and a King really was the most knowing or able (*Can-ning*). It so happened the Jocelin was the exact contemporary of Ivanhoe, and so Carlyle could make frequent use of that book, which, like most of his contemporaries, he read as far more favorable to the Middle Ages than it was. None of Scott's criticism of chivalry, for example, seems to have come through to him, and Gurth, the thrall of Cedric the Saxon whom Scott describes with mild acerbity as having a brass collar round his neck, Carlyle sees as perfectly happy. "Gurth's brass collar did not gall him," says Carlyle. "Cedric *deserved* to be his master. The pigs were Cedric's, but Gurth too would get his parings of them. Gurth had the inexpressible satisfaction of feeling himself related indissolubly, though in a rude brass-collar way, to his fellow-mortals in this Earth. He had superiors, inferiors, equals." He did not have liberty, but then " 'Liberty to die by starvation' is not so divine!"

There is no question but that Carlyle was favorable to the Middle Ages, but there is really very little in *Past and Present* that is specifically medieval. The life in the monastery is not noticeably interdependent, and the Catholic religion is almost embarrassingly absent. Abbot Samson, who is a rude, practical, overbearing peasant with amazing spiritual and physical force, seems more like a pre-incarnation of Cromwell, or of Carlyle's father, than a medieval Abbot. Indeed, the thing that seems most powerfully to have drawn Carlyle to his material was not the contrast between Bury St. Edmunds and the workhouse but the contrast between the treatment of Cromwell's corpse and the enshrined and embalmed body of St. Edmund. For far and away the most dramatic scene in *Past and Present* is that in which Samson and eleven of his fellows, in the dead of night, open the coffin of their patron saint and reverently look in upon the relic (two of them touching it) before they transfer it to its newly enriched shrine. Saints are the Heroes of the Middle Ages, and those ages knew how to worship them aright. Cromwell's body, on the other hand, after having been buried in Westminster Abbey, was, at the Restoration, torn from its coffin and hanged on the gallows at Tyburn from 10 A.M. until sunset. The head was then cut off with an axe by the common hangman and mounted on a pole on top of Westminster Hall—the rest of the body being buried in a pit beneath the gallows. This, said Carlyle, is the way the modern world treats its Heroes, and in a chapter entitled "Two Centuries" he traces the spiritual desiccation of England not from the twelfth century but from the seventeenth.

The second episode in Jocelin's narrative in which Carlyle is most deeply interested in the election of Samson as Abbot. An election, says Carlyle, "is a most important social act; nay, at bottom, the one important social act. Given the men a People choose, the People itself, in its exact worth and worthlessness, is given. . . . Nor are electoral methods, Reform Bills and such like, unimportant. A People's electoral methods are, in the long-run, the express image of its electoral *talent*." The electoral methods of the monastery were superficially very complicated but at bottom very simple: good men simply got together and chose the one they thought best in the sight and fear of the Lord. It happened that the one they chose was of low birth, and in this too he was like Cromwell, who rose from a country squire to be the most powerful and "the Ablest Man in England, the King of England." Burns, on the other hand, was allowed to weigh out malt in eighteenth-century England.

When Carlyle treated Cromwell in *Heroes and Hero-worship*, he put him in the very last chapter along with Napoleon under the title "The Hero as King." This is surprising because all the other heroes are in chronological order. Indeed, the work has a historical thesis that the divine spirit, incarnating itself in Heroes, accommodates itself to the degree of civilization of the age, so that one goes through the series: Hero as Divinity (Odin), as Prophet (Mahomet), as Poet (Dante and Shakespeare), as Priest (Luther and Knox), as Man of Letters (Johnson, Rousseau, and Burns), and as King (Napoleon and Cromwell). Carlyle insists, despite the apparent secularization, that there is no falling off in the central heroic stuff, merely an accommodation of the divine to the spirit of the age. But it is obvious that the King is not the old-fashioned King by divine right of which Charles I and Louis XVI were a faint relic, but the new post-revolutionary King who comes to impose an order upon Sansculotism. He is, then, a King of the future, not of the past, and the fact that England had its revolution in the seventeenth century does not matter in this essentially philosophical development.

The association of Cromwell with Napoleon was not original with Carlyle; it was, indeed, a commonplace in his century. For, as we have already seen, Cromwell had been so maligned by all parties immediately following the Restoration that he was, in Pope's words, "damn'd to everlasting fame." Throughout most of the eighteenth century he was regarded as a monster both in private and in public life. Two Nonconformist biographies early in the century somewhat modified this view, but then there was nothing for three-quarters of a century until Napoleon's career suddenly "explained" Cromwell to both the British and the Continental public. The antiquarians meanwhile had been printing a great many documents, and there was a sudden flurry of new biographies, none of which really changed the traditional view. Carlyle, who had been suffering through these documents for nearly twenty years and who had arrived at the conclusion that Cromwell was England's greatest national leader, wished to publish a new biography of his own, but reluctantly decided that the only way was to let the facts speak for themselves. He thus edited in two (later three) volumes the letters and speeches of Cromwell (1845) with a voluble commentary so that not even the dullest could miss the point. The result was a great triumph. The Lord Protector's character and personality stood clear for the first time both of the distorting lies of his detractors and also of the accumulated rubbish of the historians, and, as Hilaire Belloc says, a new myth was born. For such was the growing affluence and power of the Nonconformists, such the hatred of the Tractarians, and such too the feeling that England was being called to imperial greatness, that Cromwell was raised to the position of a national hero. "He stood somehow, consciously or unconsciously, for the English people." "He was a practical mystic," said Lord Rosebery, "the most formidable and terrible of all combinations, uniting an inspiration derived from the celestial and supernatural with the energy of a mighty man of action. . . . no hypocrite but a defender of the faith, the raiser and maintainer of the Empire of England."

With Cromwell, the Once and Future King, Carlyle came to the end of his historical myth, and the six volumes on Frederick the Great were really unnecessary. Frederick was the last real King *before* the Revolution, a Reality in an age of shams, and that is doubtless the reason for Carlyle's interest in him. Feeling more and more out of phase with his age himself, he wanted to see how one had managed who was completely out of phase. But Frederick, as Carlyle admitted, was "a questionable hero." The two elements of a Hero were vision and will. Cromwell mediated the vision of John Knox to the English people, but Frederick did not mediate that of Luther, merely of Voltaire and his own Realpolitik. More and more Carlyle emphasizes will in his heroes at the expense of vision, doubtless because he is impatient that the New Era does not come. How long will it take? "Will *one* century of constant fluctuation serve us," he asks in 1831, "or shall we need two?" By *Sartor Resartus* he has concluded that two would be a bargain. "Two centuries; hardly less;" he exclaims in *The French Revolution*, "before Democracy go through its due, most baleful, stages of *Quack*ocracy; and a pestilential World be burnt up, and have begun to grow green and young again." But by the end of *Frederick the Great* he declares, "Centuries of it yet lying ahead of us . . . ! Say Two Centuries yet,—say even Ten of such a process: before the Old is completely burnt out, and the New in any state of sightliness. Millennium of Anarchies!"

Obviously, the new Industrial Age in which the Captains of Industry are directed by the Scientists did not have to wait a thousand years. It is here already. But that is only the lesser side of the world that Carlyle envisioned. He envisioned a world based on social justice in which religion

would be a living reality again. But it would be religion with a difference—
a religion in which "Man is still Man" and Nature is not fallen but erect.
"The Universe, I say, is made by Law; the great Soul of the World is just
and not unjust. Look thou, if thou have eyes or soul left, into this great
shoreless Incomprehensible: in the heart of its tumultuous Appearances,
Embroilments, and mad Time-vortexes, is there not, silent eternal, an All-
just, and All-beautiful; sole Reality and ultimate controlling Power of the
whole? This is not a figure of speech; this is a fact. The fact of Gravitation
known to all animals, is not surer than this inner Fact, which may be known
to all men." Carlyle's use of *fact* where we would say *value*, and *Reality* where
we would say *God*, is a part of his Natural Supernaturalism. Heaven and
Hell, he declares, "are not a similitude, nor a fable nor semi-fable: . . . they
are an everlasting highest fact!" One may say that they *were* a fact until
Carlyle and his generation demystified them and made them into a fable,
and the effort now to take the psychological or moral truth which that fable
represents and transform it back into a fact is not easy. It is Mill's problem
all over again. Having been catapulted from the Metaphysical into the Positive stage, it is difficult to climb back up into the Metaphysical. We can see
Carlyle trying to do it by his capital letters, which attempt to make Real
Entities out of subjective feelings, by his Biblical language and assumption
of the garb and mien of Jehovah, and by his creation of a band of Heroes,
who are his version of the Visible Church. But it will not do: he cannot be
both inside history and outside it. He cannot believe both that every age has
its own validity in the historic process and also that there are some ages,
such as the eighteenth century, that have "no history at all." He cannot have
his Heroes both Representative Men and Unrepresentative Men. He cannot
say that Belief is of transcendent importance, with the strong implication
that it does not matter what one believes, and still urge his countrymen to
believe this or that particular thing. He cannot see religion both as relative
to the state of society it is in and as of absolute significance to those within
that state. He cannot say that Might makes Right, even in the long-range
sense that the real forces in the world do tend to legitimize themselves in
history, and at the same time thunder against the Might that has made Wrong.
He has effected a quasi-divinization of history and a quasi-secularization of
God, and it is difficult to assimilate the one to the other. "Man lives at the
conflux of two eternities," Carlyle was fond of saying. He obviously had a
deep-seated need to live at the conflux, but also to feel that there were
eternities before and after.

In some of his later works Carlyle tended to see history not as a matter
of alternating periods but of radiating lineal descent. He found in Norse

mythology the metaphor of the tree of Igdrasil, which expressed his deeply felt sense that nothing in the past is lost.

> I like, too, that representation they have of the Tree Igdrasil. All Life is figured by them as a Tree. Igdrasil, the Ash-Tree of Existence, has its roots deep-down in the kingdoms of Hela or Death; its trunk reaches up heaven-high, spreads its boughs over the whole Universe: it is the Tree of Existence. At the foot of it, in the Death-Kingdom, sit Three *Norns*, Fates,—the Past, Present, Future; watering its roots from the Sacred Well. Its 'boughs,' with their buddings and disleafings,—events, things suffered, things done, catastrophes,—stretch through all lands and times. Is not every leaf of it a biography, every fibre there an act or word? Its boughs are Histories of Nations. The rustle of it is the noise of Human Existence, onwards from of old. It grows there, the breath of Human Passion rustling through it;—or stormtost, the stormwind howling through it like the voice of all the gods. It is Igdrasil, the Tree of Existence.

The metaphor expresses Carlyle's strong sense of the organic unity of the present with the past, of the fact that nothing true in the past is ever lost. Therefore, the past, whether analogous to the present or not, is at least relevant to the present. "Let us search more and more into the Past; let all men explore it, as the true fountain of knowledge; by whose light alone, consciously or unconsciously employed, can the Present and the Future be interpreted or guessed at. For though the whole meaning lies far beyond our ken; yet in that complex Manuscript, covered over with formless inextricably-entangled unknown characters,—nay, which is a *Palimpsest*, and had once prophetic writing, still dimly legible there,—some letters, some words, may be deciphered."

Chronology

1795   Thomas Carlyle is born on December 4 in Ecclefechan, Scotland, to James Carlyle, a stone mason, and Margaret Aitken Carlyle. He is the eldest child in a family characterized by their father's piety, frugality, and reverence for hard work.

1809–13   Carlyle attends Edinburgh University intent on Mathematics as his major field of study. He leaves, however, without taking a degree.

1814–18   Carlyle decides to break with family tradition and not become a member of the clergy. He earns his living as a tutor at Annan School and as schoolmaster of Kirkcaldy School.

1821–25   Carlyle meets Jane Welsh. He tutors privately and publishes "Life of Schiller" (1823) in *London Magazine*. He meets Coleridge at Highgate.

1826–31   Carlyle marries Jane Welsh. They settle at first in Edinburgh and then in Craigenputtock, Scotland. "Signs of the Times" (1829) and the important early essay "Characteristics" (1831) both appear in the *Edinburgh Review*.

1833–34   After much difficulty Carlyle publishes *Sartor Resartus* in *Fraser's Magazine*. He is visited by Ralph Waldo Emerson for the first time.

1834–36   Carlyle and his wife move to Chelsea and their marriage undergoes the first of many difficult periods. Although he begins work on *The French Revolution*, the manuscript of the first volume is inadvertently burned at the home of John Stuart Mill and Carlyle spends a number of years rewriting it.

1837–43	Carlyle publishes *The French Revolution* (1837) which wins him much deserved and much sought-after attention. He goes on to publish *On Heroes, Hero-Worship and the Heroic in History* (1841), and *Past and Present* (1843).
1845–51	Carlyle edits the *Letters and Speeches of Oliver Cromwell* (1845). He also publishes the more flamboyant of his *Latter-Day Pamphlets* (1850) and *The Life of John Sterling* (1851).
1858–65	Carlyle writes and publishes his massive *History of Friedrich II of Prussia, Called Frederick the Great* (1865) in six volumes.
1866	Carlyle is appointed Rector of Edinburgh University. Jane Welsh Carlyle dies.
1874–75	Carlyle receives the Prussian Order of Merit from Bismarck but declines an English baronetcy offered by Disraeli.
1881	Thomas Carlyle dies on February 5 and is buried in Ecclefechan.

Contributors

HAROLD BLOOM, Sterling Professor of the Humanities at Yale University, is the author of *The Anxiety of Influence*, *Poetry and Repression*, and many other volumes of literary criticism. His forthcoming study, *Freud: Transference and Authority*, attempts a full-scale reading of all of Freud's major writings. A MacArthur Prize Fellow, he is general editor of five series of literary criticism published by Chelsea House.

JOHN HOLLOWAY is Professor of Modern English at Cambridge University. His recent critical writings include *Poetry and the Self* and *Narrative and Structure*. He has also published several volumes of verse including *Planet of Winds*.

ALBERT J. LaVALLEY is a professor in the Department of Drama at Dartmouth College. He is the editor of several works on film criticism, including *Focus on Hitchcock* and *Mildred Pierce*, as well as a volume on *Twentieth Century Interpretations of* Tess of the D'Urbervilles.

GEORGE LEVINE is the Kenneth Burke Professor of Literature at Rutgers University. His books include *The Endurance of* Frankenstein and *The Realistic Imagination*. He was recently a research fellow at Cambridge University.

BRIAN JOHN is the author of *Supreme Fictions: Studies in the Work of William Blake, Thomas Carlyle, W. B. Yeats, and D. H. Lawrence*.

PHILIP ROSENBERG lives and works in New York City. He has written literary criticism, the novel *Contact on Cherry Street*, and several works of investigative journalism on crime and police work, including *Point Blank* and *Badge of the Assassin*. He is currently working on a new novel.

JOHN PHILIP FARRELL is Associate Professor of English at the University of Texas, Austin. *The Fiction of Community* is his work-in-progress on the image of community in a number of nineteenth-century novels and plays.

163

GEOFFREY H. HARTMAN is Karl Young Professor of English and Comparative Literature at Yale University. His recent books of criticism include *Criticism in the Wilderness*, *Saving the Text*, and *Easy Pieces*.

A. DWIGHT CULLER is Emily Sanford Professor Emeritus of English Literature at Yale University. He is the author of *The Imperial Intellect*: *A Study of Newman's Educational Ideal*, *Imaginative Reason*: *The Poetry of Matthew Arnold*, and *The Poetry of Tennyson*.

Bibliography

Baumgarten, Murray. "Carlyle and 'Spiritual Optics.' " *Victorian Studies* 11 (1968): 503–22.

Beaty, Jerome. "All Victoria's Horses and All Victoria's Men." *New Literary History* 1 (1970): 271–92.

Brantlinger, Patrick. " 'Romance,' 'Biography,' and the Making of *Sartor Resartus.*" *Philological Quarterly* 52 (1973): 108–18.

Brock, D. Heywood. "The Portrait of Abbot Sampson in *Past and Present*: Carlyle and Jocelin of Brakelond." *English Miscellany* 23 (1972): 149–65.

Campbell, Ian. "Carlyle and the Negro Question Again." *Criticism* 13 (1971): 279–90.

———. "Carlyle, Pichet and Jeffrey Again." *Bibliotheck* 7 (1974): 1–15.

———. "Edward Irving, Carlyle and the Stage." *Studies in Scottish Literature* 8 (1971): 166–73.

———. *Thomas Carlyle.* London: Hamish Hamilton, 1974.

Chandler, Alice. "Faith and Order: Carlyle." In *A Dream of Order*, 122–51. Lincoln: University of Nebraska Press, 1970.

Cheever, Leonard A. "A Concept of Freedom: Carlyle's and B. F. Skinner's." In *Studies in Relevance: Romantic and Victorian Writers in 1972*, edited by Thomas M. Harwell, 98–113. Salzburg: University of Salzburg, 1974.

Christensen, Allan C. "A Dickensian Hero Retailored: The Carlylean Apprenticeship of Martin Chuzzlewit." *Studies in the Novel* 3 (1971): 18–25.

Clubbe, John, ed. *Carlyle and His Contemporaries: Essays in Honor of Charles Richard Sanders.* Durham, N.C.: Duke University Press, 1976.

———. "John Carlyle in Germany and the Genesis of *Sartor Resartus*." In *Romantic and Victorian: Studies in Memory of William H. Marshall*, 264–89. Rutherford, N.J.: Fairleigh Dickinson Press, 1971.

Coulling, Sidney M. B. "Carlyle and Swift." *Studies in English Literature* 10 (1970): 741–58.

Daiches, David. "Carlyle and the Victorian Dilemma." In *More Literary Essays*, 115–32. London: Oliver & Boyd, 1968.

DeLaura, David J. "Ishmael as Prophet: *Heroes and Hero-Worship* and the Self-Expressive Basis of Carlyle's Art." *Texas Studies in Literature and Language* 11 (1969): 705–32.

Dibble, Jerry A. "Carlyle's 'British Reader' and the Structure of *Sartor Resartus*." *Texas Studies in Literature and Language* 16 (1974): 293–304.

————. *The Pythia's Drunken Song: Thomas Carlyle's* Sartor Resartus *and the Style Problem in German Idealist Philosophy*. The Hague: Martinus Nijhoff, 1978.

Dilthey, Wilhelm. "*Sartor Resartus*: Philosophical Conflict, Positive and Negative Eras, and Personal Resolution." *Clio* 1 (1972): 40–60.

Donovan, Robert A. "Carlyle and the Climate of Hero-Worship." *University of Toronto Quarterly* 42 (1973): 122–41.

Dunn, Richard J. "David Copperfield's Carlylean Retailoring." In *Dickens the Craftsman*, edited by Robert Partlow, 95–114. Carbondale: Southern Illinois University Press, 1970.

————. " 'Inverse Sublimity': Carlyle's Theory of Humour." *University of Toronto Quarterly* 40 (1970): 41–57.

Fielding, K. J., and Rodger L. Tarr, eds. *Carlyle Past and Present: A Collection of New Essays*. London: Vision Press, 1976.

Fleishman, Avrom. "Carlyle's Sartor: The Open Secret." In *Figures of Autobiography*, 121–37. Berkeley: University of California Press, 1983.

Gilbert, Elliot L. " 'A Wondrous Contiguity': Anachronism in Carlyle's Prophecy and Art." *PMLA* 87 (1972): 432–42.

Goldberg, Michael. "From Bentham to Carlyle: Dickens' Political Development." *Journal of the History of Ideas* 33 (1972): 61–76.

————. *Carlyle and Dickens*. Athens: University of Georgia Press, 1972.

Harding, Anthony J. "Sterling, Carlyle and German Higher Criticism: A Reassessment." *Victorian Studies* 26 (1983): 269–85.

Harris, Kenneth Marc. *Carlyle and Emerson: Their Long Debate*. Cambridge: Harvard University Press, 1978.

Hilles, Frederick W. "Tom Carlyle and His Mocking Bonny Jane." *Yale Review* 60 (1971): 569–76.

Hook, Andrew. *Carlyle and America*. Edinburgh: Carlyle Society, 1970.

Hopwood, Alison L. "Carlyle and Conrad: *Past and Present* and *Heart of Darkness*." *Review of English Studies* 23 (1972): 162–72.

Horst, Drescher W., ed. *Thomas Carlyle 1981: Papers Given at the International Carlyle Centenary Symposium*. Frankfurt: Lang, 1983.

Hughs, J. J., and Peter M. Horowitz. "Organic Biography: The Death of Art." *Journal of British Studies* 12 (1973): 86–104.

Ikeler, A. Abbott. *Puritan Temper and Transcendental Faith: Carlyle's Literary Vision*. Columbus: Ohio State University Press, 1972.

James, Jerry D., and Charles S. Fineman, eds. *Lectures on Carlyle and His Era*. Santa Cruz: University Library of Santa Cruz, 1982.

Jay, Paul. "Carlyle and Nietzsche: The Subject Retailored." In *Being in the Text*, 92–114. Ithaca: Cornell University Press, 1984.

John, Brian. "Yeats and Carlyle." *Notes and Queries* 17 (1970): 455.

Kenny, Blair G. "Carlyle and *Bleak House*." *Dickensian* 66 (1970): 36–41.

Kusch, Robert W. "The Eighteenth Century as 'Decaying Organism' in Carlyle's *The French Revolution*." *Anglia* 89 (1971): 456–70.

————. "Pattern and Paradox in *Heroes and Hero-Worship*." *Studies in Scottish Literature* 6 (1969): 146–55.

Landow, George P. " 'Swim or Drown': Carlyle's World of Shipwrecks, Castaways, and Stranded Voyagers." *Studies in English Literature* 15 (1975): 641–55.

LaValley, Albert J. *Carlyle and the Idea of the Modern*. New Haven: Yale University Press, 1968.

Levine, George. *The Boundaries of Fiction: Carlyle, Macaulay, Newman*. Princeton: Princeton University Press, 1968.

Mellor, Anne K. "Carlyle's *Sartor Resartus*: A Self-Consuming Act." In *English Romantic Irony*, 109–34. Cambridge: Harvard University Press, 1980.

Metzger, Lore. "*Sartor Resartus*: A Victorian *Faust*." *Comparative Literature* 13 (1962): 316–31.

Moore, Carlisle. "Thomas Carlyle and Fiction: 1822–1834." In *Nineteenth-Century Studies*, edited by Herbert Davis, William C. DeVane, and R. C. Bald. 1940 Rpt. Darby, Pa.: Folcroft Library Editions, 1973.

Morgan, Peter F. "Carlyle and Macaulay as Critics of Literature and Life in the *Edinburgh Review*." *Studia Germanica Gandensia* 12 (1970): 131–44.

Morrison, N. Brysson. *True Minds: The Marriage of Thomas and Jane Carlyle*. London: J. M. Dent, 1974.

Nicholson, Frederick J. *Thomas Carlyle and Hugh MacDiarmid*. Edinburgh: Carlyle Society, 1973.

Oddie, William. *Dickens and Carlyle: The Question of Influence*. London: Centenary Press, 1972.

Peach, Linden. "The True Face of Democracy?: Carlyle's Challenge to Whitman's Idealism." In *British Influence on the Birth of American Literature*, 162–93. London: Macmillan, 1982.

Rosenberg, Philip. *The Seventh Hero: Thomas Carlyle and the Theory of Radical Activism*. Cambridge: Harvard University Press, 1974.

Seigel, Jules P., ed. *Thomas Carlyle: The Critical Heritage*. London: Routledge & Kegan Paul, 1971.

Sigman, Joseph. "Adam-Kadmon, Nifl, Muspel, and the Biblical Symbolism of *Sartor Resartus*." *ELH* 41 (1974): 233–56.

———. " 'Diabolico-angelical Indifference': The Image of Polarity in *Sartor Resartus*." *Southern Review* (Australia) 5 (1972): 207–24.

Smith, Sheila M. "Blue Books and Victorian Novelists." *Review of English Studies* 21 (1970): 24–40.

Starzyk, Lawrence J. "Arnold and Carlyle." *Criticism* 12 (1970): 281–300.

Swanson, Donald R. "Carlyle and the English Romantic Poets." *Lock Haven Review* 11 (1969): 25–32.

Symons, Julian. *Thomas Carlyle: The Life and Ideas of a Prophet*. New York: Oxford University Press, 1952.

Tarr, Rodger L. *A Bibliography of English Language Articles on Thomas Carlyle, 1900–1965*. Bibliographical Series Number 7. Columbia, S.C.: University of South Carolina Department of English, 1972.

———. *Thomas Carlyle: A Bibliography of English Language Criticism 1824–1974*. Charlottesville: University of Virginia Press, 1976.

Tennyson, G. B. *Carlyle and the Modern World*. Edinburgh: Carlyle Society, 1971.

———. "Carlyle: Beginning with the Word." In *The Victorian Experience: The Prose Writers*, edited by Richard Levine, 1–21. Athens, Ohio: Ohio University Press, 1982.

————. *Sartor Called Resartus: The Genesis, Structure, and Style of Thomas Carlyle's First Major Work*. Princeton: Princeton University Press, 1965.

Thurman, William R. "Carlyle, Browning, and Ruskin on One Purpose of Art." *South Atlantic Bulletin* 37 (1972): 52–57.

Tilloston, Geoffrey. "Carlyle." In *A View of Victorian Literature*, 55–111. Oxford: Oxford University Press, 1978.

Trowbridge, Ronald L. "Thomas Carlyle's Masks of Humor." *Michigan Academician* 3 (1970): 57–66.

West, Paul. "Carlyle's Bravura Prophetics." *Costerus* 5 (1972): 153–95.

Wilkinson, D. R. M. "Carlyle, Arnold, and Literary Justice." *PMLA* 86 (1971): 225–35.

————. "Carlyle's Creative Disregard." *Melbourne Critical Review* 5 (1962): 16–26.

Wilson, John R. "*Sartor Resartus*: A Study in the Paradox of Despair." *Christianity and Literature* 23 (1974): 9–27.

————. " 'Signs of the Times' and 'The Present Age': Essays in Crisis." *Western Humanities Review* 26 (1972): 369–74.

Witte, William. *Carlyle and Goethe*. Edinburgh: Carlyle Society, 1972.

Workman, Gillian. "Thomas Carlyle and the Governor Eyre Controversy: An Account with Some New Material." *Victorian Studies* 18 (1974): 77–102.

Young, Kenneth. "The Literature of Politics." *Transactions of the Royal Society of Literature* 37 (1972): 134–52.

Acknowledgments

"Introduction" © 1986 by Harold Bloom. Parts II and III originally appeared under the title "Emerson: The American Religion" in *Agon: Towards a Theory of Revisionism* by Harold Bloom, © 1982 by Oxford University Press, Inc. Reprinted by permission.

"The Life of Carlyle's Language" (originally entitled "Carlyle") by John Holloway from *The Victorian Sage: Studies in Argument* by John Holloway, © 1953 by John Holloway. Reprinted by permission.

"*The French Revolution*: Change and Historical Consciousness" by Albert J. LaValley from *Carlyle and the Idea of the Modern: Studies in Carlyle's Prophetic Literature and Its Relation to Blake, Nietzsche, Marx, and Others* by Albert J. LaValley, © 1968 by Yale University. Reprinted by permission of Yale University Press.

"*Sartor Resartus* and the Balance of Fiction" by George Levine from *The Boundaries of Fiction: Carlyle, Macaulay, Newman* by George Levine, © 1968 by Princeton University Press. Reprinted by permission of Princeton University Press. This essay first appeared in *Victorian Studies* 8.

"The Fictive World: *Past and Present*" (originally entitled "The Fictive World of Thomas Carlyle") by Brian John from *Supreme Fictions: Studies in the Work of William Blake, Thomas Carlyle, W. B. Yeats, and D. H. Lawrence* by Brian John, © 1974 by McGill-Queen's University Press. Reprinted by permission of the author and publisher.

"A Whole World of Heroes" by Philip Rosenberg from *The Seventh Hero: Thomas Carlyle and the Theory of Radical Activism* by Philip Rosenberg, © 1974 by the President and Fellows of Harvard College. Reprinted by permission of Harvard University Press.

"Transcendental Despair: *The French Revolution*" (originally entitled "Carlyle: The True Man's Tragedy") by John P. Farrell from *Revolution as Tragedy: The Dilemma of the Moderate from Scott to Arnold* by John P. Farrell, © 1980 by Cornell University. Reprinted by permission of the publisher, Cornell University Press.

"Enthusiastic Criticism" (originally entitled "The Sacred Jungle: Carlyle, Eliot, Bloom") by Geoffrey H. Hartman from *Criticism in the Wilderness: The Study of*

Literature Today by Geoffrey H. Hartman, © 1980 by Yale University. Reprinted by permission of Yale University Press.

"Mill, Carlyle, and the Spirit of the Age" by A. Dwight Culler from *The Victorian Mirror of History* by A. Dwight Culler, © 1985 by Yale University. Reprinted by permission of Yale University Press.

Index